THE EXPERIENTIAL LIBRARY

CHANDOS
INFORMATION PROFESSIONAL SERIES
Series Editor: Ruth Rikowski
(email: Rikowskigr@aol.com)

Chandos' new series of books is aimed at the busy information professional. They have been specially commissioned to provide the reader with an authoritative view of current thinking. They are designed to provide easy-to-read and (most importantly) practical coverage of topics that are of interest to librarians and other information professionals. If you would like a full listing of current and forthcoming titles, please visit www.chandospublishing.com.

New authors: we are always pleased to receive ideas for new titles; if you would like to write a book for Chandos, please contact Dr Glyn Jones on g.jones.2@elsevier.com or telephone +44 (0) 1865 843000.

THE EXPERIENTIAL LIBRARY

Transforming Academic and Research Libraries through the Power of Experiential Learning

Edited by

PETE McDONNELL

AMSTERDAM • BOSTON • HEIDELBERG • LONDON
NEW YORK • OXFORD • PARIS • SAN DIEGO
SAN FRANCISCO • SINGAPORE • SYDNEY • TOKYO

Chandos Publishing is an imprint of Elsevier

Chandos Publishing is an imprint of Elsevier
50 Hampshire Street, 5th Floor, Cambridge, MA 02139, United States
The Boulevard, Langford Lane, Kidlington, OX5 1GB, United Kingdom

Copyright © 2017 P. McDonnell. Published by Elsevier Ltd. All rights reserved.

No part of this publication may be reproduced or transmitted in any form or by any means, electronic or mechanical, including photocopying, recording, or any information storage and retrieval system, without permission in writing from the publisher. Details on how to seek permission, further information about the Publisher's permissions policies and our arrangements with organizations such as the Copyright Clearance Center and the Copyright Licensing Agency, can be found at our website: www.elsevier.com/permissions.

This book and the individual contributions contained in it are protected under copyright by the Publisher (other than as may be noted herein).

Notices
Knowledge and best practice in this field are constantly changing. As new research and experience broaden our understanding, changes in research methods, professional practices, or medical treatment may become necessary.

Practitioners and researchers must always rely on their own experience and knowledge in evaluating and using any information, methods, compounds, or experiments described herein. In using such information or methods they should be mindful of their own safety and the safety of others, including parties for whom they have a professional responsibility.

To the fullest extent of the law, neither the Publisher nor the authors, contributors, or editors, assume any liability for any injury and/or damage to persons or property as a matter of products liability, negligence or otherwise, or from any use or operation of any methods, products, instructions, or ideas contained in the material herein.

British Library Cataloguing-in-Publication Data
A catalogue record for this book is available from the British Library

Library of Congress Cataloging-in-Publication Data
A catalog record for this book is available from the Library of Congress

ISBN: 978-0-08-100775-4 (print)
ISBN: 978-0-08-100778-5 (online)

For information on all Chandos Publishing
visit our website at https://www.elsevier.com

Working together to grow libraries in developing countries

www.elsevier.com • www.bookaid.org

Publisher: Glyn Jones
Acquisition Editor: George Knott
Editorial Project Manager: Tessa De Roo
Production Project Manager: Omer Mukthar
Designer: Maria Inês Cruz

Typeset by MPS Limited, Chennai, India

DEDICATION

For Chris

CONTENTS

Contributor Biographical Sketches	xiii
Foreword	xxv
Preface	xxvii
Acknowledgment	xxxv

PART I THE EXPERIENTIAL LIBRARY: NEW PATHS FOR INFORMATION LITERACY INSTRUCTION

1. Integrating Experiential Learning Into Information Literacy Curriculum — 3
J. Mavodza

1.1	Kolb's Theory of EL	4
1.2	IL Curriculum and EL at Zayed University	6
1.3	Revisiting the Application of EL Theory	12
1.4	Concluding Thoughts	13
	References	13

2. Experiential Learning in a Faculty of Education Library — 15
C. Laverty

2.1	Experiential Learning Trends in Higher Education	15
2.2	The Path to EL in an Education Library	16
2.3	EL Design in the Academic Library	19
2.4	Reflections	21
	References	24

3. Beyond Object Lessons: Object-Based Learning in the Academic Library — 27
A.R. Barlow

3.1	History	28
3.2	OBL Theory	30
3.3	OBL in Higher Education	31
3.4	OBL in Academic Libraries	32
3.5	Library Instruction for OBL	34
3.6	Beyond Object Lessons	40
	References	41

4. **Taking the Class Out of the Classroom: Libraries, Literacy, and Service Learning** — 43
   J. Blodgett

   4.1 Service Learning and the Academic Library: Opportunities Abound — 43
   4.2 The Course — 45
   4.3 What the Students Learned About the Community — 48
   4.4 What the Students Learned About Themselves — 49
   4.5 What I Learned, Moving Forward — 50
   References — 52

5. **Training Student Drivers: Using a Flipped Classroom Model for IL Instruction** — 53
   E.A. Sanders, A.H. Balius and S.A. Sanders

   5.1 Connecting IL, Research Skills, and Employability — 53
   5.2 IL, EL, and Flipped Classroom — 55
   5.3 Synergy Between Flipped Classroom and EL — 57
   5.4 EL Exercises — 60
   5.5 EL Project — 63
   5.6 Road Conditions — 67
   5.7 End of the Road — 70
   References — 70

6. **Handheld Learning: Authentic Assessment Using iPads** — 73
   K. Viars, M.A. Cullen and A.R. Stalker

   6.1 First, Some Context — 73
   6.2 Using iPads in the Classroom — 77
   6.3 The Future of Authentic Assessment — 82
   Acknowledgment — 85
   References — 85

PART II THE EXPERIENTIAL LIBRARY: PROGRAMS, COLLECTIONS, SPACES, STAFF DEVELOPMENT AND TRAINING

7. **"Out of the Vault": Engaging Students in Experiential Learning Through Special Collections and Archives** — 89
   C.J. Anderson and C. Brand

   7.1 Experiential Learning in a Special Collections and University Archives Context — 90

7.2	Out of the Vault Series	91
7.3	Student-Curated Exhibits	93
7.4	Students Workers as Experiential Learners	95
7.5	Conclusion	100
References		101

8. Game On! Experiential Learning With Tabletop Games   103
L. Hays and M. Hayse

8.1	Games Galore: Tabletop Gaming as Experiential Learning	103
8.2	Let the Games Begin: Tabletop Games in the Library	105
8.3	Setting up the Game: Center for Games & Learning	106
8.4	Faculty at Play: Community of Practice	109
8.5	Students at Play: Case Studies	109
8.6	Choosing a Strategy: Tabletop Game Selection	111
8.7	High Score: Lessons Learned	113
References		114

9. Building Knowledge Together: Interactive Course Exhibits in the Academic Library   117
S. Fralin, B. Mathews and L. Pressley

9.1	The Beginnings	117
9.2	The Idea Takes Shape	118
9.3	Building the Program	119
9.4	The Pedagogy	119
9.5	Chickering and Gamson	120
9.6	Bloom's Taxonomy	121
9.7	Library's Learning Outcomes	122
9.8	The Design Process	123
9.9	Case One: Soviet History for the Networked Age	123
9.10	Case Two: Photography in Focus	127
9.11	Tips on the Process	131
9.12	Costs/Supplies	131
9.13	Assessment	133
9.14	Future	133
9.15	Conclusion	134
References		134

10. Going Vertical: Enhancing Staff Training Through Vertically Integrated Instruction   135
E.N. Decker and J.A. Townes

   10.1 Workplace Learning   135
   10.2 Going Vertical: Vertically Integrated Instruction   138
   10.3 Solutions and Recommendations   143
   10.4 Future Directions in Library Workplace Learning   144
   References   146

11. From Training to Learning: Developing Student Employees Through Experiential Learning Design   147
H. Bussell and J. Hagman

   11.1 Student Employees in Libraries: An Emphasis on Training   147
   11.2 Current Student Employment Practices at the Ohio University Libraries   150
   11.3 Adapting Student Employment Practices to Incorporate EL   151
   11.4 Challenges and Issues to Consider   155
   11.5 Concluding Thoughts   158
   References   158

PART III THE EXPERIENTIAL LIBRARY: INNOVATION AND MULTI-LIBRARY COLLABORATIONS

12. Home Grown: Lessons Learned From Experiential Learning Partnerships in an Academic Library   163
C. Groves and A. Shealy

   12.1 Setting the Stage for Experiential Learning at Walker Library   163
   12.2 Staffing at Walker Library   164
   12.3 Library Relevance and Innovation   166
   12.4 Libraries Embrace Ethnographic Studies   168
   12.5 Future Directions   173
   12.6 Final Lessons   173
   References   174

13. Grasping a Golden Opportunity: Librarian Support for Students on Summer Internships   175
C. Seeman and S. Ziph

   13.1 Business Curriculum and the Role of the Internship in Business Education   176

13.2	Action Learning at Ross School of Business	178
13.3	Service Orientation of Kresge Library Services	180
13.4	Using Materials for Action and Experiential Learning Programs: Best Practices	182
13.5	Internship Service Opportunities for Libraries	183
13.6	Conclusion	185
References		185

14. The New Hampshire Human Library Project: Breaking Barriers and Building Bridges by Engaging Communities of Learners   187
C.W. Gamtso, M. Mannon and S. Whipple

14.1	Beginnings	187
14.2	What Is a Human Library?	187
14.3	The Opportunity of EL	188
14.4	The New Hampshire Human Library Collaboration	189
14.5	"Closing the Book": Endings and New Beginnings	198
References		200

15. Conclusion: An Experiential Librarian's Creed   203
P. McDonnell

15.1	Why a Creed?	203
15.2	Finally… What Can Libraries Do to Support Experiential Education?	207
References		208

Index   *209*

CONTRIBUTOR BIOGRAPHICAL SKETCHES

Christopher J. Anderson (Drew University)
Christopher J. Anderson is Head of Special Collections, Archives and Methodist Librarian at the Drew University Library in Madison, New Jersey. He is also the Librarian for the General Commission on Archives and History for the United Methodist Church. He coaches baseball at Drew and hosts *The Drew Vault*, a weekly Internet radio show on special collections and university archives. Prior to Drew, Chris was faculty at several colleges and seminaries in the New York City area. He has a PhD in American Religion and Culture from Drew and an MLIS from Syracuse University. He is particularly interested in experiential learning and outreach in a special collections and archive environment and has published and presented on this topic.

Angela H. Balius (Southeastern Louisiana University)
Angela H. Balius currently works as a Reference/Instruction Librarian at Southeastern Louisiana University. She holds a BS in Journalism from the University of Southern Mississippi and MLIS from the University of Alabama. She works as the evening reference librarian in addition to teaching information literacy in Library Science 102, a 1-h for-credit course. She has coauthored an annotated bibliography on experiential learning in academic libraries and attended a series of four workshops on experiential learning offered at Southeastern Louisiana University. She also presented on experiential learning in academic libraries and on the new ACRL Framework (LOUIS User's Conference 2015).

Amy R. Barlow (Rhode Island College)
Amy R. Barlow is Assistant Professor and Reference Librarian at Rhode Island College. Prior to that, she was the Humanities Liaison at Wheaton College (Norton, MA), where she supported multiple object-based learning assignments. She is an educator, librarian, and technologist with master's degrees in US History and Library and Information Studies. In 2012, Amy was an ACRL Member of the Week and ALA Emerging Leader. Recent presentations at NERCOMP Annual Conference 2015 and the 43rd Annual LOEX Conference demonstrate her affinity for active and problem-based learning theory. She is published in *Weave: Journal of Library User Experience*, *Reference and User Services Quarterly*, and has a forthcoming paper in *LOEX Conference Proceedings 2015*.

Jayne Blodgett (University of Northern Colorado)

Jayne Blodgett is Assistant Dean of Libraries at the University of Northern Colorado. She is interested in how technical and public services can best work together to meet the ever-changing needs of students and faculty. Prior to moving to UNC, she worked as Assistant Library Director at the University of Minnesota, Morris, where she had the opportunity to teach a number of FYS classes, including a class focused on libraries and literacy. She served in the chair positions of the Minnesota ACRL chapter from 2012 to 2016. She holds an MA in English Literature from the University of Wisconsin-Eau Claire and an MLIS from Dominican University.

Cassie Brand (Drew University)

Cassie Brand is Methodist Associate and Special Collections Cataloger at Drew University. She is also working on a doctorate at Drew University in History and Culture, with a concentration in Book History, expanding on the work she did while completing her MLS from Indiana University. Her goal is to use both intellectual history and descriptive bibliography together to study the book as a whole. Much of her research focuses on the intersection between text and form, looking at the ways in which they complement or fight against each other, in addition to looking at ways to enhance and improve library services in special collections. Her favorite part of the job is introducing new people to rare books, bringing primary sources into the classroom, and mentoring students.

Hilary Bussell (The Ohio State University)

Hilary Bussell is Assistant Professor and Social Sciences Librarian at The Ohio State University. Previously, she was the eLearning Librarian at Ohio University in Athens, OH. She holds an MLIS from the University of Illinois at Urbana-Champaign and an MA in Philosophy from Loyola University Chicago. In 2014, she participated in the first cohort of scholars at the Institute for Research Design in Librarianship. She has presented and published on graduate student research needs, iPad use in libraries, and library support for distance learners. Her research interests include emerging technologies, information literacy, and the OER movement.

Mary Ann Cullen (Georgia State University, Perimeter College)

With 10 years of experience in academic libraries, Mary Ann Cullen is the Director of Library Services for Georgia State University's Alpharetta campus library (formerly Georgia Perimeter College) and Perimeter College Online. She holds an MS degree in Library Studies from Florida State University and an MS degree in Psychology from the University of Georgia. She has presented at local, state, and national conferences about innovative ideas in library instruction for face-to-face and distance learners. Her research interests include information literacy and assessment, distance library services, and open educational resources.

Emy Nelson Decker (Georgia Institute of Technology)

Emy Nelson Decker is the NextGen Public Services Manager at the Georgia Tech Library. She holds an MLIS from Valdosta State University and an MA in art history from the University of Chicago. Emy's current interests are centered on emerging technologies as well as new uses of existing technologies within the modern academic library setting. In addition to presenting in venues such as the American Library Association and the Association of College & Research Libraries, she has published numerous refereed journal articles and book chapters within the library field. She is also the coeditor of the *Handbook of Research on Disaster Management and Contingency Planning in Modern Libraries*.

Scott Fralin (Virginia Polytechnic Institute & State University)

Scott Fralin is the Exhibit Specialist and Event Operations Coordinator at the Virginia Tech Libraries. He works directly with the faculty and students to design and build the Course Exhibits described in the book. Scott is excited about providing examples and case studies of previous exhibits to illustrate how they came to be, as well as providing a framework for others to use in order to create similar programs in their own libraries. Scott and his coauthors Brian Mathews and Lauren Pressley presented "Building Knowledge Together: Interactive Course Exhibits as Project-Based Learning" at The Innovative Library Classroom Conference in May 2015.

Carolyn White Gamtso (University of New Hampshire at Manchester)

Carolyn White Gamtso is an Associate Professor and Head of Reference and Instruction at the University of New Hampshire at Manchester Library. She is interested in information literacy initiatives, and helped develop the UNH Manchester Research Mentor Program, which trains class-linked tutors to assist students with library research. She enjoys working with faculty to create interactive, experiential information literacy workshops. Professor Gamtso's research interests include information literacy, faculty collaboration, and peer tutoring in the library. She has shared her research in the area of library instruction at local, regional, national, and international conferences, and has coauthored several articles and a book chapter that discuss information literacy projects and practices.

Christy Groves (Middle Tennessee State University)

Christy Groves earned her Bachelor's from the University of Tennessee, Knoxville (UTK), in 1993, graduating summa cum laude. In 1995, she graduated from UTK with a Masters of Library Science and began her professional library career in Indiana. After working as a Reference Librarian, a Science Library Branch Manager and Science Librarian, and then Head of Access Services, she accepted her current position as Department Chair of User Services at the James E. Walker Library, Middle Tennessee State University.

For over 20 years she has been directly involved in recruitment, supervision, and development of library faculty and staff. She has led a number of service excellence initiatives and embraces trends and technologies that support ongoing library relevance and student success. Her research interests include library management, staff development, and entrepreneurship in libraries. In addition to serving as a regular columnist for *Tennessee Libraries*, most recently her work has appeared in two monographs, *The Generation X Librarian* and *The Entrepreneurial Librarian*, and in *College and Research Libraries News*.

Jessica Hagman (Ohio University)

Jessica Hagman is the Social Media Coordinator and Subject Librarian for Scripps College at Ohio University. She holds an MA in Library and Information Science from the University of Wisconsin-Madison and an MA in Organizational Communication from Ohio University. She has previously published and presented on the use of social media in academic libraries and the use of a needs assessment to develop library services for graduate students. Beyond these areas, her research interests also include identity and identification among instruction librarians, the subject of her recent master's thesis in Organizational Communication.

Lauren Hays (MidAmerica Nazarene University)
Lauren Hays is the Instructional and Research Librarian at MidAmerica Nazarene University. She holds an MLS from Emporia State University, and an MS in Educational Technology and a Graduate Certificate in Online Teaching and Learning, both from the University of Central Missouri. In 2014 and 2015, she served as the Principal Investigator on an IMLS Sparks! Ignition Grant to create a library-based Center for Games & Learning. Her research interests include the scholarship of teaching and learning, information literacy, and educational technology. She was awarded the 2015 New Professional Award from the Kansas Library Association.

Mark Hayse (MidAmerica Nazarene University)
Mark Hayse holds an MA in Religious Education, and a PhD in Educational Studies. His dissertation topic was "Religious Architecture in Videogames: Perspectives from Curriculum Theory and Religious Education." He is the Faculty and Staff Development Coordinator and the Director of the Honors Program at MidAmerica Nazarene University. In 2007, he was awarded the Alpha Chi Donald S. Metz Award—Faculty Member of the Year for Distinctive Academic Contributions. Mark has written numerous scholarly publications on games and gaming and regularly presents on these topics. He has spent 20 years in youth work, with an ongoing emphasis on games and recreation, and has researched how games can be used in education.

Corinne Laverty (Queen's University)
Corinne Laverty is Teaching & Learning Specialist at the Queen's University Centre for Teaching and Learning. She holds a teaching degree, MLIS, and a PhD in Information Science (Wales, UK). Her research interests are in the development and assessment of information literacy curricula, support for the scholarship of teaching and learning, and professional development models for faculty and librarians. She received the 2013 Academic Librarianship Award from the Ontario Confederation of University Faculty Associations.

Melissa Mannon (Goffstown High School)
Melissa Mannon has served as a high school librarian for the past 4 years, teaching and cultivating diverse information literacy skills while fostering a sense of community, sense of place, appreciation for diversity, and love for life-long learning. She previously worked for 12 years as an archives and cultural heritage consultant, fostering information literacy through projects, public speaking, teaching, publishing, and social media engagement. Before that, she was employed in public libraries and museums. Ms. Mannon holds an MSLS from Simmons College and is currently matriculating in the CAGS program at Plymouth State University. An important part of her work at the high school involves collaborating with a science museum in New Hampshire to engage in a complex STEM learning initiative within her library. The organizations hope this project will serve as a model for New Hampshire librarians, teachers, and museum professionals to boost experiential learning opportunities in public schools. In 2015, her school library was recognized for its "Outstanding Library Program" by the New Hampshire School Library Media Association and a people's choice winner for innovation in the national "Follett Challenge."

Brian Mathews (Virginia Polytechnic Institute & State University)
Brian Mathews is the Associate Dean leading the Learning Division at the Virginia Tech Libraries. He proposed the original framework for course exhibits based on work at the Georgia Tech Libraries. He offers insight into the origins of the program and the guiding vision that provides direction for the exhibits to the day. Brian has written extensively on innovative library practices including "Engines for Change: Libraries as Drivers of Engagement" (2014), "Flip the Model: Strategies for Creating and Delivering Value" (2013), and "Think like a Startup: a White Paper to Inspire Library Entrepreneurialism" (2012). He is also the author of two books: *Marketing Today's Academic Library* and *Encoding Space*. Brian and his coauthors Scott Fralin and Lauren Pressley presented "Building Knowledge Together: Interactive Course Exhibits as Project-Based Learning" at The Innovative Library Classroom Conference in May 2015.

Judith Mavodza (Zayed University)
Judith Mavodza is Associate Professor, Instruction Reference Librarian at Zayed University, Abu Dhabi, United Arab Emirates. Her current work includes instruction and work as liaison librarian for supporting the

research needs of the academic community. Her areas of research interest include reference and instruction, marketing and assessment of library services, professional development of librarians, and knowledge management. A published author of several scholarly journal articles and book chapters, she is a member of the Information Literacy Network (ILN) of the Gulf Region, and participates in events of the UAE Advanced Network for Research and Education. She holds a BSc (Honours) Sociology from the University of Zimbabwe (Harare), a Post-Graduate Diploma in Library Studies from the University College London (UK), MA in Library Studies from the University of London (UK), and a Doctor of Literature and Philosophy in Information Science from the University of South Africa (Pretoria).

Pete McDonnell (Bemidji State University)
Pete McDonnell is Systems/Distance Learning/Circulation Librarian at Bemidji State University's A.C. Clark Library, in Bemidji, Minnesota. He received his MLIS from the University of Illinois at Urbana-Champaign, and has an MS in Experiential Education from Minnesota State University, Mankato. His professional research interests include experiential learning, organizational development, and support of student learning through library technology. Over the past decade, he has developed and facilitated percussion-based experiential exercises (also known as drum circles) for students, library staff, and faculty, and at professional library conferences, along with his colleague Keith Russell from the University of Kansas. He has written on topics such as the intersections between experiential learning and academic libraries, and librarian professional development, for the *Unabashed Librarian, College & Research Libraries News*, as well as on his blog at http://thecircleisacircuit.blogspot.com. He is a member of the American Library Association, Association of College and Research Libraries, and the Association for Experiential Education. He enjoys spending his free time reading, hiking, making music, playing drums and other percussion toys, and spending time with his wife and their cats in the forests of Northern Minnesota.

Lauren Pressley (University of Washington)
Lauren Pressley is Director of UW Tacoma Library and Associate Dean for University of Washington Libraries. She has written and presented extensively on topics related to teaching and pedagogy and has diverse experience with library instruction including workshops, credit-bearing instruction,

online learning, embedded librarianship, faculty development, and informal learning. She has presented at ACRL and at regional conferences on learning, pedagogy, and the student experience. Lauren and her coauthors Scott Fralin and Brian Mathews presented "Building Knowledge Together: Interactive Course Exhibits as Project-Based Learning" at The Innovative Library Classroom Conference in May 2015.

Keith Russell (University of Kansas)
In the mid-1970s, Keith Russell was a staff development specialist in the General Libraries at the University of Texas at Austin. Since then he has continued to learn, develop, and use experiential exercises. For the past 12 years he has been promoting the use of group drumming for experiential learning in libraries—to reinforce training about communication and diversity, to improve teamwork, to celebrate group accomplishments, to relieve stress, and to change a group's behavior. His area of research and scholarship as a library faculty member at the University of Kansas was professional and organizational development, and his work specialty was Life Sciences Librarian. He retired in Feb. 2015.

Elizabeth A. Sanders (Southeastern Louisiana University)
Elizabeth A. Sanders currently works as a Reference/Instruction Librarian at Southeastern Louisiana University. She holds an MA in English from the University of Arkansas and an MLIS from Louisiana State University. She has previously taught composition classes and currently teaches information literacy in Library Science 102, a 1-h for-credit course. She has coauthored an annotated bibliography on experiential learning in academic libraries and attended a series of four workshops on experiential learning offered at Southeastern Louisiana University. She has presented on experiential learning in academic libraries (LOUIS User's Conference 2015). Her research interests include information literacy, the connection between the writing and the research processes, and popular culture.

Stephen A. Sanders (Southeastern Louisiana University)
Dr. Stephen A. Sanders has been Coordinator of Library Science 102, a 1-h for-credit course, since 2012. He is author of "Through a Mirror Darkly: A Postmodern Approach to Teaching Expertise, Authority, and Bias" in the ACRL publication *Not Just Where to Click: Teaching Students How to Think about Information* (Mar. 2015). He has presented on bibliographic instruction

topics at: LOEX Annual Conference (2013): LUC (LOUIS User's Conference) (Oct. 2013, Oct. 2014); and the Louisiana Library Association (2013). He received a BA (with Honors) from the University of Arkansas, and the MLIS degree from Louisiana State University. He also holds seminary degrees (M.Div., Th.D.) from New Orleans Baptist Theological Seminary. He served as a US Army chaplain (endorsed by the Christian Church [Disciples of Christ]) in both Afghanistan and Iraq.

Corey Seeman (University of Michigan)
Corey Seeman is the director of Kresge Library Services (Ross School of Business at the University of Michigan, Ann Arbor). Prior to that position, Corey served as Assistant Dean at the University of Toledo, a training consultant at Innovative Interfaces, and a librarian and archivist at historical libraries including the National Baseball Hall of Fame in Cooperstown. Corey has written and presented on customer service and change management within libraries, especially academic ones. He also maintains the Library Writer's Blog (http://librarywriting.blogspot.com/).

Ashley Shealy (Middle Tennessee State University)
Ashley Shealy is a Reference & Instruction Librarian at James E. Walker Library, Middle Tennessee State University (MTSU). Prior to joining the library faculty at MTSU, she served as Reference & Instruction Librarian at Wingate University (NC). She earned her Masters of Library Science from the University of North Carolina at Chapel Hill in 2010 and has presented on various issues related to library instruction, student success, and library/writing center partnerships, most recently at the Georgia International Conference on Information Literacy in Savannah, GA. Her research interests include pedagogy, assessment of library instruction, undergraduates and digital literacy, and experiential and active learning in libraries. Currently she also serves as the Associate Editor of *Tennessee Libraries*, the official journal of the Tennessee Library Association.

Amy R. Stalker (Georgia State University, Perimeter College)
Amy R. Stalker is a reference and instruction librarian at Georgia State University, Perimeter College (formerly Georgia Perimeter College) in Atlanta, Georgia. She earned her MLIS degree from Valdosta State University, and is an active member of the Georgia Library Association, including the Public Relations Committee. Her research interests include reference services, information literacy instruction, and readers' advisory in academic libraries.

Jennifer A. Townes (Georgia College & State University)
Jennifer A. Townes is the Scholarly Communication Librarian at Georgia College & State University in Milledgeville, Georgia. She holds an MSLS from the University of North Carolina at Chapel Hill. She has presented on robotic telepresence (Association of College and Research Libraries) and information literacy (North Carolina Library Association). Jennifer's research interests lie in information literacy, assessment, and faculty collaboration. She is also the coeditor of the *Handbook of Research on Disaster Management and Contingency Planning in Modern Libraries*.

Karen Viars (Georgia State University, Perimeter College)
Karen Viars is a reference and instruction librarian at Georgia State University, Perimeter College (formerly Georgia Perimeter College) in Atlanta, Georgia. In addition to the MLIS, she also holds an MS degree in instructional design and technology, and her instructional design work has been used nationally by Fortune 500 companies. She is the winner of the Georgia Library Association 2009 Academic Library Division award for her paper "Instructional Design in Academic Libraries: Implications for the Future" and has published peer-reviewed articles and chapters. Her research interests include instructional design in academic libraries, reference services, and assessment.

Sandy Whipple (Goffstown Public Library)
Sandy Whipple has been the Adult Services and Outreach Coordinator at the Goffstown Public Library for 8 years. In this position, she fulfills her desire to challenge, inspire, and engage the community in new ways. While she champions what would be considered traditional library services, she is also seen as somewhat of a maverick in her approach to public programming. Partnering with a variety of arts and service organizations, including the American Friends Service Committee, the Afghan Women's Writing Project, and Liberty House, as well as local businesses and nonprofits, she thrives on offering unique experiences and opportunities for the residents of Goffstown. In 2015, the Goffstown Public Library was awarded the Lloyd Green Humanity Achievement Award for their contributions to the community and Sandy was honored as the recipient of the READS Award of Excellence from the Reference and Adult Services Section of the NH Library Association. This award recognizes outstanding contributions by an individual who has been instrumental in improving library service to adults.

Sally Ziph (University of Michigan)
Sally Ziph is a Business Reference & Instruction Librarian at Kresge Library Services (Ross School of Business at the University of Michigan, Ann Arbor). Prior to Kresge, Sally worked as a Reference & Instruction Librarian at the Mardigian Library, University of Michigan-Dearborn.

FOREWORD

It is a tremendous honor to be asked to write the Foreword to this important work. What most stands out about the volume you now hold in your hands (or read on your mobile device)—what makes it special and unique in the Library Science literature—is that it brings together "reports from the field" on the applications of experiential learning (EL) in academic libraries, and is written by the very librarians working on the front lines of the ever-changing learning organization. We can all hope this benchmark work sets the stage for future applications which will benefit library users, library staff, and the community the library serves. Indeed, the potential for innovations arising from the cross-pollination of these two seemingly disparate areas is great. Twenty-first century librarians and library staff can use the processes of EL to achieve (and even exceed) defined goals. And the more we all know and share, the better off we'll all be in an unknown, exciting future.

Experiential learning, as both theory and methodology, has a long history, but interest in it has definitely escalated in recent years, from the classroom to the boardroom, and everywhere in between. Each reader brings to EL her or his own informal and formal experiences with it over time, from early childhood into adulthood. Some are molded and shaped by EL in later stages of life, through workplace training programs, higher education coursework, and life experiences in general. As instructional designers or developers of library programming and services, we are called to apply what we have learned as we provide experiential opportunities for others. With that in mind, I urge readers to contemplate their own relationship to EL, in order to learn more from this work, and to use and adapt what they find within this book's pages.

In my case, EL was an important component of K-12 art, math, and science courses. When I went to college, it was to train as a biology teacher, and EL was an important component of classical biological education and teacher certification. When I became a staff development specialist in the mid-1970s at the University of Texas General Libraries, my past training was helpful in getting the job, and I took advantage of several workshops on designing and utilizing library-related experiential learning exercises. Throughout my career, most of the library, management, and leadership workshops I have participated in, and sometimes given, have had experiential components. As a library faculty member at the University of Kansas, my main scholarly interests and activities were in professional and organizational effectiveness. Within that broad area, I have been particularly intrigued by applications of group drumming for improving teamwork and facilitating change.

It was through the experiential applications of group drumming that I met Pete McDonnell, who initiated this volume, serves as editor, and who has made his own contributions in the design and utilization of percussion exercises. His interest in group drumming for team building and learning led him to the Internet, where he discovered that at least one other librarian was using group drumming in library settings—me. Pete and I would occasionally meet for coffee to talk about our interests in libraries, group drumming, and EL in general. That in turn led to joint presentations at state and regional library conferences. We complement each other in significant ways, since he is a musician in addition to being a librarian, and his experiential exercises reflect a more musical approach. I, on the other hand, am proof positive that anyone with the motivation, even without any musical background, can learn to facilitate a group drumming experience. Both of us are oriented toward experiential learning as a profession. Indeed, both of us are or have been members of the Association for Experiential Education, and Pete has a Master's degree in the subject—uniquely suiting him to serve as editor of this volume.

It is my hope that this work stimulates even more experimentation with EL in library settings. I also encourage those doing the experimenting to report both successes and failures to the broader library community—in the literature and at workshops and conferences. And if other disciplines and professions adopt some of the processes and techniques we discover in libraries, so much the better for everyone.

Keith Russell
Librarian Emeritus
The University of Kansas

PREFACE

Experiential learning (EL), as both an educational theory and a collection of practical methods, has become a powerful force in higher education over the last quarter century. Indeed, one could argue that it has played a large role in transforming how teaching and learning is conducted in the 21st century. Over the same period of time, libraries have undergone great changes, as their parent institutions, organizational structures, technologies, and user needs have evolved. Amidst all of this upheaval, it will come as no surprise that EL practices and techniques are finding a larger place in the everyday work of academic and research libraries.

As has been argued in the Library and Information Science (LIS) literature by Lewis (2007), Stamatoplos (2009), and others, academic libraries must continue to transform themselves in order to provide relevant services and collections to their user communities, while at the same time achieving closer alignment with institutional priorities. The literature also suggests that academic libraries must continue to focus on engagement with students and their learning, especially as the transition from print to digital continues and new technologies impact the way libraries support students and faculty.

The central claim of this book, supported by illustrative examples of how libraries are embracing EL, is that EL will increasingly become a key component of what academic and research libraries can offer the learning enterprise. As they continue to undergo transformations, reach out and engage with students and their learning, and as they achieve tighter integration with institutional missions, this book posits that academic and research libraries are indeed becoming more "experiential" institutions.

EXPERIENTIAL LEARNING—WHAT DOES IT MEAN FOR ACADEMIC LIBRARIES?

Not surprisingly, students in today's college and university classrooms have increasing access to a variety of impactful learning experiences. Numerous experience-based practices and methods are now widely implemented in colleges and universities throughout the United States, Canada, and the world—active learning, service learning, problem and inquiry-based learning, reflective portfolios, internships and practicums, credit for prior learning, to name but a few. However, EL in higher education is not a new development: it has its roots in the progressive and cooperative education movements of the late 19th and early 20th centuries, most notably represented in the work of the American social philosopher and educational theorist John Dewey. As we move further into the 21st century, amidst the calls from many quarters (parents, taxpayers, and employers) for institutions of higher education to become more accountable and affordable, the power of EL to transform students' academic experiences and support their transition from college to the workforce is becoming even more apparent.

For the purposes of this book, EL (also sometimes called experiential education) is defined as a learner-centered educational theory and methodology which places experience at the forefront of learning. Instead of viewing teachers as the "sage on the stage" and students as passive receptacles to be filled with information and wisdom, EL places the emphasis on the student's active integration of subject knowledge and learning, through development and application of skills. It is often accompanied by reflective observation of the learner's interaction with the material studied. The character of EL is sometimes encapsulated in the phrase "learning by doing." But, to go beyond this phrase, EL in its most effective forms also engages the learner in a transformational journey, moving her through a cycle of *concrete experience, reflective observation, abstract conceptualization*, and *active experimentation*, in order to integrate learning for overall personal development.

This definition of EL draws its main inspiration from the ideas of John Dewey and David A. Kolb, two of the leading lights in the field of experiential education. Dewey, the social philosopher and progressive educator who came to prominence early in the 20th century as a leading figure in the progressive education movement (and whose ideas are almost synonymous with experiential education), can be seen as David Kolb's intellectual forebear; Kolb has carried John Dewey's EL torch into the 21st century.

An early view of Dewey's ideas on EL can be seen in his *My Pedagogic Creed* (1897), a work in which he laid down a foundation for experiential education through a series of "I believe" statements. In that work, one can feel Dewey's emphasis on the interests and experience of the learner as having as much weight (or more) than the "higher authority" of the school and the society at large. Through such statements as "I believe that interests are the signs and symptoms of growing power.... I believe they represent dawning capacities...I believe that only through the continual and sympathetic observation of childhood's interests can the adult enter into the child's life and see what it is ready for" (Dewey, 1897), one can grasp a sense of the importance of developing students' native capacities to learn from experience. Interested readers should consult Dewey's *Experience and Education* (1938) for a concise yet integrative statement of his philosophy of education, made at the end of his long career.

In addition to shifting the focus from what is learned to the learner's relationship to it, Dewey's theory also views education as more than simply the transmission of information and the fitting of students to current societal needs; education is viewed *as a process*: "I believe, finally, that education must be conceived as a continuing reconstruction of experience; that the process and goal of education are one and the same thing." (Dewey, 1897). The goal of this process is twofold: it aims at both the learner's individual development through experience, as well as his or her integration into a democratic social fabric: "I believe that education is a process of living and not a preparation for future living" (Dewey, 1897). In *My Pedagogic Creed* (1897), Dewey argues that education must be authentic to "forms of life that are worth living for their own sake," and thus should fit both the student's individual needs and character, as well as the overall social life of the community.

Much of the development of EL theory in the past 30 years has gained impetus and direction by the work of David A. Kolb. Since his widely cited synthesis of EL theory, *Experiential Learning: Experience as the Source of Learning and Development*, was published in 1983 (and which is in its second edition as of this writing), many publications, journal articles, and research studies have explored the explanatory power and usefulness of the theory in various disciplines and professional fields. Kolb not only synthesizes and updates the work of Dewey and other thinkers, but also draws from wide-ranging fields, such as educational psychology, philosophy, physiology, and leadership/management, in developing the structure of what he calls Experiential Learning Theory (ELT). In 1980, Kolb founded a nonprofit organization to advance EL research and practice. This organization now maintains a very extensive online bibliography of the ELT literature (Kolb and Kolb, 2015); interested readers may find up-to-date and relevant resources there.

Kolb is most well-known for creating a model of the learning process, based on the ideas of the "learning cycle" and "learning styles." As mentioned above, the learning cycle describes a transformational process, one which encompasses four main areas of interaction between the learner, his or her skills and abilities, and the subject at hand: concrete experience, reflective observation, abstract conceptualization, and active experimentation. Kolb's theory also posits the idea of "learning styles," which are inclinations and preferences that direct the learner's approaches to subject material and knowledge generation. The four learning styles and the type of knowledge they generate are termed Diverger, Assimilator, Converger, and Accommodator, and each one is based on the activity of one of the four areas of the learning cycle. Overall, Kolb argues that when one is aware of one's preferred mode of learning, she can then also branch out into the other learning styles, all in the service of richer, more authentic learning (Kolb, 2014).

EL, as developed by Dewey, Kolb, and others, offers both a coherent theory and a collection of tested, practical methods, which educators and library professionals can use to energize student learning. These powerful pedagogies have been successfully applied in a wide variety of disciplines—business and management, law, science and engineering, library science, and a host of others. Practicums, internships, service learning, and active and hands-on learning strategies are now more than ever integrated into teaching and learning, touching the lives of many students. The literature on EL in general is quite large—Kolb's online bibliography alone lists nearly 4000 references within its 589 pages! (Kolb and Kolb, 2015).

If one accepts that EL is now a more prominent feature of the landscape of higher education, one may well ask—are academic and research libraries really becoming more experiential places? Is there such a thing as an "experiential library"? While a growing body of the LIS literature has been devoted to exploring EL in the context of preparing students in graduate LIS programs, much less has been written about academic and research library support for EL of college students in general. Understandably, much of what has been written on this aspect of the topic has focused on integrating experiential methods into information literacy (IL) instruction; for representative examples, see articles by Bodi (1990) and Riddle (2003). Other authors, such as York et al. (2010), have examined the integration of EL into library services, through partnerships with students that also help the library achieve its own goals. Interestingly enough, a recent bibliography on EL and academic libraries by contributors Elizabeth Sanders and Angela Balius (2015) reflects the growing interest in this topic; readers would be wise to consult their bibliography for current EL applications in academic libraries. By and large, the literature reflects that libraries are starting to support this important endeavor—but more needs to be done. If the growth of innovative, experience-based library programs and services over the last several years is any indication, academic and research libraries have indeed taken up the call to innovate, to become more responsive to student and institutional needs. The time seems ripe, then, for both an overview and in-depth look at what is being done to support, nurture, and grow the experiential library.

PURPOSE AND SCOPE OF THIS BOOK

At a time when EL in academic and research libraries is on the rise, a work such as this will hopefully serve multiple purposes. As mentioned above, the application of EL theories and methods into library work has already been reported in the LIS literature. As a contribution to this stream of research, the book will hopefully serve as both an update and a complement to the valuable articles and studies which have already appeared. One of the main purposes for the book is to serve as a "one-stop shop" of theoretical and research-based information, case studies, and hard-won practical knowledge, from libraries using the EL approach. It will range over the landscape of current EL applications in libraries, and will point out places where library professionals can leverage their skills to nourish innovative services, collections, and programs. The information contained in the book should be useful to students in LIS programs wanting a survey of this emerging topic, as well as to beginning and experienced library professionals; library-related academic and professional programs could also be well-served by the book, as a course textbook or selection of readings.

It is also hoped that this work may open up potential synergies between the LIS and experiential education disciplines. For example, when library work or IL is viewed through an EL lens, or when EL programs integrate concepts and methods from library science, both fields may end up benefiting in new, unexpected ways. Viewed in this light, the book may serve as a springboard for cross-disciplinary exploration of questions, research, and methodological approaches. Those working in libraries will find here much that is relevant to current discussions and debates surrounding relevance, IL, and libraries' support of lifelong learning and student achievement. On the other hand, it is also hoped that this work may appeal to those working on the front lines of experiential education, or those who may be looking to expand their knowledge of experiential applications in nonclassroom settings.

As a concept and methodology, this book will cover EL as it is currently being applied in academic and research libraries, though there is some cross-over into other types of libraries—most notably public, elementary, and secondary school libraries. Academic libraries from a variety of institutions are represented in these pages, from a large Carnegie I research institution, mid-sized universities and colleges, to community colleges, as well as collaborations between academic, public, and school libraries. The chapters—ranging from exciting student-driven course exhibits (see chapter: Building Knowledge Together: Interactive Course Exhibits in the Academic Library), to collaborative experiential programming such as the "Human Library" (see chapter: The New Hampshire Human Library Project: Breaking Barriers and Building Bridges by Engaging Communities of Learners)—provide practical and lively overviews of their slice of the EL "pie." No matter at what level, the book's chapters will appeal to library professionals who are interested in learning ways to diversify their service offerings and collections, or who desire to connect with their primary clientele in new ways. As the coming chapters will illustrate, libraries have implemented EL in a myriad of ways, which is helping to transform libraries into more experiential institutions.

CHAPTER OVERVIEW

The first section of the book, "New Paths for Information Literacy Instruction," focuses on the ties between EL and IL instruction. Judith Mavodza begins by highlighting EL theory as it applies to IL integration into the curriculum of Zayed University (United Arab Emirates). In doing so, she shows how EL can inform curriculum design and pedagogical strategies at the local level, as well as how it can be enacted more broadly. Next, Corinne Laverty presents a case study of an Education library that redesigned its instruction program around inquiry-based projects that have practical, immediate application in the classroom. This chapter serves as a clarion call for librarians to partner with discipline-based faculty to design meaningful learning experiences, ones which encourage both self-directed and collaborative inquiry. Amy Barlow's chapter on object-based learning explores how this emerging pedagogy can infuse new life into IL instruction, where subject librarians can leverage their deep knowledge and skills with one-of-a-kind collections for increased student engagement. In "Taking the Class out of the Classroom: Libraries, Literacy, and Service Learning", Jayne Blodgett illuminates the impacts service learning has on students' learning of IL, and shows how this pedagogy can be used to improve student engagement in library-based First Year Seminar courses. Next, Elizabeth Sanders, Angela Balius, and Stephen Sanders tackle the implementation of a "flipped" classroom model in credit-based IL courses for real-world learning, and will share lessons from their experience of "training student drivers" in the library instruction classroom. To round off the first section of the book, Karen Viars, Mary Ann Cullen, and Amy Stalker explore the subject of "authentic assessment" of student learning through technology-rich, interactive, and ultimately better-assessed IL instruction.

In the second section of the book, "Programs, Collections, Spaces, Staff Development and Training", Christopher Anderson and Cassie Brand discuss bringing special, archival, and rare collections "out of the vault" and into students' hands and their scholarship. They also focus on ways to bring more impactful learning to their student employees, and provide advice on ways to extend the value of sometimes-overlooked archival collections. In a piece on their US Institute of Museum and Library Services-funded Center for Games & Learning, Lauren Hays and Mark Hayse "get their game on," as they share successes and failures in collecting, promoting, and advocating for the use of tabletop games as a means to enhance students' 21st Century Skills. In "Building Knowledge Together: Interactive Course Exhibits in the Academic Library," Scott Fralin, Brian Mathews, and Lauren Pressley show how libraries can partner with discipline-based faculty to transform and reinvigorate existing library spaces, through museum-like exhibits created by student scholars in their courses. Next, Emy Nelson Decker and Jennifer Townes detail an exciting workplace learning initiative they've termed "vertically integrated library instruction," which harnesses the power of both formal and informal learning to spread the wealth of staff knowledge. They'll also share tips on how to replicate the program in any size of library. To round out this section, readers will learn from Hilary Bussell and Jessica Hagman, two librarians on the front lines of incorporating EL into student training programs. Through problem-based learning and reflective portfolios, they are bringing a renewed emphasis on *learning* to these programs.

In the book's final section on "Innovation and Multilibrary Collaborations," Christy Groves and Ashley Shealy ask the questions: How does a library sustain and grow its experiential initiatives? Can they be built to provide students with authentic work and engaging learning experiences, while at the same time benefit the library? They present lessons-learned on innovating their library through intensive EL collaborations. Next, Corey Seeman and Sally Ziph focus on the intersection of EL and library services, through graduate student internship support in their Business school library. They make the case that libraries can provide responsive and nimble support to students making their way in the world. Carolyn Gamtso, Melissa Mannon, and Sandy Whipple then explore the first-ever "Human Library" event in New Hampshire, describing the unique synergies that can happen when academic, public, and school libraries band together to provide learning opportunities for students and the community at large. In the book's concluding chapter, "An Experiential Librarian's Creed," Pete McDonnell summarizes the key themes of the book and provokes thoughts on the future of EL in libraries, through the lens of the editor's journey as an "experiential librarian."

REFERENCES

Bodi, S., 1990. Teaching effectiveness and bibliographic instruction: the relevance of learning styles. Coll. Res. Libr. 51 (2), 113–119, <http://crl.acrl.org/content/51/2/113.full.pdf+html> (accessed 20.11.15).

Dewey, J., 1938. Experience and Education. Macmillan, New York, NY.

Dewey, J., 1897. My Pedagogic Creed. E. L. Kellogg & Co, New York, NY.

Kolb, D.A., 2014. Experiential Learning: Experience as the Source of Learning and Development, second ed. Pearson Education Ltd, Upper Saddle River, NJ.

Kolb, A., Kolb, D.A., 2015. Experiential Learning Theory Bibliography, Vol. 1–4 (1971–2014). Experience Based Learning Systems, Inc. Website. <http://learningfromexperience.com/lfe_research_lib_doc_type/bibliography/> (accessed 20.11.15).

Lewis, D.W., 2007. A strategy for academic libraries in the first quarter of the 21st century. Coll. Res. Libr. 68 (5), 418–434, <http://crl.acrl.org/content/68/5/418.full.pdf+html> (accessed 20.11.15).

Riddle, J.S., 2003. Where's the library in service learning? Models for engaged library instruction. J. Acad. Libr. 29 (2), 71–81.

Sanders, E.A., Balius, A., 2015. Experiential learning and academic libraries: an annotated bibliography. Codex J. La. Chap. ACRL 3 (3), 49–74, <http://journal.acrlla.org/index.php/codex/article/view/110> (accessed 20.11.15).

Stamatoplos, A., 2009. The role of academic libraries in mentored undergraduate research: a model of engagement in the academic community. Coll. Res. Libr. 70 (3), 235–249, <http://crl.acrl.org/content/70/3/235.full.pdf+html> (accessed 20.11.15).

York, A., Groves, C., Black, W., 2010. Enriching the academic experience: the library and experiential learning. Collab. Libr. 2 (4), 193–203.

ACKNOWLEDGMENT

Heartfelt thanks goes out to:

Keith, for being a mentor and a friend,

Craig at CAIRNS in Martin, South Dakota, for a beautiful place to reflect, read, and write,

My parents and all my family, for their continued (and continual) support,

Mary, Sam, and Franny, for understanding.

PART I

The Experiential Library: New Paths for Information Literacy Instruction

CHAPTER 1

Integrating Experiential Learning Into Information Literacy Curriculum

J. Mavodza
Zayed University, Abu Dhabi, United Arab Emirates

The theoretical foundations of a discipline are the basis around which research and development of the discipline are focused for generating ideas (Bawden, 2008). This chapter sets out to understand the integration and relevance of the experiential learning (EL) theory to information literacy (IL) instruction in general, and in the context of a specific environment in particular, Zayed University (ZU) (Abu Dhabi, United Arab Emirates). Moving out again from that specific context, it is hoped that what we have learned here at ZU can be applied generally to academic libraries as a whole.

Using theory, rather than personal opinion or common sense, is based on the fact that it employs objective knowledge, a map that is not dictated by an individual person's approach to experience (Polanyi, 1962). Mitchell and Jolley (2007) specify the benefits of using theory, as opposed to the use of common sense, in doing research:

> theory tends to be more consistent than common sense..., usually doesn't contradict itself..., tends to be more consistent with existing facts than common facts..., is not restricted to making commonsense or intuitively obvious predictions..., summarizes and organizes a great deal of information..., focuses research..., is broad in scope...can be applied to a wide range of situations, researchers can generate a wide variety of studies from a single theory...[and] explains facts with only a few core ideas.

The Free Dictionary online (2015) defines a theory as "an organized system of accepted knowledge that applies in a variety of circumstances to a specific set of phenomena; a belief that can guide behavior." This chapter directs this discussion to academic activities at ZU that revolve around the EL theory, service learning, and how those are integrated in IL instruction.

1.1 KOLB'S THEORY OF EL

EL offers the foundation for an approach to education and learning as a lifelong process that is based on intellectual traditions of social psychology, philosophy, and cognitive psychology. Kolb (1984) developed the theory of EL based on reviewing the work of education theorists Dewey (1938), Piaget (1954), and Lewin (1957). As a result, the theory has elements of these philosophers' thinking, but extends and modifies their ideas into a theory of learning. Some aspects of EL can be adapted directly for use in the classroom, especially in the area of instructional design based on cognitive development. It pursues a framework for examining and strengthening the critical linkages among education, work, and personal development. It is a system of competencies for describing job demands and corresponding educational objectives, and emphasizes the interdependence that can be developed between the classroom and the "real world" with EL methods (Kolb, 1984, p. 4; Lewis and Williams, 1994, p. 5).

From Dewey (1938), Kolb (1984) was most interested in his publication *Experience and Education*, where there was a strong emphasis on the concept of experience and feedback in education. Kolb regards some of the interpretations in higher education of Dewey's theories on education with caution, but emphasizes the validity of experience as a method for learning. Commenting on Dewey's work, Kolb (1984, p. 5) mentions that "the challenges his approaches were developed to meet, those of coping with change and lifelong learning, have increased even more dramatically."

Kolb (1984) highlights Lewin's work in the development of a four-stage learning cycle made up of the formations of abstract concepts and generalizations, testing the concepts, concrete experience, and observations and reflections. Lewin (1957) was involved in experimental work with organizations and training situations which led to his belief that the most effective learning takes place where there is interactive tesion and conflict between immediate, concrete experience and analytic detachment. This happened by bringing together "here-and-now concrete experience to validate and test abstract concepts" (Kolb, 1984, p. 21). According to Lewin (1957), feedback processes provide the basis for evaluating the viability of a process.

Piaget (1954) focused his attention on the nature of adult thought and how it develops. His interest on the stages of development led him to the theory that intelligence was directly linked to experience and concept, reflection, and action. "Stated most simply, Piaget's theory describes how intelligence is shaped by experience. Intelligence is not an innate internal characteristic of the individual but arises as a product of the interaction between the person and his or her environment" (Kolb, 1984, p. 12). Piaget's research led to his theories of stages of cognitive development that ended with adolescence, but subsequent researchers have extended the idea into adult learning for lifelong development. This contributes to Kolb's ideas about EL in higher education.

From research and studying preceding education theorists, Kolb (1984) refers to a theory of double-knowledge where there is a distinction between apprehension and comprehension. Parallels can be seen with Bruner's (1985, 1990) two modes of thinking. "Experiential learning is based on a dual-knowledge theory: the empiricists' concrete experience, grasping reality by the process of direct apprehension, and the rationalists' abstract conceptualization, grasping reality via the mediating process of abstract conceptualization" (Kolb, 1984, p. 101). Kolb places knowledge gained through apprehension on an equal level as knowledge gained through comprehension. According to Kolb, who is expressing Kant's analysis of the relation between apprehension and comprehension:

> Apprehensions are the source of validation for comprehensions ("thoughts without content are empty"), and comprehensions are the source of guidance in the selection of apprehensions ("intuitions without concepts are blind")
> **Kolb (1984, p. 106).**

From an interpretation of the Kantian perspective, Kolb suggests four different forms of knowledge illustrated in Table 1.1, that is, divergent, assimilative, convergent, and accommodative. Firstly, experience grasped through apprehension and transformed through intention results in divergent knowledge. Secondly, experience grasped through comprehension and transformed through intention results in assimilative knowledge.

Table 1.1 Kolb's forms of knowledge

Forms of knowledge	Mode of grasping knowledge	Result
Apprehension	Intention	Divergent knowledge
Comprehension	Intention	Assimilative knowledge
Comprehension	Extension	Convergent knowledge
Apprehension	Extension	Accommodative knowledge

Thirdly, when experience is grasped through comprehension and transformed through extension, the result is convergent knowledge. And finally, when experience is grasped by apprehension and transformed by extension, accommodative knowledge is the result.

Kolb reiterates that learning requires both a grasp and a representation of experience, as well as some transformation of that representation. Figurative grasp alone or operative transformation alone are not sufficient. Thus, it is this interactive process that produces learning. At various iterations, the student is engaged in Kolb's EL cycle, depending on the level and intensity of the lesson, as well as the amount of informational connections to the content of the class curriculum.

1.2 IL CURRICULUM AND EL AT ZAYED UNIVERSITY

For student success, ZU has identified learning outcomes known as Zayed University Learning Outcomes (ZULOs). These include critical thinking and quantitative reasoning, global awareness, IL, English and Arabic language, leadership, and technological literacy. The student-based approach practiced at ZU depends on the ability of the student to find and evaluate information (classic IL skills) and deduce the most reasonable conclusions, that is, critical thinking. Actually, none of the ZULOs is independent of the others. This is especially important where the academic background of most students at ZU varies from public and private schools in the United Arab Emirates (UAE). According to the results of research by McKinnon et al. (2013):

> Public schools in this study generally espouse a more traditional style of teaching (more teacher directed, lecture based and whole-class instruction) while private schools tend to use more contemporary methods (more student-centered, inquiry based, small group and discussion based).

Much care has therefore to be taken to create lessons that are inclusive of every student's academic background. When this is translated into implications on library use and IL skills instruction, Martin (2013) mentions that the circumstances of the UAE, while unique in many ways, are reflective of many countries where there has not been a strong history of library services nor indeed a culture of reading, and where there is a paucity of understanding of the value of libraries and library professionals. That makes it important to integrate IL seamlessly with the rest of the learning process. This is what Kolb (1984, p. 198) refers to as the "perceptually complex learning environment" that entails defining and understanding concepts, collecting relevant information, and being able to do actual research on an assigned topic.

Successful classes are a result of a collaborative effort to develop an IL project that results in integration of IL in student education. At ZU, collaboration of librarians and academic advisers has engendered course-integrated IL instruction, workshops for faculty on how to effectively integrate IL in course design, and the development of an IL session for the Academic Bridge Program, Colloquy 120, 140, and 150 (see Fig. 1.1). Colloquy 120 is specifically tailored to contribute towards the requirements of a community service project, and the IL part is integrated as the student searches for, uses, and cites information resources for that assignment. This is a service learning model intended to enhance the relevance of lessons learned to real-life situations as an experiential teaching

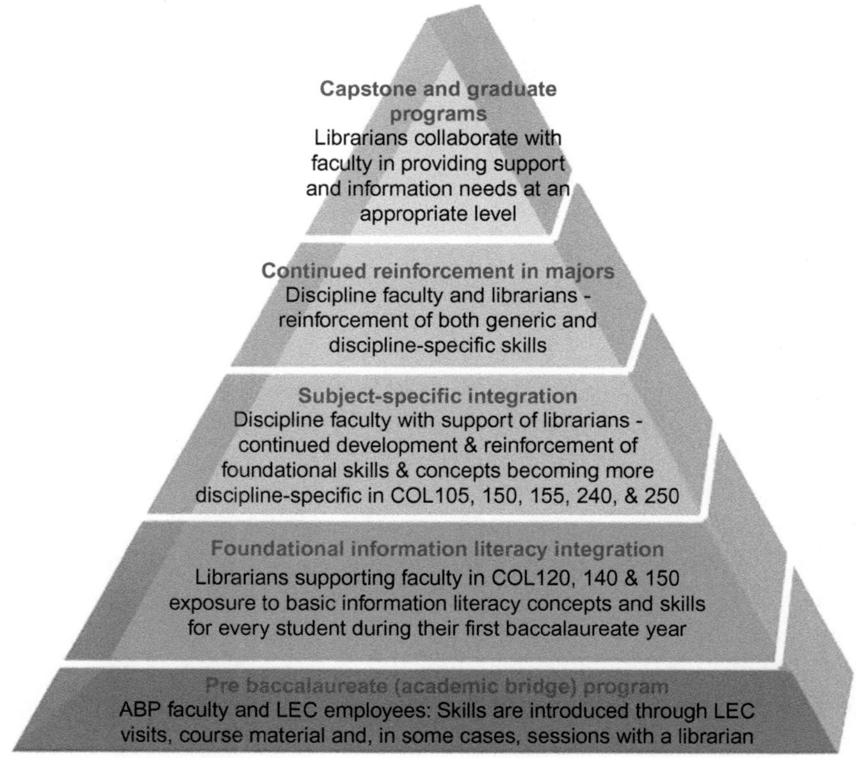

Capstone and graduate programs
Librarians collaborate with faculty in providing support and information needs at an appropriate level

Continued reinforcement in majors
Discipline faculty and librarians - reinforcement of both generic and discipline-specific skills

Subject-specific integration
Discipline faculty with support of librarians - continued development & reinforcement of foundational skills & concepts becoming more discipline-specific in COL105, 150, 155, 240, & 250

Foundational information literacy integration
Librarians supporting faculty in COL120, 140 & 150 exposure to basic information literacy concepts and skills for every student during their first baccalaureate year

Pre baccalaureate (academic bridge) program
ABP faculty and LEC employees: Skills are introduced through LEC visits, course material and, in some cases, sessions with a librarian

Figure 1.1 Zayed University IL curriculum integration. *Zayed University IL Library Guide at http://zu.libguides.com/il.*

method. Kolb (1984, p. 197) refers to this as an affective environment, whereby learning happens by experiencing concrete events (such as realizing what it is like to be a professional), while testing the application of ideas discussed in the classroom.

EL happens in a social context, because it is based on experience. It is the process that links education, work, and personal development (Kolb, 1984, p. 4). Experience is expressed both consciously and subconsciously. If a student is given the chance to use personal experience or service experience in the context of actual learning, a door may be opened for deeper and transformative learning to occur. One of the most practical ways for achieving that is through internships, apprenticeships, and community-based projects. This is what Lewis and Williams (1994, p. 7) refer to as "field-based experiential learning." *High-Impact Educational Practices: A Brief Overview* (Zayed University, 2015a), a document from the ZU website, mentions that field-based EL with community partners is an instructional strategy—and often a required part of the course. Cumulating service learning experiences provide EL opportunities. This approach is intended for students to be engaged with the community and identify specific problems that they can take appropriate responsibility for and help alleviate or solve. "These programs model the idea that giving something back to the community is an important college outcome, and that working with community partners is good preparation for citizenship, work, and life" (Zayed University, 2015a). The document also mentions workplace internships as another form of EL. The ZU library has occasionally hosted some students involved in internship programs.

The goal of a service learning approach is to help guide students in evaluating their role and actions vis-à-vis the project(s), as well as to build a knowledge base through experiencing situations and reading about the issues at hand. It is even more important at ZU, where most of the students may never have been in the employment sector, and so lack previous working experience. But, "when the learner is intent on meaningful learning/wants to understand the material for herself" (Moon, 2004, p. 87), then reflective learning takes place. From an experiential perspective, community-based learning provides a concrete experience that, paired with critical synthesis of how the service relates to key course ideas, is aimed at stimulating student conceptual growth and learning. As suggested by Kolb (1984), this is a move away from purely abstract concepts and into the realm of reflective observation and experimentation by students in real-life situations.

Librarians at ZU apply the ACRL Information Literacy Competency Standards for Higher Education (2000). These standards guide the teaching of IL, and specify the importance of tailoring to suit the requirements of institutional goals and mission. ZU is accredited by the US Middle States Commission on Higher Education (MSCHE), whose expectations include following the guidelines set in the ACRL Standards. Ordinarily, accreditation is based on the assumption that all students had an opportunity to use the *Big6* model (task definition, information-seeking strategies, location and access, use of information, synthesis, and evaluation) (Story-Huffman, 2014) in their K-12 schooling. Because that is not always necessarily the case in the UAE, the *Big6* becomes a framework within which to deliver content, using ACRL guidelines. It helps in the process of content development. For example, topics that are covered in the IL class focus on Task Definition-*Big6 #1*. The librarian and professor develop relevant class activities (such as brainstorming) to help identify topics and their related concepts. At this stage, clarification of terms is also essential, as this is an English as a Second Language (ESL) context.

Examples of topics covered in the service learning process include environmental issues such as pollution, recycling, and overuse of water/electricity; health-related matters such as diabetes, obesity, thalassemia, cancer; people with special needs such as those with autism, Down syndrome, physical disabilities; also, topics such as women's rights, addiction, human trafficking, loss of culture and heritage, child welfare, and so on. These topics are targeted for their direct interest to the UAE population, and usually the students can relate to some of them directly. As such, what social and personal interest they provoke makes the topics relevant to their academic lives. That forms the basis for each student's choice of service learning area.

Students, with guidance from their instructors/professors, research and select organizations that they can potentially visit for a service experience. For example, one who is interested in waste recycling could be enlightened by visiting the Centre for Waste Management, to see what is involved in the technology. However, before proceeding, the student has to find reliable library resources about recycling; the student has to also find sources about the topic from the Centre's website. Already, that means the student has used a reference source to understand the meaning of the topic, and then has consulted a website for more information. At each stage, the student is being encouraged to use different types of reliable information sources. As they search, the librarian and the professor jointly give guidance on how and where to search, how to correctly give credit to originators of ideas and information, and how to properly format papers in the preferred style at ZU. It is at this stage that, in addition to the use of library databases, effective use of additional sources such as Google (e.g., Google Scholar) are introduced. That is because trying to totally disengage students from the Google phenomenon is pointless, when they can get some of what they need through it. In fact, when the individual's Google Scholar account settings are updated to recognize the library as a resource, the students realize that some of the required full-text articles are actually accessible through their library.

The only challenge may be that the number of hours allocated to the service learning experience may not necessarily be sufficient, since individual student learning styles also have an impact. This is one of the reasons that an activity such as *Action 2015 Service Learning Week* (Zayed University, 2015b), a cocurricular project based on the ZU curriculum, raised funds to assist refugees in two Middle Eastern countries. Such an activity encourages in many students a curiosity about geography, resulting in enhanced general knowledge, as well as a desire to be involved in the wider world. According to Kolb (1984, p. 197), this is an environment where actions have real consequences, and the combination of the learner's initiative and developing knowledge base, helps to alleviate a real-life problem.

As of 2015, the new ACRL *Framework for Information Literacy for Higher Education* has been introduced as a way of refocusing IL to work with discipline *Threshold Concepts*, boosting the ACRL Standards. At ZU, the *Framework* and many of its evolving implications are still a topic for study by librarians. However, it "redefines the boundaries of what librarians teach and how they conceptualize the study of information within the curricula of higher education institutions" (ACRL, 2015). Its provisions do not interfere with the IL program in place at ZU, especially as it also now redefines IL to include "the reflective discovery of information" for student success (ACRL, 2015). The fact that it suggests helping students to view themselves as information producers supports the service learning agenda, as students can identify with the products of their efforts. In reference to reflective thinking in an academic environment, Moon (2004, p. 83) points out that "evidence of learning or change of behavior may be expected to result from the process of reflection." At ZU, this evidence is usually expressed when the student writes about his or her service learning project, and his or her ability to find and use information effectively is usually reflected in the quality of the completed assignment. Actually, according to the ACRL (2012) website, the use of EL activities is considered a best practice in IL instruction.

In ZU's current model, each discipline on campus has an IL component which is one of the ZULOs. For example, the Public Health department would require its students to take a class that highlights IL concepts using relevant topics. During this time students study location and access, *Big6 Stage 3*, and the librarian presents the various Public Health databases and journal titles that are accessible through the library. For this approach to work, the professor and librarian identify specific assignments and activities that match the learning objectives for both the discipline and the ACRL Standards, again tied together through the use of *The Big6*.

Team-teaching, with both the professor and librarian delivering content, helps the students realize that library instruction is relevant to their coursework. Librarians and professors use an "Information Literacy Matrix" to make sure students are learning requisite IL skills at the appropriate level. Instructors and librarians have the common goal of enabling student learning, and IL is a skill that is intended to serve students beyond graduation. In fact, ACRL clearly indicates that the development of IL skills extends "beyond formal classroom settings" and can happen on the job. As illustrated in Fig. 1.1, successful integration is a continuous refinement of goals, outcomes, and learning opportunities for the professor, the librarian, and the student.

The university also integrates IL into the curriculum by requiring a session in research methods for students in their major. At this point, the ZULOs will have developed into disciplinary Major Learning Outcomes (MALOs). This is provided by a liaison librarian, who identifies the curriculum's goals, content, and skills, and then ties them to standards-based outcomes identified in the ACRL Standards. When a unit, such as the College of Education, engages student teachers in practicum experiences, the librarian responsible is completely immersed in making sure the requisite library resources and support are available. This approach is expressed by Becker (2009) as the best suited for teaching Millennials, and it requires an IL librarian who understands the programs that are underway and who can thus support the students effectively.

In addition, a ZU "Learning Assessment Map" has been created to help all educators to focus on the ZULO's goal, using experiential and service learning. Such an approach has been discussed by Lewis and

Williams (1994, p. 9) as essential in harnessing experience for improved student learning. Furthermore, as librarians help students get resources relevant for their projects, they are also learning and reflecting on student progress and how to support them better. This is reinforced by Brookfield (1995, 2007), who believes that when teachers model reflective teaching methods, they are likely to have motivated, critically reflective students. However, this in turn requires open-mindedness, receptiveness to constructive criticism, and a healthy dose of self-confidence to make decisions and to voice opinions.

1.3 REVISITING THE APPLICATION OF EL THEORY

EL theory, as with many other theories, is subject to interpretation, resulting in possible misunderstanding of the theory. Kolb (2015a), however, has developed a website, Experience Based Learning Systems, Inc. (http://learningfromexperience.com/), which can serve to unbundle the meaning of the theory and provide guidelines on its effective use.

While Kolb (1984) admits that EL theory is a result of investigating perceptions based on self-rating by the participants, the fact that it successfully puts together several perspectives (e.g., Dewey, 1938; Piaget, 1954; Lewin, 1957) cannot be dismissed as insignificant. This is particularly relevant to the current fast-changing information and technology environment, where instructional design is being tailored to suit student needs and preferences. The results of research at ZU by Rahal and Palfreyman (2009, pp. 13—14) revealed that the favorite learning style of some of the students studied, other than auditory, was visual word and visual picture styles (lecturing with graphic support). Additionally, this study revealed learning-by-talking and visual-word mode (reading) to be minority pursuits. The research confirms the importance of student educational style, and academic background—highlighting the importance of instructional design that is sensitive to a variety of learning styles and student experiences. In the case of ZU, it is noteworthy that the learning styles of students may not necessarily be identical to those originally studied by Kolb. However, the Learning Style Inventory (LSI), now Version 4 (Kolb, 2015b), is inclusive of a broader range of styles. Additionally, the nature of EL theory is that it can be applied to a wide range of situations. While there is no "perfect theory," the ability to critique Kolb's ideas may result in more suitable varieties of EL theory.

1.4 CONCLUDING THOUGHTS

The program at ZU demonstrates that it is possible to tailor the ACRL IL Standards to suit institutional requirements regardless of geographical location, just as implied in the text of the Standards. IL can be incorporated into the initial stages of a service learning assignment that is driven by the EL model, as is happening at the ZU Colloquy stages. Given varying student learning styles, Kolb's experiential theory can be viewed as a suitable approach for institutions that are increasingly called on to match student success with postgraduation outcomes. In the case of ZU, the limited work experience that many students have at the time of enrolling into university has made inroads for the use of EL and service learning as a foundation for future growth. The fact that a student may never have worked formally does not necessarily mean that they do not have life experiences which can be harnessed for relevance to real-life work situations.

The student-centered education described above requires educators to be more highly involved with how learning takes place, including accommodating different learning styles of students, modeling, monitoring good academic behavior, and conducting assessment. The implication for campus administrators is that the process works best with a small student—instructor ratio, that is, smaller class sizes, as well as the requisite library resource base. In addition, the continuously evolving teaching and learning environment requires faculty to be actively involved with research and publishing. That also demands faculty time away from teaching activities, and there are other kinds of support that faculty can benefit from, for example, financial support, promotion, and other types of recognition. In the end, however, it is the match between student experiences and actual learning which should enhance lifelong learning and work readiness at the point of graduation.

REFERENCES

Association of College and Research Libraries, 2012. Characteristics of programs of information literacy that illustrate best practices: a guideline. <http://www.ala.org/acrl/standards/characteristics> (accessed 29.10.15.).

Association of College and Research Libraries, 2015. Framework for Information Literacy for Higher Education [Homepage of ALA]. <http://www.ala.org/acrl/standards/ilframework> (accessed 15.06.15.).

Bawden, D., 2008. Smoother pebbles and the shoulders of giants: the developing foundations of information science. J. Inf. Sci. 34 (4), 415—426.

Becker, C.H., 2009. Student values and research: are millennials really changing the future of reference and research? J. Libr. Adm. 49 (4), 341–364.

Brookfield, S.D., 1995. Becoming a Critically Reflective Teacher. Jossey Bass, San Francisco, CA.

Brookfield, S.D., 2007. Becoming a critically reflective teacher. <http://www.stephenbrookfield.com/Dr._Stephen_D._Brookfield/Workshop_Materials_files/BCRT_Wkshp_Pkt.pdf> (accessed 07.10.15.).

Bruner, J., 1985. Vygotsky: a historical and conceptual perspective. In: Wertsch, J.V. (Ed.), Culture, Communication and Cognition: Vygotskian Perspectives. Cambridge University Press, Cambridge, pp. 21–33.

Bruner, J., 1990. Acts of Meaning. Harvard University Press, London.

Dewey, J., 1938. Experience and Education. Collier-MacMillan Canada Ltd., Toronto.

Free Dictionary, 2015. Theory. <http://www.thefreedictionary.com/theory> (accessed 16.12.15.).

Kolb, D.A., 1984. Experiential Learning: Experience as the Source of Learning and Development. Prentice Hall, Englewood Cliffs, NJ.

Kolb, D.A., 2015a. Experience-based learning systems. <http://learningfromexperience.com/> (accessed 12.08.15.).

Kolb, D.A., 2015b. Learning style inventory. <http://learningfromexperience.com/tools/kolb-learning-style-inventory-lsi/> (accessed 12.08.15.).

Lewin, K., 1957. Action research and minority problems. In: Lewin, G.W., Allport, G. (Eds.), Resolving Social Conflicts. Selected Papers on Groups Dynamics. Harper & Brothers, New York, NY, pp. 201–216.

Lewis, L.H., Williams, C.J., 1994. Experiential learning: past and present. New Dir. Adult Contin. Educ. 62, 5–16.

Martin, J., 2013. Feasibility study: the development of graduate programs in information management at Zayed University, UAE. <https://drjanetmartin.files.wordpress.com/2013/10/final-report-july-2013.pdf> (accessed 07.06.15.).

McKinnon, M., Barza, L., Moussa-Inaty, J., 2013. Public versus private education in primary science: the case of Abu Dhabi schools. Int. J. Educ. Res. 62, 51–61, <http://dx.doi.org/10.1016/j.ijer.2013.06.007> (accessed 07.01.15.).

Mitchell, M.L., Jolley, J.M., 2007. Advantages of using theory to generate ideas. In: Research Design Explained. <http://www.jolley-mitchell.com/Appendix/Theory_Appendix/Using_Theory.htm> (accessed 07.01.15.).

Moon, J., 2004. A Handbook of Reflective and Experiential Learning. RoutledgeFalmer, London.

Piaget, J., 1954. The Construction of Reality in the Child. Basic Books, New York, NY.

Polanyi, M., 1962. Personal Knowledge: Towards a Post-Critical Philosophy. University of Chicago Press, Chicago.

Rahal, T., Palfreyman, D., 2009. Assessing learning styles of students at Zayed University. Learn. Teach. Higher Educ. Gulf Perspect. 6 (2), 1–32.

Story-Huffman, R., 2014. Big6 in higher education: considering the ACRL standards in a Big6 context. <http://big6.com/pages/lessons/articles/big6-in-higher-education-considering-the-acrl-standards-in-a-big6-context.php> (accessed 31.10.15.).

Zayed University, 2015a. High-impact educational practices: a brief overview. <http://www.zu.ac.ae/main/en/_assessment_resource/Learning_Assessment/index.aspx> (accessed 12.08.15.).

Zayed University, 2015b. Action 2015 service learning week. <http://www.zu.ac.ae/main/en/news/2015/March/action2015.aspx> (accessed 12.08.15.).

CHAPTER 2

Experiential Learning in a Faculty of Education Library

C. Laverty
Queen's University, Kingston, ON, Canada

2.1 EXPERIENTIAL LEARNING TRENDS IN HIGHER EDUCATION

There is a significant shift in teaching and learning practices within higher education as a result of new education directions set by governing bodies. Institutions are encouraged to differentiate themselves based on each school's unique qualities and to revolutionize their approaches to teaching and learning environments, including the expansion of experiential education (Council of Ontario Universities, 2012, 2014). In a discussion of high-impact educational practices, Kuh (2008) identifies service and community learning as an instructional strategy that gives students direct experience with curriculum-specific issues alongside problems in a community. Many universities have introduced experiential learning (EL), even though they are grappling with how to define, develop, and assess it (McGill University, 2014; O'Toole, 2007; Ryerson University, 2012).

The Association of Experiential Education (n.d.) defines EL as "… a philosophy that informs many methodologies in which educators purposefully engage with learners in direct experience and focused reflection in order to increase knowledge, develop skills, clarify values, and develop people's capacity to contribute to their communities." Although EL is traditionally associated with "learning by doing," in formal settings such as cooperative placements, field trips, internships, study abroad, and service learning, the idea of what constitutes "experience" is expanding to encompass less formal learning scenarios.

Definitions of EL are in flux, resulting in various approaches to integrating this type of learning within the curriculum (Wurdinger and Carlson, 2010). Some universities hold broad conceptions of experiential education such as "the strategic, active engagement of students in opportunities to learn through doing, and reflection on those activities, which empowers them to apply their theoretical knowledge to practical endeavors in a multitude of settings inside and outside of the classroom" (Simon Fraser University, 2015). Others, especially in the sciences and health sciences, focus on community involvement outside the classroom: "Experiential Education provides opportunities for students to gain academically relevant experience in a community, research, or professional setting. This combination of academic and real world learning helps students to further develop the necessary qualities and skills that will be transferrable to future career paths" (McMaster University, n.d.).

Libraries are also contributing to EL initiatives. Credit-related examples from Queen's University in Ontario include:

- First-year engineering students design projects with the Library as client; learning outcomes include finding, assessing, and citing information.
- Professional students in education identify teaching and learning design problems, and explore and prototype possible technology-enabled solutions.
- Third-year art history students create library collection guides related to their field of interest.
- Senior history students complete a digital humanities, collection curation, and archival research internship, in partnership with Queen's University Archives.
- Inquiry@Queen's is an undergraduate conference enabling students to communicate their research results through presentations, posters, and written publications.

These examples highlight the diversity of disciplinary initiatives at one institution; moreover, they all focus on learning opportunities internal to the university and the library. Although EL may traditionally be associated with active participation within a community service or organization, librarians should not be constrained in developing new interpretations of EL within a library setting. The examples above include new ways of thinking about what constitutes a learning experience in the academic library. Library as client, as a place for collection analysis, inquiry-based learning, research, or as a forum for sharing experiences are all possible.

2.2 THE PATH TO EL IN AN EDUCATION LIBRARY

In Bachelor of Education programs, a teaching practicum can be equated with EL. It provides students with an opportunity to learn by teaching and observing in the classroom, applying theory to practice, and reflecting on teaching skills. The prototype for the library experience described in this chapter was an existing alternative practicum available to all candidates within the program, and generally completed outside the regular elementary or secondary-school classroom. Each placement is linked to the content of a credit-based course within the program such as arts-based education, literacy, study abroad, or teaching exceptional children. Candidates are encouraged to engage in settings such as international schools, community projects, learning associations, and nongovernmental organizations. The practicum runs three consecutive weeks and requires 30 hours of work each week. Other teacher education programs offer alternative placements and these include examples of experiential education (Dillon et al., 2007; Hildenbrand and Shultz, 2015; Maynes et al., 2013). However, despite research that underpins their value—such as a major provincial study citing exemplary school libraries and teacher-librarians as a critical element in the educational outcomes of the school (Klinger et al., 2009)—these programs do not typically involve libraries and librarians.

The idea for EL in the Queen's Education Library was sparked in 2005 when the two education librarians learned, through their work with teacher candidates and curriculum instructors, that there was little mention of school libraries and the role of the teacher-librarian in the program. This information was later confirmed in a formal research study (Lee et al., 2012). In meetings with local school librarians, we also learned that teacher-librarians were generally not involved with teacher candidates during their school placements. This knowledge triggered the idea for a practicum within library settings, where preservice teachers could work alongside librarians to better understand their role in developing inquiry-based learning skills and reading facility. Over the next 7 years, projects were negotiated with 150 individual students. Placements expanded into elementary and secondary school libraries, academic libraries, and learning resource centers.

During the practicum, librarians model how they support student learning, through selection of resources for research and reading, information literacy demonstrations, and designing and assessing inquiry-based assignments. Examples of projects included the creation of curriculum units, resource kits, fiction titles for English language learners within social studies, and Webquests. For students who choose to complete their practicum within the Education Library, the librarians host each project, provide planning assistance and continuous feedback throughout the 3-week period, and give a summative evaluation of each student's project. The work of each project is captured in a final report, curriculum plan, or artifact for use by other teachers and made available in print and/or online in the library catalog.

Over the past 2 years, a new approach to the alternative practicum in the library was adopted as a result of the increasing demand for teachers to have classroom-ready technology skills. Preservice and beginning teachers report being underprepared to use educational technology effectively in the classroom (Koch et al., 2012; Sang et al., 2010; Tondeur et al., 2012). A review of the literature uncovers various impediments to effective teaching in a technology-enhanced environment. Underlying barriers can include lack of technical support, access to equipment, and modeling of Information and Communications Technology (ICT) by tertiary instructors (Martinovic and Zhang, 2012; Hammond et al., 2009; Chai et al., 2014). More critical issues that impact technology use include attitudes towards technology, pedagogical beliefs that technology has a positive impact on learning (Buabeng-Andoh, 2012; Chai et al., 2014; Hammond et al., 2009), and teachers' lack of design thinking regarding technology (Tsai and Chai, 2012). Design thinking can be defined as an "analytic and creative process that engages a person in opportunities to experiment, create and prototype models, gather feedback, and redesign" (Razzouk and Shute, 2012, p. 1). Hammond also describes how a mentoring environment, where teachers and students use ICT together, can raise expectations for technology use and extend awareness through modeling and feedback (Hammond et al., 2009; Lim et al., 2011).

Given this increased focus on learning technology, the Faculty of Education began testing new approaches to integrating technology within the curriculum. Compulsory SmartBoard and iPad workshops were arranged and some curriculum classes incorporated interactive whiteboards, iPads, video production, or individual response systems. Two optional program track courses on Understanding Educational Technology and Educational Technology by Design were also introduced. These new endeavors prompted the Education Library to narrow the focus of its alternative practicum to a team-based experience focused entirely on educational technology. The goal during these 3-week sessions was to identify a specific teaching and learning design problem, explore and prototype possible technology-enabled solutions, and record a description of the design journey. Projects addressed concepts and processes that are hard to teach in a discipline, such as using music notation, developing French language vocabulary, applying algebra to real-life scenarios, or tools to support English language learners and students with exceptionalities. The librarians hosted, organized, and led the experience with support from the faculty instructor for the two educational technology courses. The library served as the place for meetings, presentations, and testing, but students also worked independently. Ten students formed the technology group in 2014 and another 13 participated in 2013.

2.3 EL DESIGN IN THE ACADEMIC LIBRARY

The learning framework for the Education Library practicum aligns well with *heutagogy*, defined as the study of self-determined learning (Hase and Kenyon, 2000). The following principles of heutagogy, outlined by Blaschke (2012) and Hase and Kenyon (2007), provide a good picture of the overall learning experience, and have much in common with EL. Learners determined what they would learn and much of the process by which their learning would take place. Learning involved experimentation and research in a resource-rich environment and was individualized as much as possible, so that areas of interest could be freely explored. Social media in the form of a wiki was used to network learners and provide a platform for self-reflection and feedback. The instructors facilitated the development of learner competencies as well as the learner's capacity to learn. The focus on building knowledge and skills in conjunction with a student's self-efficacy is described by Blaschke (2012) as "double-loop learning," because students are both addressing a problem and reflecting on the problem-solving process and how that impacts their beliefs and actions.

A description of the library experience provides context for how these heutagogic principles unfolded during the practicum. In beginning the new group practicum, the education librarians held an initial meeting with participants to give them an overview of how they would be deeply involved in the design of their own learning experience. After face-to-face introductions, each student created a page in a class wiki and recorded experiences and interests with educational technology. Discussions ensued, facilitated by the librarians and educational technology instructor, around students' experiences with educational technology in the classroom and what they hoped to gain from the practicum. Some

students were expecting formally structured classes and were surprised to take ownership of the outcomes and activities for the practicum. Following group discussions, learning outcomes and associated activities for the 3-week period were collectively determined:
- Apply a design thinking approach (identify a problem—undertake research—generate plans—produce solutions—test solutions) to learn how educational technology can address a teaching/learning challenge.

    Activities: Work through an iterative process of exploration, testing, and posing solutions.
- Evaluate the research literature as it applies to your area of interest.

    Activity: Search education databases for descriptions of how technology has been applied to support learning in specific scenarios.
- Share teaching/learning challenges and steps in your learning process with the group.

    Activity: Record project progress on individual wiki pages and receive feedback via the wiki. Present technologies that are being tested in short tech talks. Meet formally as a group for 2 hours three times a week.
- Communicate findings and design journey broadly.

    Activity: Make projects available in the online university repository so they are accessible to other teachers and present them during a culminating year-end technology fair.

There was a wide range of experience with learning technologies among group members and the open conversations about individual backgrounds and interests set the tone for a collegial learning environment. Some students became aware that they had common interests and many made suggestions about the types of technologies that could be explored. Although the librarians were facilitators, they were also learners within the group, and contributed questions and feedback as members of the whole. One of their key roles was to demonstrate how to search the research literature for examples of how technology could support learning in various classroom scenarios. Follow-up consultations addressed finding resources supporting individual projects for specific grades and subjects.

Working individually or in pairs, students explored new software, modeled it for others, and tested how it could be applied to specific learning problems. Group members viewed technologies from the perspective of the teacher and the student during the testing demonstrations. Taking on different roles proved to be instrumental in helping them conceptualize the place of educational technology in teaching. In order to enable students to apply their new learning to authentic teaching scenarios in the future, it would have been useful to actually test their technology recommendations with students in the classroom. Investigations began with the professional education literature on current practices with various types of technologies. Each project was written up in a final paper using a template designed by the students, and projects were made openly accessible with a Creative Commons license at the Education Library website: http://library.queensu.ca/research/guide/education-inquiry/tech. Projects were presented at a tech fair in the library.

Projects included examination of technologies that support:

Literacy
- Tools to promote reading engagement across different learner populations (e.g., English language learners in middle school, reluctant readers).

English
- Analysis of tools for compiling and annotating sources as part of the resource evaluation process (note-taking, citation management, and annotation tools such as Pearltrees, Awesome Screenshot, and Evernote).

History
- Development of a Popplet incorporating multimedia, primary sources, images, and websites to support a curriculum unit on civil rights.

The Arts
- Tools for innovation and creativity (e.g., Aurasma for augmented reality in a drama class; Educreations for art; virtual simulations for science).

2.4 REFLECTIONS

After hosting this unique practicum opportunity, the librarians reflected on what constitutes good EL practice. Kolb and Kolb remark that "Experiential learning is often misunderstood as a set of tools and techniques to provide learners with experiences from which they can learn. Others have used the term to describe learning that is a mindless recording of experience" (2005, p. 193). In considering how to structure these scenarios, we can draw on Kolb's model of experiential education, which outlines the abilities needed for students to learn effectively through experience. They must engage actively in the experience, reflect on their learning, apply analytical skills to conceptualize the experience, and use problem-solving skills to apply the new learning gained from the experience (Kolb, 1984). The theory of heutagogy is an exciting complement to Kolb's model, and it served as another way to create a learner-centered collaborative environment, where students can engage in research to contextualize, extend, and evaluate their ideas. Essentially the group became a community of practice, defined as "... an inclusive and mutually supportive group of people with a collaborative, reflective, and growth-oriented approach toward investigating and learning more about their practice in order to improve students' learning" (Stoll, 2010, p. 151). The experience met the five criteria for a community of practice as defined by Stoll (2010), in that participants: shared a common sense of purpose; took collective responsibility to create classroom scenarios that would support student engagement; used reflective professional inquiry to seek new knowledge through discussion, problem-solving, observation, and analysis; worked in collaboration to review solutions and provide feedback; and learned through individual and collective knowledge creation.

Upon reflection, we noticed that conversations throughout the practicum and student impressions of the overall experience revealed several best practices:

- Time

    Budget extended and focused time for testing and researching technologies outside regular class hours.

- Research Guidance

    Guide students in how to research the impact of specific technologies on student learning. Most participants will appreciate this as a way to grow their own skills, especially in use of technology in different subject areas and grade levels.

- Learning from Colleagues

    Encourage ongoing feedback and support in person and via class communication from others working on similar teaching and learning challenges. Viewing presentations by colleagues to observe the use of technologies in action can help cement the learning.

- Positive Learning Environment

    Hold regular meetings and "tech talks" in a safe, encouraging, and positive learning environment. Informal yet structured learning scenarios can help keep projects on track.

Furthermore, for librarians interested in designing programs that incorporate EL principles, we offer the following advice based on our experience of the library program.

- Involve students in what they want to learn and how they will learn it.

    Students' work was self-directed and they were required to take initiative, make decisions, and be accountable for the teaching challenges and solutions they explored. In the early stages, it would be useful to discuss EL as a process, rather than as a set of outcomes.

- Use social media and classroom conversations as platforms for sharing ideas and feedback.

    The in-class writing time and regular group meetings for project presentations were appreciated. Longer-scheduled writing periods in the wiki would have been beneficial, however. Round-table discussions revealed curiosity and creativity at play and were facilitated to engage all voices. Also, supportive relationships developed as the process unfolded: each learner to others, to their own level of understanding, and to the external classrooms they were working with in their projects. These meta-levels of engagement (self, peers, community) contributed to an authentic learning environment: students addressed real teaching challenges for real classrooms.

- Show students how to explore the research literature as a foundation for ongoing learning.

    Students benefited from a demonstration where librarians described why they selected specific research starting points and how searches evolve, as they learn more about a topic. This iterative cycle helped students to view research as a learning process in itself, rather than as a finite step at the start of the project.

- Establish a safe and inclusive learning environment.

    Written responses offering suggestions and questions, and private librarian consultations with students, reinforced the development of one-on-one relationships. Regular project meetings gave each member of the group a chance to lead discussions and participate in them as a valued contributor.

- Investigate the principles of heutagogy and communities of practice as a basis for the learning experience.

    Utilizing these theories, with their focus on a positive self-directed and group environment, can help create a successful learning experience.

- Become a learner within the group.

    While the librarians helped to facilitate discussion and support research, they contributed to open dialogue and communication within their learning community.
- Design assessments collaboratively.

    Final projects were prepared in a template that was constructed collaboratively and which included a section for students' advice to other teachers.
- Support the sharing of final projects through open access.

    Students were not expecting to make their work available to others on this scale, but it helped them to view their own work as a valued contribution to the collective learning venture.

Librarians can view EL as a natural platform for inquiry-based learning that connects course curriculum to community issues and initiatives in practice. By having librarians lead this experience within the library, we were able to demonstrate a leadership role, and are now recognized by students as educators in our own right and by other instructors as partners in course programming and support. The experience has given us confidence that the library extends beyond collections and services and integrates well with collaborative learning initiatives.

On reflection, it is useful for an educator's growth to enter a learning situation knowing that she will and should experience uncertainty, because the outcomes of experience cannot be completely predicted. Librarians should see themselves as learners and participate in the serendipitous learning opportunities and challenges that inevitably arise. We should also be aware that we bring our own idea of learning expectations to this work, and that these preconceptions can sometimes inhibit students in making the experience their own. It is important that students take away a personal experience that is memorable and distinct. To achieve this goal, they will have to have wondered and contemplated, engaged in creative thinking, brought new ideas to life, and ultimately interpreted something anew. To accomplish all this, a learning environment that is safe and supportive, but infused with expert, guided facilitation, is paramount.

REFERENCES

Association of Experiential Education, n.d. What is EE? <http://www.aee.org/what-is-ee> (accessed 29.08.15.).

Blaschke, L.M., 2012. Heutagogy and lifelong learning: a review of heutagogical practice and self-determined learning. Int. Rev. Res. Open Distance Learn. 13 (1), 56–71.

Buabeng-Andoh, C., 2012. Factors influencing teachers' adoption and integration of information and communication technology into teaching: a review of the literature. Int. J. Educ. Dev. Using ICT 8 (1), 136−155.

Chai, C.S., Koh, E., Lim, C.P., Tsai, C., 2014. Deepening ICT integration through multilevel design of technological pedagogical content knowledge. J. Comput. Educ. 1 (1), 1−17.

Council of Ontario Universities, 2012. Transforming Ontario Universities. <http://cou.on.ca/reports/transforming-ontario-universities/> (accessed 02.10.15.).

Council of Ontario Universities, 2014. Bringing life to learning at Ontario Universities. <http://cou.on.ca/reports/bringing-life-to-learning/> (accessed 02.10.15.).

Dillon, D., O'Connor, K., Strong-Wilson, T., Rudd, C., 2007. Improving teacher education in changing times through experiential education. Paper Presented at the Annual Conference of the Canadian Society for Studies in Education, Saskatoon, May 27. <https://www.mcgill.ca/edu-e3ftoption/files/edu-e3ftoption/CSSE08_Presentation2.pdf> (accessed 02.10.15.).

Hammond, M., Crosson, S., Fragkouli, E., Ingram, J., Johnston-Wilder, P., Johnston-Wilder, S., et al., 2009. Why do some student teachers make very good use of ICT? An exploratory case study. Technol. Pedagogy Educ. 18 (1), 59−73. Available from: http://dx.doi.org/10.1080/14759390802704097.

Hase, S., Kenyon, C., 2000. From andragogy to heutagogy. <http://www.psy.gla.ac.uk/~steve/pr/Heutagogy.html> (accessed 30.11.15.).

Hase, S., Kenyon, C., 2007. Heutagogy: a child of complexity theory. Complicity: Int. J. Complexity Educ. 4 (1), 111−117.

Hildenbrand, S.M., Schultz, S.M., 2015. Implementing service learning in pre-service teacher coursework. J. Exp. Educ. 38 (3), 262−279. Available from: http://dx.doi.org/10.1177/1053825915571748.

Klinger D.A., Lee E.A., Stephenson G., Deluca C. and Luu K., 2009. Exemplary school libraries in Ontario: a study by Queen's University & People for Education. Ontario Library Association; Toronto. < http://www.peopleforeducation.ca/wp-content/uploads/2011/12/Exemplary-School-Libraries-in-Ontario.pdf> (accessed 9.7.16.).

Koch, A., Heo, M., Kush, J.C., 2012. Technology integration into pre-service teacher training. Int. J. Inf. Commun. Technol. Educ. 8 (1), 1−14. Available from: http://dx.doi.org/10.4018/jicte.2012010101.

Kolb, D., 1984. Experiential Learning: Experience as the Source of Learning and Development. Prentice Hall, Englewood Cliffs, NJ.

Kolb, A.Y., Kolb, D.A., 2005. Learning styles and learning spaces: enhancing experiential learning in higher education. Acad. Manag. Learn. Educ. 4 (2), 193−212.

Kuh, G.D., 2008. High-Impact Educational Practices: What They Are, Who Has Access to Them, and Why They Matter. Association of American Colleges and Universities, Washington, DC.

Lee, E.A., Reed, B., Laverty, C., 2012. Preservice teachers' knowledge of information literacy and their perceptions of the school library program. Behav. Soc. Sci. Librar. 31 (1), 3−22. Available from: http://dx.doi.org/10.1080/01639269.2012.657513.

Lim, C.P., Chai, C.S., Churchill, D., 2011. A framework for developing pre-service teachers' competencies in using technologies to enhance teaching and learning. Educ. Media Int. 48 (2), 69−83.

Martinovic, D., Zhang, Z., 2012. Situating ICT in the teacher education program: overcoming challenges, fulfilling expectations. Teach. Teach. Educ. 28 (3), 461−469. Available from: http://dx.doi.org/10.1016/j.tate.2011.12.001.

Maynes, N., Hatt, B., Wideman, R., 2013. Service learning as a practicum experience in a pre-service education program. Can. J. High. Educ. 43 (1), 80−99.

McGill University, Teaching and Learning Services, 2014. Guidelines for Assessment of Experiential Learning. Teaching and Learning Services, McGill University, Montreal. <https://www.mcgill.ca/tls/files/tls/guidelines_-_assessment_of_experiential_learning_1.pdf> (accessed 02.10.15.).

McMaster University, n.d. Experiential education. <http://www.science.mcmaster.ca/scce/experiential> (accessed 02.10.15.).

O'Toole, K., 2007. Assessment in experiential learning: the case of a public policy internship. Educ. Res. Perspect. 34 (2), 51–62.

Razzouk, R., Shute, V., 2012. What is design thinking and why is it important? Rev. Educ. Res. 82 (3), 330–348. Available from: http://dx.doi.org/10.3102/0034654312457429.

Ryerson University. The Learning and Teaching Office, 2012. Best Practices in Experiential Learning. The Learning and Teaching Office, Ryerson University, Toronto. <http://www.ryerson.ca/content/dam/lt/resources/handouts/ExperientialLearningReport.pdf> (accessed 02.10.15.).

Sang, G., Valcke, M., van Braak, J., Tondeur, J., 2010. Student teachers' thinking processes and ICT integration: predictors of prospective teaching behaviors with educational technology. Comput. Educ. 54 (1), 103–112. Available from: http://dx.doi.org/10.1016/j.compedu.2009.07.010.

Simon Fraser University, 2015. Defining experiential education at SFU. <http://www.sfu.ca/experiential/?page_id=56> (accessed 02.10.15.).

Stoll, L., 2010. Professional learning community. In: Peterson, P., Baker, E., McGaw, B. (Eds.), International Encyclopedia of Education, third ed. Elsevier, Oxford, pp. 151–157.

Tondeur, J., van Braak, J., Sang, G., Voogt, J., Fisser, P., Ottenbreit-Leftwich, A., 2012. Preparing pre-service teachers to integrate technology in education: a synthesis of qualitative evidence. Comput. Educ. 59 (1), 134–144. Available from: http://dx.doi.org/10.1016/j.compedu.2011.10.009.

Tsai, C.C., Chai, C.S., 2012. The "third"-order barrier for technology-integration instruction: implications for teacher education. Australasia J. Educ. Technol. 28 (6), 1057–1060.

Wurdinger, S.D., Carlson, J., 2010. Teaching for Experiential Learning: Five Approaches that Work. Rowman & Littlefield Education, Lanham, MD.

CHAPTER 3

Beyond Object Lessons: Object-Based Learning in the Academic Library

A.R. Barlow
Rhode Island College, Providence, RI, United States

> For Things, to be considered, they must be such as have been either of general Use or Pleasure to Mankind.
>
> **William Temple (1731).**

Object-based learning (OBL) is an experiential pedagogy concerned with the close and tactile study of material *things*, such as artworks, specimens, texts, and artifacts. It is an approach for "learning about, with, and through objects" (Paris, 2002, p. xiv). Like its historical antecedents, *object lessons* and *object teaching*, contemporary OBL practice draws its strength from the power of sensory experience. It is not unusual for educators to invite their students to look, listen, touch, and even taste during OBL. Each mode of sensory engagement holds the potential to provoke emotion, curiosity, and meaning. Though popular with art and museum educators, OBL is best described as a niche pedagogy in higher education. Its acceptance, however, is growing, as faculty discover its ability to engage students in authentic learning (see Fig. 3.1).

Academic librarians should be acquainted with the principles and practice of OBL as well. OBL presents exciting opportunities for library instructors to partner with faculty, teach research concepts, and enliven their lessons. OBL can bolster the use of campus collections in teaching and scholarship, demonstrating that there is more to research than text. And object-based projects serve to diversify forms of knowledge production on campus. Because objects are visually stimulating and generally silent—you can't always quote from them, for example—they are excellent candidates for digital presentation formats, such as interactive online

Figure 3.1 Wheaton College students, Liam Grace-Flood and Audrey Spina, working with Herbert Haseltine's *Arab Foal (Filly)*, supported by collection assistant Abe Ziner. The sculpture was a bequest of Monawee Allen Richards, Class of 1934. *Photo credit: Flynn Larsen.*

exhibits, images, and videos. Media presentations may be intellectually and logistically accessible in ways that student research papers are not. They can be shared with a wider audience via Internet publishing. In this way, campus stakeholders and the general public can learn more about an institution's current research interests.

3.1 HISTORY

Educators have long advocated for the benefits of experiential learning. In 1543, Andreas Vesalius prefaced the first modern anatomy text, *De Humani Corporis Fabrica*, with an argument for hands-on medical education. As Professor of Anatomy at Padua, Vesalius not only insisted on performing dissections himself, he brought human bone and tissue (obtained by cutting down the bodies of hanged criminals) into the classroom. He required students to examine the "dissected particles," asking them to compare firsthand observation against their readings of ancient medical texts, many of which were built on false assumptions about the human body. In *Fabrica*, Vesalius noted that hands-on anatomical study gave students "a little more trust in their rational faculties and their eyes...than to the writings of Galen." The young physicians were enthralled, "writing hither and thither to their friends about these truly paradoxical things" (Vesalius, 1543, pp. 136—7). Vesalius' methods trained young doctors to detect errors in the classical medical curriculum, and gave them the confidence to openly challenge the medical authority on which it was built.

While the handling of specimens became a cornerstone of scientific education, learning through physical study has come in and out of practice in other disciplines. During the 18th and 19th centuries, university departments amassed incredible collections pertaining to the study of art, archeology, and geology. These collections reflected the research interests of both faculty and students, as they traipsed the globe collecting and classifying materials for their burgeoning fields of study (Chatterjee, 2011). The result was a physical curriculum devised for teaching and learning at the university. At the same time, elementary education reformers, such as Johann Heinrich Pestalozzi and Henry Barnard, promoted the advantages of tactile learning for children. They centered their arguments for object teaching on the concept of *anschauung*, the idea that sensory experience is essential for learning. During an object lesson, students would be asked to touch a substance, such as glass or slate, and describe its qualities: smooth, hard, cold, etc. The instructor would use those concrete understandings to teach abstract concepts for the development of language and composition skills. By the end of the century, object teaching was mainstream to the extent that it was lampooned by the *New York Times*:

> Of late years, what is called "object teaching" has become very popular among those who have charge of public schools. "Object-teaching" was invented by Mr. Squeers, the able and accomplished principal of "Dotheboys Hall." When Mr. Squeers had taught one of his pupils that botany means "a knowledge of plants," he ordered him to go into the garden and learn to know plants by weeding the vegetable bed. Later instructors have but developed into broader proportions... In physiology as well in history Miss Thomson [a burlesque dancer] has no rival as a teacher...when the children are, for example, required to spell "l-e-g, leg," and have defined it according to Webster...the teacher will thereupon impress the leading facts in regard to leg upon their minds in accordance with the best system of object-teaching.
> **Object-Teaching in Melrose (1878).**

During the 20th century, object teaching and use of collections fell from popularity. With the expansion of higher education and subsequent growth in class size, few faculty expected students to examine physical objects as a means of understanding subject matter. University collections came to be viewed as cabinets of curiosity, rooms of wonder with little relevance to the curriculum. It wasn't until public museums overhauled their engagement strategies in the 21st century—resulting in OBL research and education programs that championed visitor interaction with objects—that faculty began to look at their university collections with renewed interest (Hannan et al., 2013).

3.2 OBL THEORY

OBL shares a branch with other experiential learning modalities, such as active and problem-based learning. All sprout from inquiry-based learning, an experiential pedagogy with a record of scholarship dating to the 1970s. Inquiry-based learning turns the traditional classroom inside out. Students make decisions about their learning, while the teacher plays a facilitative and supportive role. In inquiry-based learning, the instructor will commonly present a scenario from which students are expected to develop questions, find evidence, and draw conclusions. The degree of instructor support is determined by an assessment of how much prior knowledge students bring to the class, as well as how much exposure they have had to inquiry-based learning itself. When deployed carefully, inquiry-based learning personalizes a student's connection to subject matter (Rockenbach, 2011). It can motivate and promote critical thinking (Lane, 2007).

OBL is a specialized type of inquiry distinguished by its focus on physical materials and sensory experience. Pioneered by art and museum educators, OBL makes a case for the educational value of visual, tactile, olfactory, and auditory engagement with objects. Research in the Museum Studies field demonstrates that hands-on interaction with objects triggers emotion, aids memory retention, and facilitates understanding (Chatterjee, 2008). Data from Eilean Hooper-Greenhill's groundbreaking book, *Museums and Their Visitors* (1994), indicate that object handling can lead to recall rates as high as 90%. To put this into perspective, subjects retain 30% of what they see, 20% of what they hear, and 10% of what they read (Hooper-Greenhill, 1994, p. 145). Hooper-Greenhill's findings are reinforced by research that specifically compares the benefits of exposure to real objects against digital surrogates. That research suggests that digital images, though convenient and often high quality, do not aid retention on the level of kinesthetic interaction with objects (Simpson and Hammond, 2012). Real objects, like the carved Chinese tiger pictured in Fig. 3.2, activate visual, spatial, linguistic, kinesthetic, and interpersonal intelligences. They invoke the mind—body connection.

Figure 3.2 Close-up of a carved stone Chinese tiger donated by Dr. Harry Kozol in honor of his wife, Ruth Massell Kozol (Class of 1925) and his daughter, Barbara Kozol Schwab (Class of 1954). The tiger's provenance was researched by students as part of an assignment for their First-Year Seminar.

3.3 OBL IN HIGHER EDUCATION

An emerging body of scholarship explores the potential for OBL practice in higher education. Much of this research is summarized by Leonie Hannan, Rosalind Duhs, and Helen Chatterjee in their paper, "Object-Based Learning: A Powerful Pedagogy for Higher Education" (2013), and presented in the form of case studies in the first book dedicated to this subject, *Engaging the Senses: Object-based Learning in Higher Education* (Chatterjee and Hannan, 2015). Taken together, these studies demonstrate how educators are applying OBL to teach subject-specific knowledge and instill transferable skills across disciplines and academic levels. Given the current momentum, it is not too surprising that we can find creative examples of OBL on dozens of campuses, both domestic and international, such as University of Pennsylvania, Macquarie University, and Hong Kong Institute of Education.

My own interest in OBL began while teaching history at a community college in 2010. One of my courses, *History 122: World Civilizations II*, was a survey of key events in global history from the early modern period to the present. In addition to the textbook, the assigned readings included a thematic selection of primary source documents. For example, students read excerpts from The Sadler Commission's Report on Child Labor (1832) and Esteban Montejo's *Biography of a Runaway Slave* to gain insight into the lives of 19th century laborers. Both texts dealt with themes of historical significance to the community: the former echoed the industrial past of the region and the latter had been translated and published by a local press. Despite this, students seemed detached and overwhelmed by the scope of the course. Perceiving their struggle, I created two object-based assignments designed to refocus their attention and get them interested in doing history.

The first assignment was an in-class OBL activity focused on modeling inquiry and building student confidence. I brought a vibrant Mexican amate bark painting from a private collection into class. Students examined the artwork, handling it and noting its signature and date. Students then worked in groups to formulate questions, and together we searched the Web for more information. The painting, which depicted a joyous agricultural scene, was most likely produced in the 1970s for the tourist market. Students returned to their groups, where they reconsidered a course reading—the testimony of a Maya plantation laborer—comparing his perspective to that of the artist. The ensuing discussion was lively, ranging from the historical accuracy of crops to the idealization of agricultural work.

Following the in-class exercises, students were assigned independent work. They were required to pair a document, selected from a list of four, with either an image or object held locally. Their task was to establish some connection between their sources through close reading, analysis, and basic information gathering. Most students chose to pair their documents with images of artworks, but a minority opted to investigate local material culture such as a mill house, furniture, and tools. Each student wrote a brief paragraph explaining the historical relationship, and made his or her case to the class (see Fig. 3.3). The project culminated in a discussion of a hypothetical book project: If students were to publish an anthology of primary sources, which of their objects would they include as visual support for the documents? Students responded strongly to the idea, and took their job as editors seriously. Since then, I have longed to collaborate with students on such a project and gather feedback about their experiences. For the time being, I continue to integrate OBL into instruction through my role as an academic librarian.

3.4 OBL IN ACADEMIC LIBRARIES

The archival community has a strong tradition of encouraging faculty to integrate original source material into the curriculum. Archival collections may include, but are not restricted to: rare books, manuscripts, art objects, equipment, costumes, recordings, taxidermy, and all manner of materials contributed by academic departments, alumni, students, and

Figure 3.3 Jillian Carkin, Class of 2014, presents her research on the provenance of Wheaton College's *Greek Black-Figure Attic Amphora*, purchased in 1981 with the Newell Bequest Fund.

donors. With this wealth of material at their fingertips, it is not surprising that archivists have been leaders of OBL practice in academic libraries. In fact, guidelines published by The Society of American Archivists advise professionals to model their collections and policies on the concept of an educational laboratory, a collaborative space where students learn procedures for handling materials, explore different types of sources, and gain knowledge in academic subjects (Core Archival Functions, 1999).

In a 2002 issue of *portal: Libraries and the Academy*, Ann Schmiesing (Professor of German and Scandinavian Studies) and Deborah Hollis (Associate Professor/Special Collections) shared examples of OBL-style assignments that they created for students at University of Colorado Boulder (Schmiesing and Hollis, 2002). One case study detailed their efforts to deepen students' understanding of Enlightenment society by giving them access to texts from the period. Students worked in teams to document the physical characteristics of several 18th-century books, including quality and feeling of paper, dimensions, layout, typeface, illustrations, and bindings. The activity inspired plenty of questions, setting the stage for a discussion about what a book's physical aspects can reveal about its production and readership. Schmiesing and Hollis' approach seems especially suitable for undergraduates, as they may lack the intellectual background necessary to analyze texts written in unfamiliar languages, handwriting, and formats.

Recent archivist—faculty collaborations demonstrate a sustained interest in OBL. In 2011, Harvard University's Jeffrey Hamburger, Professor of German Art and Culture, discussed his experiential methods for teaching students to work with historical materials. Hamburger invited students to a session in the Houghton Library where they learned to handle medieval manuscripts. For their major research project, Hamburger gave them a choice: (1) Write a paper, or (2) Craft a book that either renders a modern text in a medieval format or a medieval book in modern format. According to Hamburger, the book project was more demanding and conveyed practical skills (Talking About Teaching, Part III, 2011). Hamburger's project is one of several examples highlighting the innate relationship between sensory learning and the Maker movement.

Conservator Barbara Adams Hebard and Professor Virginia Reinburg designed a similar assignment for a course entitled *Early Printed Books: History and Craft* (Fall 2014) at Boston College. They transformed Hebard's conservation lab in The John J. Burns Library of Rare Books and Special Collections into a classroom makerspace. That's where Hebard facilitated a series of workshops featuring books published before 1800. During the sessions, students received training covering the methods, tools, and materials used by bookbinders from the time period. Once students mastered the necessary folding, sewing, and tooling techniques, Hebard had them create reproductions of early books, such as puzzle purses, vellum pamphlets (substituting paper for vellum to keep costs down), and girdle books (Hebard, 2015). In its ability to convey historical concepts and developments, the physical experience of producing early books may trump even the most talented lecturer. And through the making process students gained real, artisanal skills. It is also worth noting that The John J. Burns Library reaffirmed its relevance by redefining its conservation work area as a makerspace.

3.5 LIBRARY INSTRUCTION FOR OBL

With so many players already at the table—curators, faculty, archivists, and students—what role is there for the instruction librarian in OBL? I will argue that instruction librarians are uniquely positioned to partner with faculty to provide a range of support for OBL on campus. More than that, we can incorporate its practices into our own teaching, in order to advance information literacy concepts, even when the class is not engaged in a more formalized object-based project. And, through reference consultation and advocacy, we can encourage our learning communities to treat objects as sources of information for research and scholarship.

The role of the instruction librarian has been evolving for some time. We spend fewer hours on the reference desk and more time integrating into the curriculum. We are versed in the theory and practice of education, the application of which helps us to meet our pedagogical goals. Many library instructors are involved with technology-enabled learning initiatives on campus. In fact, the work of an instruction librarian may belong to a wide spectrum of overlapping specialty areas, such as educator, instructional designer, information technologist, information specialist, and subject liaison (Cole, 2014). And yet, despite all of the potential locus points for creativity, instruction librarians can feel dissatisfied and less than sure about their effectiveness in the classroom. For some, role ambiguity *is* the problem. Being overextended is a real issue; it limits time for professional development and experimentation. Others are stymied by external expectations of material to be covered during library instruction. Perhaps the librarian is asked to help with students with a "market basket" assignment: the type that requires two books, three peer-reviewed articles, and one reliable website for an annotated bibliography. Is it possible to meet a library instructor who hasn't struggled against the constraints of the traditional research paper? And who, as a result, hasn't fallen into the comfortable groove of lecturing and messing around with databases once or twice? Those of us who are guilty of it know that we don't need an assessment technique to measure student engagement. We can survey the room with our eyes.

OBL is one potential catalyst for shaking up the repertoire. After a lifetime of looking at websites and paging through textbooks, students are generally enthusiastic about access to real artworks, manuscripts, scientific equipment, artifacts, and even ordinary household objects. Harvard historian, Professor Laurel Thatcher Ulrich, remarked that "students get terribly excited when you put them in touch with real stuff...the object itself becomes the hub of a wheel of exploration, with spokes of inquiry radiating out in many directions" (Talking About Teaching, Part III, 2011). As a librarian, I have observed that the specificity of an object imposes important limits on inquiry, making the task of research more manageable for students. An object's finite nature has the power to focus the mind and inspire pointed thought. Its boundaries, both real and constructed, can help a researcher to demarcate what is relevant to understanding and what is not. This is an excellent starting point for research.

At Wheaton College in Norton, MA, Leah Niederstadt has enhanced several of her art history courses through research centered on OBL. As Assistant Professor of Museum Studies and Curator of the Permanent Collection, Niederstadt is in the unique position of having oversight and access to a sizable collection of art objects. Niederstadt integrates materials from the Permanent Collection into all of her courses, usually in the form of experiential learning exercises that require students to research a single object. While developing her *Introduction to Museums Studies* course for 2014, Niederstadt devised an assignment that required students to trace the provenance of selected objects (see Fig. 3.4). They would share their findings through the creation of a collaborative digital exhibit. To ensure support for her course, Niederstadt organized a collaborative team consisting of an instruction librarian, digital initiatives librarian, and archivist.

The planning resulted in a series of research and technology workshops facilitated by librarians. Wheaton's Digital Initiatives Librarian, Amy Bocko, and I facilitated two of these workshops. The first was a 90-minute session that introduced students to research methods, search tools, and issues surrounding image copyright and fair use. I started class by modeling a method for researching provenance. Using the example of a painting in Wheaton's Permanent Collection, I took students through an inquiry process that began with mining pertinent documents held by

Figure 3.4 Student working with documents in object file for Herbert Haseltine's *Arab Foal (Filly)*. Photo credit: Flynn Larsen.

the college. After identifying key pieces of information from primary source materials, the students brainstormed questions, which led into my demonstration of search techniques for article databases and other web-based tools. We then shifted gears, so that Bocko could show students how to find and evaluate supporting images for their digital exhibitions. The second research workshop was a just-in-time session tailored to needs and questions that had surfaced during research consultations with me or conversations with Niederstadt.

Supporting the distinct information needs of students working with one-of-a-kind objects cannot be accomplished during one-shot library instruction. There is no prescribed methodology for researching objects, no database or peer-reviewed journal that holds all of the answers. To learn about objects, students will need to be incredibly resourceful in their efforts to identify and exhaust all of the potential sources of information at their disposal. Niederstadt makes this point in her assignment guidelines:

> *It is important to remember that research is a process, one that can be exciting, frustrating, satisfying, and tedious. You will find that records are often incomplete, either because documents have been lost, modified, or destroyed or have not been made public, or because many types of information were never recorded in the first place. The latter is particularly true with objects deemed "anthropological" or "ethnographic" and/or for artwork produced outside of Europe or North America. On any research project, you are certain to encounter dead ends or to have gaps that cannot be filled. This is especially true for provenance research. Therefore, some students may be unable to identify the complete provenance for the object they select. In such cases, I expect you to hypothesize as to where the object may have been and to support your hypothesis with evidence from your research. You will have to be creative and wide-ranging in your search for sources. You will need to use books, exhibition catalogues, archival and collection records, academic journals, popular press, census records, genealogy websites, and other resources, both in print and digital formats. You may even have to contact museums or auction houses in search of information. When you hit a dead end, ask for help from the many resources available.*
>
> **Niederstadt, Provenance Assignment Guidelines for ARTH 230, Wheaton College (2014).**

Through this process, students learn to conduct original research, which helps them to avoid plagiarism, and gives them experience working in a professional manner. Having to consult with peers, professors, and librarians teaches students that research is responsive and social. And, at some stage, students may be delighted to realize that they are making discoveries, and that they are foremost experts on their objects. Each new ability helps students to close the gap between their skills and those cited by employers as being areas of weakness among new college graduates, including: (1) engaging others in the research process; (2) retrieving information using a variety of formats; and (3) exploring a topic with dogged persistence (Head and Wihby, 2014).

The following recommendations may serve to help instruction librarians in meeting their own OBL goals, while at the same time enriching collaborative relationships with discipline-based faculty:

- With its emphasis on resourcefulness, OBL activities allow library instructors to challenge the pervasive academic belief in *good* and *bad* sources, shifting the focus to more flexible concepts of *authority* and *knowledge production*.
- Library instructors who are familiar with the pedagogical advantages of OBL should talk about it during consultation with faculty, rather than waiting to be approached.
- Although it is sometimes the case that faculty will reach out to their liaisons to request support for OBL, many faculty may not understand how we can help. Therefore, in consulting with faculty, librarians should be prepared to listen and discuss course learning outcomes, relevant objects and collections, as well as the logistics of working with objects.
- Larger OBL assignments enable librarians to experiment with various modes of instruction, embed into a course, and maybe even learn students' names.

Keep in mind that, from a faculty perspective, teaching with objects requires adoption of new pedagogy, changes to curriculum, reduced time for lecturing, and increased collaboration with curators and librarians. There are practical concerns too. What about the challenges presented by stationary classroom design, large class size, student-to-object ratio, security, note-taking, absences, and access to objects outside of class? It is perhaps not surprising that digital images, which can be easily integrated into a lecture, are an attractive alternative. Professor Joe Cain, a practitioner of OBL at University College London, recommends several helpful strategies for resolving some of these issues (Cain, 2011):

- Faculty are more likely to integrate objects into their courses when approached directly by knowledgeable library and archives staff who can make specific suggestions based on the curriculum.

- Not all faculty are comfortable diving into new pedagogical frameworks. It is more likely that OBL will find a home on campuses that support faculty through dialogues and training workshops, and led by staff who are versed in the theory and practice of teaching with collections.

Collaborations with faculty around OBL may be jumping-off points for discussions of digital knowledge production and web publishing. At Wheaton College, Niederstadt made the decision to integrate technology into OBL assignments after attending a talk sponsored by Library and Information Services (LIS) entitled *Teaching Naked*, by José Antonio Bowen. Niederstadt collaborated with Pete Coco and Jenni Lund, both in the LIS Research and Instruction Department, to create two OBL assignments with digital outputs: interactive, web-based timelines and Google Earth maps (Coco and Niederstadt, 2014). Both projects culminated in an Omeka site (pictured in Fig. 3.5) used to share OBL, shed new light on the college's artworks, and were accessible to a large audience, thereby fulfilling Niederstadt's goal of service learning for her students.

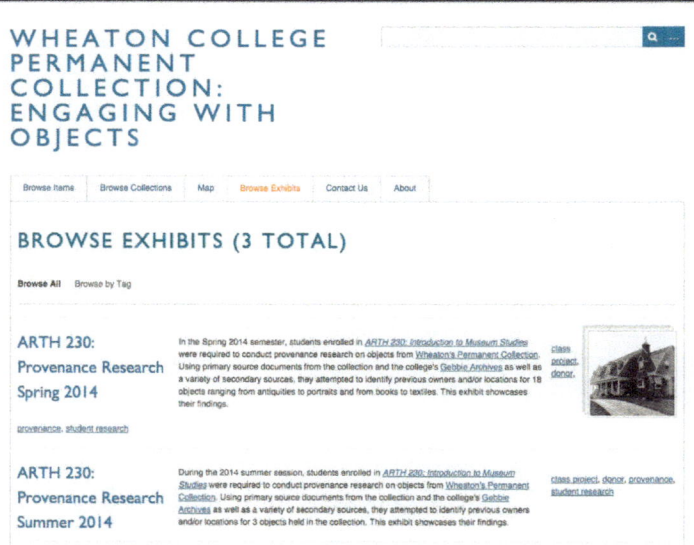

Figure 3.5 Omeka site created to share object-based learning using the Wheaton College Permanent Collection.

Outside of the classroom, such collaborations can lead to better digital asset management on campus, with the effect of improving the impact and reach of OBL. Access to high-quality digital surrogates allows students to review objects at their own pace outside of class time, and centralized image management platforms bring objects from disparate campus collections into one searchable environment. Faculty from various departments will discover specialized collections, and find themselves attracted to materials outside of their disciplines. And, maybe they will even reach out to their colleagues in the library to talk about integrating objects from these wonderful collections into their curriculum.

3.6 BEYOND OBJECT LESSONS

Perhaps one of the most compelling cases for OBL comes from students. They report that they like learning from objects, even preferring them to traditional lectures and research papers. At University College London, one student said that she learned to apply knowledge as opposed to "just imagining." In the same survey, another student wrote that he enjoyed OBL because it is "tangible and fun" (Hannan et al., 2013, p. 163). In Spring 2014, students at Wheaton College were asked to evaluate OBL projects designed by Niederstadt. A history major said, "I loved working on original research. It was much more exciting knowing that this was my own research and my object. Rather than just compiling others' thoughts on a subject, I was hunting for clues that no one else had found yet. The profound sense of ownership made the research addicting" (Barlow and Niederstadt, 2015).

Having worked with that student, I will confess that I found it addicting myself. Watching students get excited about research and helping them to track-down information inspired my interest in doing more with OBL. Since then, I have been speaking with practitioners of OBL in the museum education community, as well as experimenting with small-scale activities during library instruction. For example, I recently organized an art history "petting zoo" comprised of different types of source material, such as exhibition catalogues, primary documents, monographs, anthologies, and academic journals. Students were instructed to flip through sources from each category (marked 1—5), and to select one volume. With my guidance, they worked in pairs to explore and describe their materials. Through hands-on examination most, but not all, were able to correctly characterize their source types. Students then transitioned from the physical world to the digital, as they looked for additional information about their volumes in the online catalogue and in Google Books. The faculty member was pleased to see students interacting with physical library materials; I could cover basic concepts relating to academic sources and align them to the research assignment; and students remained engaged throughout the class. I believe that small risks and teaching experiments open the door to more substantial librarian—faculty collaborations. And in the final analysis, OBL creates opportunities to engage students in deeper experiential learning.

REFERENCES

Barlow, A., Niederstadt, L., 2015. Digital humanities at work: a collaborative model for creating student scholars. Presented at the NERCOMP Annual Conference, Providence, RI. <http://www.educause.edu/sites/default/files/library/presentations/NC15/SESS29/Digital_Humanities_At_Work_NERCOMP_2015.pdf> (accessed 15.07.15.).

Cain, J., 2011. Practical concerns when implementing object-based teaching in higher education. Univ. Mus. Collect. J. 3, 197—201.

Chatterjee, H., 2008. Touch in Museums: Policy and Practice in Object Handling. Berg, Oxford.

Chatterjee, H., 2011. Object-based learning in higher education: the pedagogical power of museums. Univ. Mus. Collect. J. 3, 179—181.

Chatterjee, H., Hannan, L., 2015. Engaging the senses: Object-based learning in higher education. Ashgate Publishing, Farnham, Surrey.

Coco, P., Niederstadt, L., 2014. Digital projects and the First Year Seminar: making blended learning work at a small liberal arts college. The Academic Commons. <http://www.academiccommons.org/2014/08/25/digital-projects-and-the-first-year-seminar-making-blended-learning-work-at-a-small-liberal-arts-college/> (accessed 15.07.15.).

Cole, J., 2014. Instructional roles for librarians. In: Blevins, A., Inman, M. (Eds.), Curriculum-Based Library Instruction: From Cultivating Faculty Relationships to Assessment, Medical Library Association Books. Rowman & Littlefield, Lanham, MD, pp. 3—10.

Core Archival Functions, 1999. SAA guidelines for college and university archives. <http://www2.archivists.org/governance/handbook/section9/list-of-saa-sections> (accessed 20.08.15.).

Hannan, L., Duhs, R., Chatterjee, H., 2013. Object-based learning: a powerful pedagogy for higher education. In: Boddington, A., Boys, J., Speight, C. (Eds.), Museums and Higher Education Working Together: Challenges and Opportunities. Ashgate Publishing, Farnham, pp. 160—168.

Head, A., Wihby, J., 2014. At sea in a deluge of data. The Chronicle of Higher Education. <http://chronicle.com/article/At-Sea-in-a-Deluge-of-Data/147477/> (accessed 11.08.15.).

Hebard, B.A., 2015. History in the making. Boston College Libraries newsletter. <http://www.bc.edu/libraries/newsletter/2015spring/book.html> (accessed 11.08.15.).

Hooper-Greenhill, E., 1994. Museums and Their Visitors. Routledge, London.
Lane, J., 2007. Inquiry-based learning. Schreyer Institute for Teaching Excellence at Penn State. <http://www.schreyerinstitute.psu.edu/pdf/ibl.pdf> (accessed 01.09.15.).
Object-Teaching in Melrose. 4 May 1878. New York Times 4.
Paris, S., 2002. Perspectives on Object-Centered Learning in Museums. Routledge, London.
Rockenbach, B., 2011. Archives, undergraduates, and inquiry-based learning: case studies from Yale University Library. Am. Arch. 74, 297–311.
Schmiesing, A., Hollis, D., 2002. The role of special collections departments in humanities undergraduate and graduate teaching. A case study, portal: Libraries and the Academy 2 (3), 465–480.
Simpson, A., Hammond, G., 2012. University collections and object-based pedagogies. Univ. Mus. Collect. J. 5, 75–81.
Talking About Teaching, Part III: Using the University's collections, 2011. Harvard Magazine. <http://harvardmagazine.com/2011/04/teaching-and-learning-collections> (accessed 16.8.15).
Vesalius, A., 1543. De Humani Corporis Fabrica. In: Clendening, L. (Ed.), Source Book of Medical History (W. Hotchkiss, Trans.). Dover, New York, pp. 128–151.

CHAPTER 4

Taking the Class Out of the Classroom: Libraries, Literacy, and Service Learning

J. Blodgett
University of Northern Colorado, Greeley, CO, United States

The University of Minnesota, Morris (UMM), is a small, public, residential liberal arts college located in West Central Minnesota. While part of the University of Minnesota system, each system campus has its own Carnegie classification and mission. In addition to being a selective public liberal arts college, UMM is committed to sustainability and social justice, having its own Office of Community Engagement (OCE), which coordinates the campus volunteer and service learning programs in a number of disciplines such as art and Spanish.

My interest in service learning is rooted in my own commitment to volunteerism and social justice. Additionally, in thinking about teaching a course on libraries and literacy, service learning seemed the perfect pedagogical tool for taking the values and theories of librarianship from the classroom to the "real world." A colleague, Heather James (Marquette University), and I first designed this course as a study abroad class to El Salvador. We researched options and decided on an NGO based in Chicago, working with schools in El Salvador. The organization, Contextos (www.con-textos.org), works in a number of schools around El Salvador, training teachers and developing libraries and literacy programs. Due to unforeseen circumstances we were unable to teach the class, but I was able to adapt the proposal to fit UMM's First Year Seminar program, offering Beyond Shushing: Libraries and Literacy in the 21st Century in the fall of 2013.

4.1 SERVICE LEARNING AND THE ACADEMIC LIBRARY: OPPORTUNITIES ABOUND

Service learning has become more popular in higher education over the last 20 years, with many schools seeing the advantages of community engagement programs for the school and the student. Academic libraries have been slower to embrace service learning, especially in for-credit undergraduate programs. While there is ample literature about libraries' involvement in service learning classes through information literacy instruction or as the collaborating partner, and there is a growing body of literature on the importance of service learning classes to graduate LIS programs, there are fewer examples of academic libraries at undergraduate institutions offering for-credit library-related service learning classes.

John Riddle questioned library commitment to service learning in the early 2000s (Riddle, 2003), and Westney echoed his concerns 3 years later (Westney, 2006), but in the past 10 years libraries have become active supporters of service learning. Service learning allows a student to put the theories discussed in the classroom into practice in the "real" world, and it allows students the opportunity to "see the relationship between those serving and being served as reciprocal, with both sides having something to gain from the experience" (Ball, 2008, p. 72). By combining "community service with academic instruction" students can focus on "critical, reflective thinking and civic responsibility" (Heiselt and Wolverton, 2009, p. 84). Students also have the opportunity to learn about current community issues and how those relate to classroom learning (Heiselt and Wolverton, 2009).

Librarians are uniquely positioned to "assist students in recognizing and strengthening the connection between their service experience and their course assignment" (Nutefall, 2014). In fact, students who work with librarians during their service learning class are more likely to use more and a wider variety of sources than those who did not work with a librarian, and they are more likely to be concerned with issues of bias in the field (Nutefall, 2009). As libraries continue to transition from being thought of as a warehouse for materials to a "dynamic institution of communication and knowledge dissemination" (Herther, 2008, p. 388), the opportunities to be involved with service learning expand. Additionally, libraries have strong connections to faculty and staff across the disciplines as well as connections to the wider public, allowing libraries to support service learning classes across the university (Herther, 2008; Yates, 2014).

Libraries support service learning in three ways—through research assistance, as host for a service learning project, and/or by teaching a library course with a service learning component. The first two options are represented in the literature primarily in undergraduate classes. For example, librarians at Eastern Washington University worked with students in communication classes to market and teach RefWorks to other students (Meyer and Miller, 2008). Libraries have also facilitated service learning opportunities with area public libraries (Heiselt and Wolverton, 2009), and computer training for individuals with intellectual disabilities (Whitaker and Albertson, 2011).

Graduate LIS programs have actively integrated service learning into their programs in order to combine practical experience with a greater understanding of societal issues, such as the digital divide and equity of access (Overall, 2010). Albertson and Whitaker concur that LIS students need to "be equipped with the tools to initiate, foster and maintain community partnerships that will benefit communities as a whole and non-dominant groups in particular" (Albertson and Whitaker, 2011). They argue that service learning in an LIS program allows the students to see the pedagogical outcomes of their studies (Albertson and Whitaker, 2011). Since libraries are focused on meeting community needs, it is only logical that students should have the opportunity to put their classroom learning to use in a service learning class. Some of the projects represented in the literature include developing websites for public libraries (Elmborg et al., 2001), computer classes for job seekers (Roy et al., 2010; Brzozowski et al., 2012), peer-tutoring (O'Brien et al., 2014), creating a library at a homeless shelter (Peterson, 2003), and creating a virtual museum of the American Indian (Roy, 2001).

There are, however, a minimal number of articles that discuss service learning classes focusing on libraries and/or literacy at the undergraduate level. Maureen Barry, editor of the Service Learning Librarian blog (http://www.libraries.wright.edu/servicelearning/) discusses the class at Wright State University which involved students in providing research for local nonprofit agencies (Barry, 2011). While I'm sure there are other undergraduate courses that combine service learning and library/literacy skills, they are not widely represented in the literature.

4.2 THE COURSE

Taught in Fall 2013, this two-credit class met for 50 minutes twice a week, which allowed me to divided the schedule, so we focused on libraries and literacy theory one day a week and service learning theory and the class project on the other day. The First Year Seminars at UMM have a very specific mission of introducing students to the type of work expected of them in college, while creating an intellectual community where they develop close relationships with their classmates and the faculty member. The course sizes are small, with a maximum size of 14 students.

Prior to starting the semester I worked with our OCE coordinator to determine which programs best fit the needs of the class and the greater Morris community. I was conscious of not making the projects too large and complex because of the limitations of only teaching a two-credit course. After discussing the course objectives and community needs, we decided on three community partners offering four projects: story time at the public library, story time with evening ESL students (K-3), library instruction at Briggs Library (UMM's library) for adults in the ESL program, and computer literacy sessions with senior citizens. A fifth project, a usage study for Briggs Library, was coordinated by the library separately from the OCE.

At the start of class, I made it clear to the students that there was a service learning project required in the course which would potentially involve work off-campus and outside of the scheduled class time. While the course description contained this information, many of the students didn't know what that meant. The idea of a semester-long group project was not enthusiastically received by everyone in the class, as a number of students mentioned in their end-of-the-semester response papers. For the first time in my teaching career, I did not let the students choose their own group. Instead, I created an online survey for them to complete after hearing presentations from each of the community partners. The survey asked questions about project preference, including a question about any projects they did not want to work on, previous experience working with the constituent populations, and concerns about working in a group. I tried to accommodate students' interests as much as I could, but I wanted to create groups that had the greatest chance for success. Since dividing the students into groups came in week three, I had a good sense of the students' strengths and weaknesses. In the end, only three projects were selected: ESL story time (K-3), computer literacy for older adults, and the Briggs Library usage study. While I was concerned about assigning groups, the students appreciated being organized by interest, and as one student noted in her final reflection paper: "This way of assigning groups keeps us from just being a group of friends that just want to be together and focuses our attention on the project's topic."

Once the groups were assigned, I handed out more specifics about the project requirements. While these were discussed in the syllabus, I created individual assignment handouts and rubrics for each component. The components were also designed to keep the students on schedule, since I didn't want them to leave everything until the end. The service learning project, including periodic reflection essays and day-to-day communication and planning, constituted 60% of their total grade. The specific assignments were:

- Email to the sponsor indicating involvement with the project and arranging an initial in-person meeting. This allowed me the opportunity to talk about how to write a professional email.
- Group charter to define the project goals and parameters, including important due dates and contact information. A sample charter was provided as an example.
- Periodic check-in reports (200–300 words) about how the project is going and any concerns with either the project itself or someone's work. A response of "Everything is fine," was not acceptable.
- Lesson plans for each session that included a Works Cited list to demonstrate the plans were pedagogically based.
- Presentation of the project, which I attended.
- Reflection paper (5–7 pages) that allowed the students to detail the work they did, how they think the project went (both the good and the bad), and what they learned about themselves and the community.

In addition to keeping them on task, the assignments allowed the students to develop valuable critical thinking and writing skills. One student noted the email assignment taught her how to be professional and still be herself: "I now know that being professional doesn't mean using advanced language, it means knowing what you are talking about and who your audience is." The lesson plan assignment required research to justify and support their plan, which also allowed me the opportunity to talk about library resources and information literacy. The two library sessions also served as research time for the other major assignment in the class—a 5–7-page research paper on the future of libraries. In addition to developing lesson plans with learning outcomes and specific activities, the students did a "dry-run" of their activities with the class. The students reported this being very helpful in seeing what would and wouldn't work as well as getting over some performance anxiety. While I was concerned about spending so much class time working on their projects, one student reported the in-class practice session was "the most useful part of the project." Furthermore, spending that time allowed them to ask questions and work through issues with others in the class. It was a useful method for demonstrating how the theoretical work we had done in class could be implemented in very practical ways, a hallmark of experiential learning.

4.3 WHAT THE STUDENTS LEARNED ABOUT THE COMMUNITY

Since a substantial difference between volunteering and service learning revolves around the reflection that takes place, the reflection papers were an important component of the class. Reflection allows the students to think about what they learned about themselves and the community. At the start of the class, I don't think the students realized how much they would enjoy their projects or understand how much they would learn about their place in the Morris community. For example, the story time group focused their readings on writing, reading, and finding books. For one session they read *Tomas and the Library Lady*, which resonated with the children at story time, as the story revolves around an immigrant child of migrant farmers. While the Mexican community in Morris is not migrant, the children enjoyed hearing a story that mirrored their own life in some way. The students also wanted to give the children and their families the opportunity to get library cards, so during the second session, all of the children, not just those in the K-3 group, came to the library to get cards and check out books. While it was a bit chaotic, it was rewarding to see how excited the students and the children were to use the library. Working with a non-native-speaking population was eye-opening for the students in this group. Each of them mentioned in their reflection papers how language barriers affect day-to-day life, especially in a small town. The one student in the group who did speak Spanish commented how uncomfortable she felt speaking Spanish to the parents because she was not fluent. It gave her insight into how difficult, frustrating, and intimidating it must be for the families who are not fluent in English to live in Morris.

The students who worked with the older adults on their computer skills at the public library were surprised by the interest the attendees had in not only working on their computer skills, but also in getting to know the students. As one student noted, "it was surprisingly a lot of fun and I learned a lot about the elders of the community and the experiences they have had in life. I have more appreciation for the rewards of teaching and reaching out to others...." One of the students, an international student from China, was very concerned about his language skills, specifically the seniors' ability to understand his English. The seniors loved the chance to hear about his life growing up in China and what he thinks of living in rural Minnesota. In a small town with a moderate town/gown problem, the senior computer literacy project was an excellent way to bridge that divide, with all parties leaving the sessions knowing more about each other, as well as about how to send photos through email.

The last group, the Briggs Library usage study, had a different experience from the other groups because they worked on-campus with the Briggs Library staff. The outreach for their group was to host two focus group sessions exploring how students use the library's physical space. While there was some marketing that had to be done, this project was not as focused on community outreach as the ESL and computer literacy classes were. The students' final reflection papers indicated that they were happy with the outcome of the project because they could see tangible results, but they missed the chance to get to know the wider community.

The service learning project helped the students see that they were doing something for someone who was depending on them. It forced the students to see that it wasn't just their grade that mattered; what they did had an impact on the broader world.

4.4 WHAT THE STUDENTS LEARNED ABOUT THEMSELVES

The students learned a great deal about working with others, not just in their individual groups, but in working with the community sponsor as well. Many of them indicated at the beginning of the project how much they hated working in small groups and how concerned they were about the amount of work expected of them. By the end of the semester, however, most had learned valuable skills to use in other classes and in their work outside of the classroom.

For example, one student working on the Briggs Library usage study discovered herself the "leader" of the group, coordinating the submission of assignments and setting the schedule. She learned that she could be "a 'take charge' kind of person. I am capable of leading people." This was a new role for her, and she was happy to learn from her group members how much they appreciated her leadership skills. Another student in the same project group learned about the importance of taking ownership of a project. She felt "there was a sense of purpose to this project…[and] it helped my work ethic." She wrote she had a "desire to please the group, not just myself or the teacher."

The students also learned the importance of organization and deadlines. One group, the students working with elders at the public library, realized they needed better organization. One student pointed out that they failed to assign each person in the group an area of responsibility, which was a recommendation I made early in the semester. In his reflection paper, this student noted "I think we should have taken the advice to make sure everyone had a role to play that would keep the group functioning well." He also mentioned that "organization was the one thing our project needed." While the computer literacy sessions went well, the group didn't have much publicity, so the turnout was quite low. This allowed them the chance to really talk with the residents who came, but it didn't meet the need of the library to reach a wider audience.

4.5 WHAT I LEARNED, MOVING FORWARD

The first and most important lesson I learned was that service learning classes are a lot more work than a traditional class, but the experiential learning the students do in the class is worth the additional effort on my part. While the traditional class preparation isn't more work than other courses I've taught, helping students coordinate three separate projects and attending each of their community sessions added time to my schedule. It was important to me, though, that I be there to support them and answer questions when they had them, especially since I was working with first-year, first-semester students who were not as familiar with UMM or the Morris community as upper-division students might have been. I know there are classes where the community partner grades the final presentation, and while I asked for feedback from the partners, it was important for me to be there to evaluate the students' work.

I was impressed by my students' hard work and by the fact that they took their projects seriously. While they didn't always do all the assignments or readings for class discussion, they were committed to delivering an excellent experience when it came to working with their constituent populations. I only had to minimally remind them to meet with their community partners, and I didn't worry they wouldn't show up on their project days.

We spent a great deal of time talking about how to avoid seeing the service learning projects, especially those working with minority populations, as the solution to larger social issues. I wanted the students to explore the larger implications of small volunteer projects. I had the students read part of Paolo Freire's *Pedagogy of the Oppressed* to open up the dialogue. I was concerned this discussion would be challenging for first-year students, but they were very interested in the topic. They seemed to understand that teaching one ESL class or helping the students find a book in the library wouldn't solve the larger issues immigrants might face. It was also clear to me during our discussions that they were keenly aware of how volunteering even for one class could open up a dialogue and create an environment where larger, more complicated issues could later be discussed. A number of the students took the skills they started to develop in class and continued to work for programs sponsored by the Office of Community Engagement. It was rewarding to see how the service learning component helped the students better understand the theoretical materials, as well as encouraged them to stay involved with the Morris community.

I vacillate between wanting the course to be four credits or two credits. This first time teaching it, the course was two credits, primarily for my own wellbeing, since I taught the class in addition to my normal workload. However, I believe that I could do much more with it as a four-credit class. In addition to the service learning project, the students had to write a research paper exploring some aspect of the future of libraries. Unfortunately, because of time limitations, their papers didn't get as much attention as they should have. When I teach this again, if it remains two credits, I want to keep a more theoretical paper as part of the class, but it will not be a full-blown research paper. My thought is to have smaller response papers based on the readings and class discussions, which should also get the students more involved with the readings.

Moving forward, I want to develop a class for upper-division students that would focus more on providing research to nonprofit groups in our region. UMM's Center for Small Towns works with rural community partners to provide research and resources for Minnesota's small towns while creating learning opportunities for faculty and students. While my course primarily worked with public libraries, a course for upper-division students would allow me to explore issues of information and digital literacy, information ethics, and other topics related more directly to access instead of services. UMM is also revitalizing its Service Learning Faculty Fellows program, and I was a member of the 2015–16 cohort. A group of five of us had the opportunity to learn more about service learning pedagogy and start planning a course to teach in the next year. As is so often the case, it was valuable to be in a room with others who have similar interests but varied approaches to teaching service learning.

I also had the chance to work with students who were interested in libraries and how they provide information access to the communities they serve. They asked insightful questions and thought deeply about the challenges and opportunities facing today's libraries. I would encourage anyone who is thinking of incorporating service learning into a library class to do so. It was a fantastic experience for all the stakeholders—me, the students, and the community partners.

If you would like to see a copy of my syllabus or have questions about the course, please feel free to contact me at jayneblodgett@gmail.com.

REFERENCES

Albertson, D., Whitaker, M.S., 2011. A service-learning framework to support an MLIS core curriculum. J. Educ. Libr. Inf. Sci. 52 (2), 152–162.
Ball, M.A., 2008. Practicums and service learning in LIS education. J. Educ. Libr. Inf. Sci. 49 (1), 70–82.
Barry, M., 2011. Research for the greater good: incorporating service learning in an information literacy course at Wright State University. Coll. Res. Libr. News 72 (6), 345–348.
Brzozowski, B., Homenda, N., Roy, L., 2012. The value of service learning projects in preparing LIS students for public services careers in public libraries. Ref. Libr. 53, 24–40.
Elmborg, J.K., Leighton, H., Huffman, H., Bradbury, J., Bryant, T., Britigan, D., et al., 2001. Service learning in the library and information science curriculum: the perspectives and experiences of one multimedia/user education class. Res. Strateg. 18, 265–281.
Heiselt, A.K., Wolverton, R.E., 2009. Libraries: partners in linking college students and their communities through service learning. Ref. User Serv. Q. 49 (1), 83–90.
Herther, N.K., 2008. Service learning and engagement in the academic library: operating out of the box. Coll. Res. Libr. News 69 (7), 386–389.
Meyer, N.J., Miller, I.R., 2008. The library as service-learning partner: A win–win collaboration with students and faculty. College & Undergraduate Libraries 15 (4), 399–413.
Nutefall, J.E., 2009. The relationship between service learning and research. Public Serv. Q. 5 (4), 250–261.
Nutefall, J.E., 2014. Why service learning is important to librarians. OLA Q. 17 (3), 16–21, <http://commons.pacificu.edu/olaq> (accessed 25.09.15.).
O'Brien, H.L., Freund, L., Jantzi, L., Sinanan, S., 2014. Investigating a peer-to-peer community service learning model for LIS education. J. Educ. Libr. Inf. Sci. 55 (4), 35.
Overall, P.M., 2010. The effect of service learning on LIS students' understanding of diversity issues related to equity of access. J. Educ. Libr. Inf. Sci. 51 (4), 251–266.
Peterson, L., 2003. Using a homeless shelter as a library education learning laboratory: incorporating service-learning in a graduate-level information sources and services in the social sciences course. Ref. User Serv. Q. 43 (4), 307–310.
Riddle, J.S., 2003. Where's the library in service learning? Models for engaged library instruction. J. Acad. Libr. 29 (2), 71–81.
Roy, L., 2001. Diversity in the classroom: incorporating service-learning experiences in the library and information science curriculum. J. Libr. Adm. 33 (3/4), 213–228.
Roy, L., Bolfing, T., Brzozowski, B., 2010. Computer classes for job seekers: LIS students team with public librarians to extend public services. Public Library Quarterly 29 (3), 193–209.
Westney, L.C., 2006. Conspicuous by their absence: academic librarians in the engaged university. Ref. User Serv. Q. 45 (4), 200–203.
Whitaker, M.S., Albertson, D., 2011. Triangulating findings from an instruction-based community engagement project. Ref. User Serv. Q. 51 (1), 49–59.
Yates, F., 2014. Beyond library space and place: creating a culture of community engagement through library partnerships. Indiana Libr. 33 (2), 53–57.

CHAPTER 5

Training Student Drivers: Using a Flipped Classroom Model for IL Instruction

E.A. Sanders, A.H. Balius and S.A. Sanders
Southeastern Louisiana University, Hammond, LA, United States

In February 2015, an event promoting Southeastern Louisiana University's Quality Enhancement Plan (QEP) sparked our interest in library applications of experiential learning (EL). Our QEP focuses on using EL to make students "real-world ready." A university workshop series introduced us to EL and inspired us to redesign our course, Introduction to Information Research (LS102).

Nearly half of our undergraduate degrees require LS102, so we teach over 1100 students annually. This 1-hour credit course is taught in Summer, Fall, and Spring for 8 weeks; each semester has two terms. Most students are first-year freshmen, but other classifications are also represented. LS102 has traditionally focused on teaching students to find, use, and evaluate information in an academic setting. The course transitions students to college-level research skills and information literacy (IL) (Sims Memorial Library, 2015; Southeastern Louisiana University, 2015).

Restructuring the course to best meet student needs has been an ongoing process. Three years ago, some LS102 instructors adopted a flipped classroom, which combined modeling and integrating EL activities into instruction. Those instructors reported improved student engagement and performance. Expanding our EL initiatives even further was logical, given Millennials' preference for experiential, exploratory, and interactive learning (Becker, 2009). It also seemed the best way to prepare students to navigate information in the longer term rather than "just a commute."

5.1 CONNECTING IL, RESEARCH SKILLS, AND EMPLOYABILITY

Librarians know the information landscape is richer, more complicated, and changing faster than ever before. IL goes beyond using libraries or performing Google searches, just as driving a car requires more than knowing "how to step on the gas pedal" (Badke, 2010). However, it remains true that "only librarians seem to be making direct connections between IL and desirable workplace skills" (Sokoloff, 2012).

Before launching our redesign, we investigated Millennials in the workplace to address this disconnect. Some literature disparages this generation, but we focused on preparing students for their future lives and careers. We wanted to avoid any generational bias. As a library staff, we represent the three generations comprising today's workforce: Baby Boomers, Generation X, and Millennials. Understanding Millennials in the workplace is also crucial as they begin to outnumber Boomers.

To understand Millennials' current work environment, we questioned what being "real-world ready" meant. Popular media gave general ideas of what employers sought, but weren't clear whether basic IL skills were expected. One report indicated workers lacked "basic employability skills" and "focus" (Bauerlein, 2013). Another stated that only 14% of employers felt new graduates were prepared for the workplace (O'Shaughnessy, 2015). The most illuminating report indicated employers sought graduates who could not only find, select, and analyze information, but also create and discuss potential solutions from it (Mello, 2015).

Next, we looked at several recent academic studies, including those produced by the Gallup-Lumina Foundation (2014), the Horizon Report (New Media Consortium, 2012), and the Association of American Colleges & Universities (2015). In these, employers highly valued skills such as critical thinking, problem-solving, and oral/written communication. The most noteworthy research connecting IL and employability came from Project Information Literacy (PIL). Head (2012) notes that employers expect new hires "to apply patience and persistence when solving information problems in the workplace." Sharkey and O'Connor's (2013) discussion of information fluency also indicates that individuals must "possess competencies for managing, integrating, creating, and communicating information, in addition to finding, using, and evaluating."

From this investigation, we see several areas where IL influences workplace skills. Millennials aren't always professionally tech savvy; if they are, IL must supplement those technical competencies (Becker, 2009; Head et al., 2013). Millennials seldom read directions, hindering their ability to deliver desired results (Becker, 2009; Twenge, 2009). They over-rely on their computers for information and rarely seek help from more experienced employees (Head et al., 2013). The "Google" mindset leads them to seek "the quickest answer" from an initial results list (Head, 2012; Head et al., 2013). Their lack of deeper research and inquiry means "they miss perspectives that would enable them to evaluate the analysis of others" (Hershatter and Epstein, 2010).

5.2 IL, EL, AND FLIPPED CLASSROOM

5.2.1 EL Pedagogy

Digital Natives, Millennials, Net Generation, Generation Me, N, Y, Z—however named, several works discuss contemporary students' distinctive traits (Oblinger and Oblinger, 2005; Feiertag and Berge, 2008; Palfrey and Gasser, 2008; Becker, 2009; Twenge, 2009; Devasagayam et al., 2012; Cole et al., 2015). Vito (2013) and Woods et al. (2011) link key generational traits, pedagogy, and classroom applications. More generally, EL "is uniquely suited" to address these characteristics and implications (Devasagayam et al., 2012).

Millennial students typically desire active and interactive learning. They favor acting over listening or reading—even to instructions (Becker, 2009; Twenge, 2009). EL, particularly when it is done well, allows students to interactively explore topics and build connections between the subject matter and its practical applications in work and society. Relatedly, students desire constant structure, clear guidelines and expectations, and rewards for effort (Twenge, 2009; Vito, 2013). EL provides meaningful structure and consistent feedback opportunities from instructors, peers, and themselves. Students have a "hypertext mindset" (Feiertag and Berge, 2008), which means expectations of constant web access, user-friendly interfaces, and instant gratification (Twenge, 2009; Hlavaty and Townsend, 2010; Vito, 2013). EL dispels these preconceptions and deepens their knowledge and expectations via challenging material.

Many Millennials have intangible, but interconnected, personality characteristics that can inhibit success in the "real world." They are often overconfident in their abilities, including research (Cole et al., 2015), but have a paralyzing fear of failure (Twenge, 2009). They also lack self-reliance, expecting constant guidance and review upon demand (Feiertag and Berge, 2008; Twenge, 2009). In short, many students lack "grit" (e.g., independence, perseverance) and other "soft skills" that employers desire (e.g., timeliness, collaboration). EL helps students develop these traits. Through testing and reflecting, students encounter gaps in their knowledge. EL doesn't punish this lack, but rather emphasizes that knowledge can be gained through action and reflection. EL gives students a place to "fail" constructively and build self-reliance.

Many believe students are tech-savvy, but Devasagayam et al. (2012) cite studies indicating this assumption is problematic. Feiertag and Berge (2008) specifically reference the digital divide as one factor for technical disparity. Even tech-savvy students must be taught how to transfer their recreational technical skills towards professional endeavors (Vito, 2013). EL tasks can help students connect their tech skills to their future careers. EL also allows students to build or to improve tech skills via tools integrated into class.

Finally, today's students need critical thinking skills in various forms, such as problem-solving, decision-making, and evaluating information. EL activities "demand rigorous engagement and involvement" that makes them "an invaluable pedagogical tool" that models a "'real-life' environment" (Devasagayam et al., 2012). EL also tackles deeply embedded myths of students, especially with IL (Cole et al., 2015). Stimulating goal-oriented students with problem-solving, evaluating, and justifying their decisions prepares them for real-world types of reasoning and exploration.

5.2.2 Flipped Classroom Pedagogy

Secondary school chemistry teachers developed the flipped classroom model in 2006. Jonathan Bergmann and Aaron Sams created video lectures accessible via YouTube for students away at sporting events. This freed class time for the hands-on portion of the course. They were so impressed with the results they wrote a book entitled *Flip Your Classroom* (2012). Librarians saw the terminology matched educational approaches they utilized (Allen, 2014). After all, our work also consists of both factual and skills-based learning.

Flipped classroom pedagogy is also consistent with EL. The teacher's mentorship demonstrates both classroom leadership and the collaborative learning process. In our case, we utilize courseware (Moodle) for background lectures and demonstrations. This allows students with sufficient background to quickly review material, while students without that advantage can easily cover new concepts.

The flipped classroom encompasses various learning tools, including lecture, demonstration, application, and group work. It encourages student—teacher interaction at the point-of-need, so we can guide students who become bogged down and discouraged during the research process (Callison, 2015). It mirrors Bloom's taxonomy, wherein lower-level skills such as knowledge, comprehension, and application are suitably taught through prerecorded lectures, thus freeing class time for the higher-order cognitive domains of analysis, synthesis, and evaluation (Allen, 2014; Callison, 2015). Also consistent with EL, the approach incorporates more active and collaborative learning. We're encouraged by recent studies indicating flipped classroom teachers are seeing improved student grades (Madden and Martinez, 2015). We believe this trend comes from students' increased responsibility for their outcomes, which in turn helps them become independent learners (Arnold-Garza, 2014).

Our freshman-level students often struggle with the self-discipline necessary to complete preliminary work for a flipped course. However, we note with Arnold-Garza (2014), that abundant literature exists to show students of various ages successfully participating in this learning environment. We've built mini-quizzes into our courseware to ameliorate this disadvantage, but we recognize this may not fit the traditional "one-shot."

In short, the flipped classroom prepares students for their careers as they apply IL skills to real-life situations. It gives them opportunities to collaboratively apply their learning to problem-solving (Arnold-Garza, 2014).

5.3 SYNERGY BETWEEN FLIPPED CLASSROOM AND EL

5.3.1 Flipped Classroom LS102—Initial Challenges

Some sections of LS102 adopted the flipped classroom model in 2012 with only 3 weeks to prepare, which presented some challenges. The LS102 coordinator redesigned the course, while simultaneously migrating course materials from blackboard to Moodle. He lacked familiarity and comfort with the flipped classroom and had concerns regarding student success in the new model. As a result, he favored highly structured class assignments and lessons.

The flipped classroom naturally creates EL opportunities, which this initial design utilized. Supplying students with preparatory materials before class allowed instructors to answer questions and to model specific skills, not basic information. Additionally, in-class assignments focused on students practicing new skills with real tools. Journal entries provided some opportunity for reflection.

However, this initial design also squandered EL opportunities. Too often, modeling devolved into lecturing. The scripted assignments perpetuated the misconception that research was simple and linear. There was no chance of failure and few challenges. As a result, students weren't prepared to engage more complex assignments later in the term. Their experiences thus weren't as authentic as they could have been. Students often appeared bored or finished assignments early. Perhaps most worrying, the lessons created more focus and dependency on instructors than desired.

5.3.2 Expanding EL—The Course Redesign

The current redesign of LS102 takes fuller advantage of the EL opportunities the flipped classroom offers. Overall, the redesign places a greater focus on students, putting them in the "driver's seat" of their education. Students participate with in-class activities and discussions, where they answer questions rather than passively listen or watch. Peer and kinesthetic learning are increased through using questions and activities to promote discussions. Assignments lack repeated directions for skills students previously encountered, which encourages thinking and retention. Assignments feature more reflection and critical thinking, asking students not only to perform tasks, but also to explain the benefit of performing them. They then use that experience to repeat the task in the future. These components also feature more writing, another skill in which students lack practice.

Additionally, we're supplementing a final exam with a Portfolio in which students research a current topic, revise previous work, and reflect on their growth. The use of the Portfolio, which combines a revised Narrowing a Topic and Bibliography with two longer reflective assignments, provides a real-world context useful both in and beyond academia. Further integrating the Portfolio divides the class equally between learning search and evaluation skills and experiencing the research process. Students are encouraged to think, to "get messy," and to have a stake in their own learning. Students have opportunities to fail and grow frustrated; their research experiences, just like in real life, don't always work the first time. While success isn't assured, they can struggle with a safety net. They can ask questions or receive guidance without getting "stuck."

5.3.3 Threshold Concepts and ACRL Framework

Our expansion of EL pedagogies into library instruction resonates with both threshold concepts, as explored in Meyer and Land (2006), and the revised "Framework for Information Literacy for Higher Education" (Association of College & Research Libraries, 2015). In particular, it highlights that research is a constructed, contextual process. Our students are accustomed to finding "the answer" that satisfies course requirements. Using assignments that build on each other and loop back, we show them that "real" learning is a dynamic, not static, process. Through this process, students learn to let go of the familiar (learning toward a test), and move into a more complex understanding that sees research as an ever-evolving, iterative process. EL—with its emphases on collaboration, group process, and revision—informs students that finding truth is a circuitous as opposed to linear activity.

We demonstrate the "troublesome" nature of knowledge because our assignments have no single path forward. Previously, we gave students "canned projects" that guaranteed success. Now students choose their own focus when finding background information and use it as a springboard into specialized literature. As students see research affecting decisions beyond finding the "right" answer, they assume an authoritative role and examine various types of authority (as reflected in the phrase "authority is constructed and contextual"). Their research is complex and full of dead ends, which parallels actual work (and life) settings. The give and take of the investigative process introduces them to how they can participate in academic conversation.

The ACRL framework states that research is a form of strategic exploration. Our Portfolio connects to this idea through work-related research that affects actual decisions. Using research questions as opposed to thesis statements reinforces this connection. We stress that the purpose of information gathering is exposure to multiple types of sources to answer a question, not marshaling random facts to support a preconceived notion. Comparing sources they currently access to those they find via the library also allows students to see how information has value, both in terms of money and power.

Increasing students' exposure to EL in the research process also enables them to gain an orientation to the "episteme" (way of knowing) of their fields. As they research a subject relevant to their future professions, they are introduced to some of the tacit assumptions that inform experts. Furthermore, they are introduced to the idea that knowledge is socially constructed and can be viewed from the inside out (as a practitioner) or from the outside in (as a student).

5.3.4 Summary

The flipped classroom allows instructors to serve as guides for students as they work. This role mirrors the formal or informal mentorship that takes place for entrance-level employees. As we look at their assignments and the areas in which they struggle, we can suggest ways to move forward—or back, if they have reached a dead end. This kind of interaction isn't possible when students complete work in a traditional course. Thus, students learn to search in a more realistic fashion while also experiencing the mentoring process that will occur in their future apprenticeships.

The more we investigated EL, the more we saw ways it interfaced with our flipped class. For example, we stressed the fact that research isn't an end, but rather a means to an end. Students were delighted to find that "wrong" answers, if used correctly, were as valuable as "right" answers. We moved from basic learning (e.g., "what button to press") to reflective observations that take place as students read, explore, discuss, and tweak their research question, search terms, and keywords. Students were empowered to experiment with both library databases and search engines. We could offer even more individualized feedback and guidance. Learning was reinforced through journals that asked students to reflect on what they learned and what they would do differently.

5.4 EL EXERCISES

5.4.1 Application

Several concerns prompted our redesign of LS102: (1) lack of critical thinking, (2) inauthentic research process, (3) disconnect from lifelong learning, and (4) lack of reflection. In short, we lacked critical IL, described as "problem-posing, multidimensional, creative, intellectual, process-based, and supportive of student agency" (McDonough, 2015). In both daily exercises and the final project, students had minimal point and click requirements, but neither evaluated nor justified choices. Their research was linear, not iterative. Students faced neither challenge nor failure. Though LS102 introduces students to our library, their lifelong learning needs require knowledge and use of other tools. Students finished their work with a disconnected sense of mastery. Increasing EL helps address all these concerns.

In particular, EL contextualizes abstract concepts with which students often struggle, such as format, information cycle, and information ethics.

For most, information ethics is limited to avoiding plagiarism. For this reason, we paid special attention to the revision of this daily assignment. The samples in Table 5.1 demonstrate how we moved beyond hypothetical situations to more exploratory, problem-solving questions. We include it as an example of a single EL exercise and hope that others, including those who perform one-shots, will find it illustrative.

The original assignment asked students to: (1) match sources to information cycle stages, (2) identify the best source type for two different information needs, and (3) identify and explain which sources would hold particular viewpoints. We found students couldn't connect the information cycle to changes in format or viewpoint. They restated details from class readings rather than demonstrating new knowledge. Most couldn't articulate why or how certain formats were used instead of others. Students were disconnected from the information cycle as an active process.

Table 5.1 Comparison of samples of the prerevised and revised Information Cycle assignments

Sample of prerevised Information Cycle assignment	Sample of revised Information Cycle assignment
Information need: This year marks the 100th Anniversary of Sir Arthur Conan Doyle's work *The Valley of Fear* (1915—2015). I know that 1915 was during the Edwardian Era. I need to research the major events going on in England during that time period. Based on the Information Cycle slides, what sources could I consult for this type of information? (2—3 sentences)	2. In 3—4 complete sentences, write a cohesive paragraph that describes how the coverage of the topic changed over time.
I want to discuss the controversy surrounding cell cloning research from *several perspectives* (e.g., a scientist, a conservative, a doctor, a Catholic). What would be my best sources *for each one* and why? (4—10 sentences)	3. Using a Google Image Search, locate an image that you could use to make your presentation. a. What type of usage rights does this image have? What does that mean? b. How would you credit or cite the image in your presentation? c. Copy and paste the URL to your image.

These samples are used under a CC BY License.

The revised assignment incorporated more EL to address these weaknesses. It actively engages students with various sources and asks them to explain changes in information over time. We also decided to tackle another abstract concept: information ethics. In earlier versions of LS102, students learned about plagiarism and citations, insufficient for the complex, prevalent need for information ethics, especially digitally. Our revised assignment introduces basic information ethics, critical to anyone creating or using online information.

In this new assignment, students work in 2–4-person groups. They are given a scenario of preparing a presentation to contextualize their work. We chose a topic familiar to our students, capitalizing on Hurricane Katrina's decennial coverage. Students are provided with three sources, each showing a different timeframe after the storm: (1) a news article (24 hour), (2) a news magazine story (month), and (3) and a scholarly article (years). Groups must collaboratively determine the audience and purpose of each article. They must also describe how information and the sources changed over time.

To incorporate information ethics, students are told they must find an image via Google to use in the presentation. Students describe their image's usage rights, cite the image, and paste the URL into the assignment. This portion of the exercise places a familiar idea (copying and pasting an image) in proper ethical context; it also introduces students to forms of licensing other than copyright.

5.4.2 Preliminary Observations

This assignment yielded mixed results. Student evaluations were inconsistent in quality. Few identified the two popular articles as news, despite indicating they were for general audiences. Some didn't recognize the scholarly source, which featured images. Most students missed the contrast of New Orleans having "dodged a bullet" in the first source to the focus it received in later articles. Nearly all students struggled with the information ethics portion, indicating revision is needed. Usage rights proved a murky issue for students.

Student behavior was also inconsistent. The majority were enthusiastic, but others demonstrated behaviors ranging from immature (e.g., cell-phone use) to inappropriate (e.g., selecting images of dead bodies). Some students rushed through the assignment to leave early rather than analyze thoughtfully.

That said, we saw several positive changes. Students were more enthusiastic and engaged. They welcomed the collaborative opportunities of the assignment. Discussions were more focused and lively, as everyone was actively involved. Many students combined personal experiences with the news stories. Overall, students were increasingly able to describe how sources moved from being primary and popular to secondary and scholarly.

5.5 EL PROJECT
5.5.1 Application

Initially, LS102 featured two interconnected final assignments. Narrowing a Topic required students to: (1) select a listed topic, (2) narrow it with one encyclopedia article, and (3) complete a search skill-refreshing exercise. Bibliography required students to: (1) compare keywords to a database thesaurus, (2) construct a search phrase, and (3) locate three different sources (book, popular, and scholarly article) using library resources.

Infusing the Portfolio with EL strengthens its value to students. The second half of our course uses the Portfolio so students can experience authentic research and can test their learning. In this assignment, students must combine problem-solving, decision-making, and reflection with searching and evaluation skills. The samples in Tables 5.2 and 5.3 illustrate our changes from a scripted to an authentic research experience, which we discuss in more detail below.

To increase lifelong learning, we "start where students are" (McDonough, 2015), through the use of Wikipedia or other online reference sources to narrow their topic. Students can find popular articles via Google or library databases. Students locate and evaluate a webpage or e-resource in addition to the other three sources. These changes connect students' prior skills and experiences with library resources.

We use a scenario that exemplifies a "real" need for research skills (e.g., preparing a professional presentation). Students choose topics related to their future profession, which increases students' responsibility and control as researchers. Critical thinking increases as decisions and evaluations examine inherent merit and appropriateness to need.

To increase reflection, we added two assignments. In Research Journal #1, students discuss their research processes, successes, problems, solutions, and share experiences through forums and discussion. In Research

Table 5.2 Comparison of samples of the prerevised and revised Narrowing a Topic assignments

Sample of prerevised Narrowing a Topic assignment	Sample of revised Narrowing a Topic assignment
1. First, we'll narrow a topic by looking at the Gale Virtual Reference Library. Using one of the following, read an overview article and then write down several ways to narrow your topic. (Topics will be assigned in class.) Look particularly for topic overview articles that contain four or more pages of information. (This may not be the first one listed!) 4. Because databases contain so much information, it is vital that you become familiar with advanced searching. This portion of the assignment will remind you of one of your best buddies—the "AND" operator. 5. Under "Library Databases," choose JSTOR. (It can be accessed from the "Favorite Databases" box in the upper right-hand side of the screen.) 6. Next select "advanced search" at the top of the page. 7. Link your two search terms using the "AND" operator. (This should be the default Boolean Operator.) 8. Use the "Narrow By" feature to select: articles, from 2008 to present, and English.	*Scenario*: You have just accepted a job in your major/field/profession. Your boss has asked you to gather resources on a topic relevant to your major/field/profession so you can prepare a presentation for your colleagues/coworkers. Your boss has provided you with a list of broad topics but wants you to decide the specific aspect to use for your presentation. At the end of two work days, you need to give your boss a specific research question for approval before you begin finding sources. 2. Find *three reference sources* (encyclopedia, dictionary, handbook, etc.) on your broad topic. You must include *one print and one digital* reference source *from the library resources*. Your print source will come from the library catalog. Useful databases to find digital reference sources for this assignment are *Credo Reference, Funk & Wagnall's Gale Virtual Reference Library,* and *SAGE Knowledge.* You may also find a digital encyclopedia or handbook from the library catalog. The third reference source is your choice. Some examples include online reference sources (Wikipedia, Encyclopedia.com, etc.), videos from the library catalog, and a second print or digital library resources.

These samples are used under a CC BY License.

Table 5.3 Comparison of samples of the prerevised and revised Bibliography assignments

Sample of prerevised Bibliography assignment	Sample of revised Bibliography assignment
First, using the MLA style, list the article you used in the Gale Virtual Reference Collection. Also include *one of the three ways* you found to narrow your broad topic. (2 points) This question has *two parts!* *First:* Enter your (selected from above) search terms into the *ProQuest Research Library* thesaurus. Are your search terms the preferred ones? Are there terms closely related to your subjects? Broader terms? Narrower terms? Don't list more than three of any category (i.e., narrower terms). (Please note: "None" is an answer, whereas leaving information out is not!). *Second:* Afterwards, when you're satisfied your terms are the best, *write below your final Boolean Search Phrase.* (2 points) Now go to *Academic Search Complete* and find a *newspaper or periodical* (in other words, "popular") article on your subject. Limit the search to full text, English, and 2008 to the present. *After* selecting an article, use the "cite" button on the right-hand side of the screen to find the *MLA* citation and place it below. (2 points)	1. Choose *one* of the three research questions from your Narrowing a Topic assignment. Use it to complete the following three activities: a. Record the original research question. *Original Research Question:* b. Underline the keywords in the above research question/ scenario. Note below any additional keywords from your readings that might be relevant to your search. c. Using all known tools (Boolean Operators, Nesting, Truncation) as necessary, create a search phrase from your keywords. *Search phrase:* 4. Using the search phrase you developed, search one or more of the library databases to find an *academic journal article*. Use all of your evaluation skills to select the *best* one available on your topic. Use that resource to complete the following activities: a. Cite the resource using *MLA Format*. b. Record any controlled vocabulary that could help you find additional, relevant resources on your topic. Briefly (1–2 sentences) explain why you selected those particular subjects. c. In at least 3–5 complete sentences, evaluate the source using the criteria and methods we discussed in class. Explain your reasoning as to why it is the best choice for this scenario, and support your statements with evidence from the source.

These samples are used under a CC BY License.

Journal #2, students identify strengths, weaknesses, and current and future development in their skills. The class "ends" with them examining their experience rather than as experts.

5.5.2 Preliminary Observations

We've seen several positive results from our EL-enriched project.

Students engaged their research processes more. The scenario successfully allowed students to combine topics of personal interest with their chosen profession, which increased motivation and persistence even in the face of difficult topics. Students embraced the opportunity to choose and explore their own topics.

As students gained awareness of the research process, their focus and research questions became sophisticated and relevant. Students improved in adjusting search phrases, using controlled vocabulary, and forming holistic knowledge. Students saw the need to adjust search behaviors to find sources. There were isolated instances of reverting to "Google behaviors"; however, students' reflections indicated skills learned in class helped them locate and evaluate sources, which encouraged continued use.

Students' work behavior changed as they recalled previously learned skills. Many students worked between classes without prompt, often motivated from in-class struggles. With their additional efforts, they received feedback and completed the task without falling behind. Moving beyond clarifying directions or seeking answers, students discussed problems and sources via numerous venues (e.g., journals, email, Reference Desk).

Reflections indicated increased student adaptability and confidence. Students usually found appropriate solutions to problems. Their confidence increased in various areas (e.g., creating search phrases, evaluating sources). Students indicated they were supplementing normal Google searching and cited successful uses in other classes. They also wrote about future need for certain skills, especially evaluation.

As instructors, we could give students more constant, individualized feedback. As hoped, more natural opportunities to discuss framework concepts appeared. For example, a diabetic student researching his condition used knowledge from his endocrinologist to justify a source's accuracy. The student used contextual authority and participated in scholarly conversation. Several students encountering "pay walls" on Google articles led to discussions of information's value.

Along with benefits came challenges. Students had difficulty identifying information formats, especially for digital materials. To them, anything online is a website. Students also struggled with differentiating the purposes of general overviews and specific information. These tendencies hindered their understanding that information formats are chosen for specific purposes.

Students actively resisted accessing a printed material via multiple tactics. Several mentioned that locating/using physical sources was difficult and impractical. Paradoxically, students expressed a desire to use more print materials throughout the course.

Our chosen topics had conceptual problems, especially if the subject wasn't well-represented in the library collection. Students with broader topics needed more time to narrow their focus but had greater flexibility when searching. Some topics were extremely popular. In one course, nearly all nursing majors selected Immunizations/Vaccinations. This fact caused problems because multiple students competed for the same sources. Some students shared with their neighbors, but such collaborations were rare.

Two additional phenomena seem noteworthy. Instructors expected students to use familiar tools; instead they utilized whatever the assignment listed first—and would remain there, even if stuck. This rigid behavior manifested in all assignments. We're unsure if assignments lacked clear steps or if students lacked strategic problem-solving skills.

Unexpectedly, student interest in government documents increased. We theorize two explanations. As a selective repository, our library has and continues adding large amounts of these sources. When learning source evaluation, government websites were discussed. Students may believe those sources require less justification for their Bibliography.

Overall, EL's benefits justified extra time and effort. Students "struggled" through authentic experiences that expanded their knowledge and skills. They improved individually and comparatively. Student reflections revealed their research strengths, weaknesses, and opportunities for future growth. Students left the class with a confident, forward-thinking mindset, prepared for lifelong learning.

5.6 ROAD CONDITIONS

5.6.1 Hits

Generally, we've found multiple benefits to increasing EL in LS102.

Students are more engaged and proactive. Encouraging participation in class discussions remains difficult, but students show more focus, ask meaningful questions, and spend more time working in and out of class. Minimizing lecture makes class less repetitive and more rigorous. Students spend more time interacting with tools, skills, and sources, both in daily exercises and in their final project. They must prepare themselves conceptually and bring questions to class to succeed in the assignments.

The flipped classes also show increased critical thinking and evaluative skills. Despite initial concerns, students rose to meet the challenge of the writing and critical thinking tasks required in the flipped LIS course. Students are reluctant to move beyond simple answers, but improve throughout the class. The exception would be Portfolio evaluations, where many students focused on completion, not depth or quality.

As instructors, we are able to offer individual, point-of-need feedback in deeper ways than before. With the revised assignments, we see more specific areas where students struggle. We sooner identify both problem areas and successful transitions.

York et al. (2010) identify three roles academic libraries assume with EL: place, client, and partner. We suggest a fourth: learner. Increasing EL has led us to undergo EL ourselves. We sooner recognize opportunities for revision and adjust consistently as needed. We've learned more about our students' current skill levels, expectations, and behavior. This knowledge facilitates ongoing investigation and adaptation.

5.6.2 Misses

We have also found some general struggles with increasing EL in LS102.

One large difficulty is time, which manifested itself in several ways: (1) revising and developing assignments, (2) switching to digital submission and file management, (3) explaining anything "extra" (e.g., citations, Moodle), (4) increased grading, and (5) students demanding more in-depth guidance.

We're still trying to resolve these difficulties but have considered several solutions: (1) fewer topic choices for assignments, (2) simplified or fewer assignment tasks, (3) more group work, and (4) formal rubrics, which we couldn't initially create due to time constraints. Of these, we've implemented (1) and (2) with some success.

Because the course builds progressively, it lacks flexibility needed to tackle setbacks. Students who miss assignments miss needed skills or background for future classwork. Technical issues affect how much students can work in class and derail the point-of-need feedback.

Despite literature warnings, we didn't account for students' lack of technical skills. Sometimes students uploaded incorrect or incomplete documents. Students who completed assignments from home had several technological problems (e.g., remote login and file compatibility issues).

In varying degrees, we still struggle with critical thinking and student motivation. Typical classroom problems remain, such as students not reading the assigned material or skipping class. Some students lack basic, professional standards. Student evaluations often focus solely on relevance or surface assumptions. Because of our profession, it's difficult to "stand back and empower others to find their own solutions" (McDonough, 2015), especially if they don't *try*.

Students expect LS102 to be an "easy A." And it is—as long as they participate. We frequently remind them that our flipped class differs from traditional coursework. It's not enough to attend class; they must engage the material on a professional level. Just as LS102 expands their understanding of information and research, so too does it plant the seeds for collegiality and good workplace decorum. We expect this difficulty to continue because (1) students must learn these skills, and (2) students may undervalue our class. To address these issues, we plan to end future sessions with students discussing that day's performance.

5.6.3 Advisories

From our experiences, we offer the following advice:
- Technology upgrades can "collide" with course redesign. Whenever possible, avoid overlap with major modifications (e.g., virtual machines, security, Moodle).
- Highly touted "money-saving" virtual machines have unique problems. Rigorously investigate feasibility and the impact of software/hardware changes.
- Students come to us with varying degrees of familiarity and experience with technology. Make generous use of, and if possible, bolster the availability of your on-campus tech resources.
- Use your library's student workers as "guinea pigs" to test assignments for clarity.
- Assume linear reading habits when inserting examples or figures into assignments.

5.7 END OF THE ROAD

We understand the hesitancy to "flip" the classroom. However, such EL methods best simulate independent research and enable our students to be real-world-ready. This approach empowers students to take the wheel and navigate towards their own research destinations.

REFERENCES

Allen, S., 2014. Shifting the instructional paradigm: articulating a set of current practices in flipped library instruction. Tenn. Libr. 64 (3), 1, <http://www.tnla.org/?page=TL64_3_shifting> (accessed 30.11.15.).

Arnold-Garza, S., 2014. The flipped classroom teaching model and its use for information literacy instruction. Commun. Inf. Lit. 8 (1), 7−22, <http://www.comminfolit.org/index.php?journal=cil&page=article&op = view&path[]=v8i1p7&path[]=183> (accessed 28.08.15.).

Association of American Colleges & Universities, Hart Research Associates, 2015. Falling short? College learning and career success. <https://www.aacu.org/sites/default/files/files/LEAP/2015employerstudentsurvey.pdf> (accessed 28.08.15.).

Association of College & Research Libraries, 2015. Framework for information literacy for higher education. <http://www.ala.org/acrl/standards/ilframework> (accessed 28.08.15.).

Badke, W., 2010. Why information literacy is invisible. Commun. Inf. Lit. 4 (2), 129−141, <http://www.comminfolit.org/index.php?journal=cil&page=article&op=view&path[]=Vol4-2010PER3&path[] = 119> (accessed 25.03.15.).

Bauerlein, M., 2013. What do U.S. college graduates lack? Professionalism. <http://www.bloombergview.com/articles/2013-05-08/what-do-u-s-college-graduates-lack-professionalism> (accessed 29.11.15.).

Becker, C., 2009. Student values and research: are Millennials really changing the future of reference and research? J. Libr. Adm. 49 (4), 341−364.

Bergmann, J., Sams, A., 2012. Flip your classroom: reach every student in every class every day. International Society for Technology in Education, Eugene, Oregon.

Callison, D., 2015. Classic instructional notions applied to flipped learning for inquiry. Sch. Libr. Mon. 31 (6), 20−22.

Cole, A., et al., 2015. Generation Z: information facts and fictions. In: Swanson, T.A., Jagman, H. (Eds.), Not Just Where to Click: Teaching Students How to Think about Information. Association of College and Research Libraries, Chicago, IL, pp. 107−137.

Devasagayam, R., Johns-Masten, K., McCollum, J., 2012. Linking information literacy, experiential learning, and student characteristics: pedagogical possibilities in business education. Acad. Educ. Leadersh. J. 16 (4), 1−18.

Feiertag, J., Berge, Z., 2008. Training Generation N: how educators should approach the Net Generation. Educ. + Train. 50 (6), 457−464.

Gallup-Lumina Foundation, 2014. What America needs to know about higher education redesign. <https://www.luminafoundation.org/files/resources/2013-gallup-lumina-foundation-report.pdf> (accessed 01.12. 15.).

Head, A., 2012. Learning curve: how college graduates solve information problems once they join the workplace. <http://projectinfolit.org/images/pdfs/pil_fall2012_workplacestudy_fullreport_revised.pdf> (accessed 28.08.15.).

Head, A., et al., 2013. What information competencies matter in today's workplace? Libr. Inf. Res. 37 (114), 74–104, <http://www.lirgjournal.org.uk/lir/ojs/index.php/lir/article/view/557> (accessed 24.08.15.).

Hershatter, A., Epstein, M., 2010. Millennials and the world of work: an organization and management perspective. J. Bus. Psychol. 25 (2), 211–223.

Hlavaty, G., Townsend, M., 2010. The library's new relevance: fostering the first-year student's acquisition, evaluation, and integration of print and electronic materials. Teach. Engl. Two-Year Coll. 38 (2), 149–160.

Madden, M.L., Martinez, I.T., 2015. The flipped library classroom at Georgia State University: a case study. Ga. Libr. Q. 52 (1), 13–20, <http://digitalcommons.kennesaw.edu/glq/vol52/iss1/9/> (accessed 30.11.15.).

McDonough, B., 2015. Beyond tools and skills: putting information back into information literacy. In: Swanson, T.A., Jagman, H. (Eds.), Not Just Where to Click: Teaching Students How to Think about Information. Association of College and Research Libraries, Chicago, IL, pp. 37–51.

Mello Jr. J.P., 2015. For tech careers it's not about what you studied, it's about what you learned. <http://www.monster.com/technology/a/tech-careers-not-about-studied-about-what-you-learned-0604> (accessed 29.11.15).

Meyer, J.H.F., Land, R. (Eds.), 2006. Overcoming Barriers to Student Understanding: Threshold Concepts and Troublesome Knowledge. Routledge, London.

New Media Consortium, 2012. Horizon report: 2012 higher education edition. <http://www.nmc.org/pdf/2012-horizon-report-HE.pdf> (accessed 15.12.15).

Oblinger, D., Oblinger, J., 2005. Is it age or IT: first steps towards understanding the Net Generation. In: Oblinger, D., Oblinger, J. (Eds.), Educating the Net Generation. EDUCAUSE, Boulder, CO, pp. 2.1–2.20. <http://www.educause.edu/research-and-publications/books/educating-net-generation> (accessed 11.11.15.).

O'Shaughnessy, L., 2015. New college grads: who employers want to hire. <http://www.cbsnews.com/news/new-college-grads-who-employers-want-to-hire/> (accessed 29.11.15.).

Palfrey, J.G., Gasser, U., 2008. Born Digital: Understanding the First Generation of Digital Natives. Basic Books, New York, NY.

Sharkey, J., O'Connor, L., 2013. Establishing Twenty-First-Century information fluency. Ref. User Serv. Q. 53 (1), 33–39.

Sims Memorial Library, 2015. Library Science 102 introduction to information research. <http://www.southeastern.edu/library/directory/ls102/index.html> (accessed 18.08.15.).

Sokoloff, J., 2012. Information literacy in the workplace: employer expectations. J. Bus. Finance Libr. 17 (1), 1–17.

Southeastern Louisiana University, 2015. General catalogue 2015–2016. 568. <https://www.southeastern.edu/admin/rec_reg/university_catalogue/current/assets/2015_2016_catalogue.pdf> (accessed 18.08.15.).

Twenge, J., 2009. Generational changes and their impact in the classroom: teaching Generation Me. Med. Educ. 43 (5), 398–405.

Vito, M., 2013. Collaborative, experiential and technology approaches for 21st century learners. Am. J. Educ. Stud. 6 (1), 47–64.

Woods, T., et al., 2011. Targeting instructional strategies to address Gen Y learner characteristics. J. Phys. Assist. Educ. 22 (2), 38–41.

York, A., et al., 2010. Enriching the academic experience: the library and experiential learning. Collab. Libr. 2 (4), 193–203, <http://collaborativelibrarianship.org/index.php/jocl/article/view/92/73> (accessed 19.03.15.).

CHAPTER 6

Handheld Learning: Authentic Assessment Using iPads

K. Viars[1], M.A. Cullen[1] and A.R. Stalker[2]
[1]Georgia State University, Perimeter College, Alpharetta, GA, United States
[2]Georgia State University, Perimeter College, Dunwoody, GA, United States

6.1 FIRST, SOME CONTEXT

Georgia Perimeter College is a public, nonresidential community college made up of five campuses and a large online "campus." The college offers associate degree programs in a variety of liberal arts majors, as well as professional programs in Nursing, Dental Hygiene, and Sign Language Interpreting. With over 20,000 students, the college prides itself on the diversity of its student body, including international students, minorities, and a wide range of ages and income levels. Approximately two-thirds of the students attend school part-time. Instead of for-credit library research classes, library instruction is integrated into the core curriculum at the discretion of the course instructors. Instruction is most often requested for English, Communications (Public Speaking), and History classes. The authors are located at the smallest of the five campuses, serving approximately 2,000 students. As of January 2016, Georgia Perimeter College consolidated with Georgia State University to form Georgia State University, Perimeter College; the authors will use Georgia Perimeter College throughout this chapter as that was the college's name when this research was conducted.

Three of the five campus libraries have a designated classroom with computer workstations for student use during a library instruction session, providing students with opportunities to improve their research skills through hands-on experience with guidance from the instructing librarian. The other two campuses, including the one where the authors work, do not have a designated library instruction classroom. Other computer classrooms on campus are rarely available for library instruction due to the campus course schedules. Instead of students coming to the library or a dedicated computer classroom for instruction, the librarian goes to the students' regular classroom. The librarian demonstrates how to use the catalog and databases via a computer station and a projector, but students do not have the opportunity to learn through experience, practice new skills, or demonstrate what they have learned.

Even without hands-on practice, many students and instructors expressed gratitude and reported that library instruction sessions helped them. However, the body language of many students in class indicated that they did not find the sessions engaging. In addition, students frequently came to the library reference desk following class, asking questions which hinted that they were struggling with the material. They were often unable even to begin their exploration of library resources, much less complete their research assignments. It was clear that our lecture-plus-demonstration technique was neither interesting to the students nor effectively helping them build the skills they needed.

In addition to making instruction more engaging for the students, we wanted to be able to assess our effectiveness as instructors. The push for assessment came from several rationales: first and foremost, we wanted to know if students were learning and to discover how we could improve our instruction. In addition, local interest in assessment was increasing, as well as in the broader fields of academic libraries and higher education. Lastly, we wanted to ensure we were providing the best experience possible for our students.

6.1.1 The Problem with Quizzes

For several semesters, we employed quizzes to assess student understanding and retention of concepts, as well as to motivate students to pay attention during class. Quizzes customized to the class and college-wide standardized quizzes were used, sometimes following and sometimes during the instruction session. While quiz results were usually good, this method fell short for several reasons. In one-shot instruction, time is a precious commodity and administering the quiz meant sacrificing instruction time. Often, the students were so rushed that test-taking skills may have been just as much a factor in the results as the content they'd learned. While some professors welcomed the quiz and gave the students class credit for taking it, others were reluctant (or refused) to have the library quiz as part of the instruction. Some students did not take the quiz seriously, while others expressed anger that there was an unscheduled quiz. Even when it was low- or no-stakes in relation to their grades, the quiz seemed to add significant stress to the experience for them. This was contrary to the positive experience we wanted them to associate with the library and librarians.

The quiz presented other problems, as well. Pedagogically, it was a disappointment, because feedback to the students was limited. We either took further class time to review the quiz, or we gave the quizzes back to the students with no opportunity to clarify the questions they missed. Other times, the quizzes were not returned to the student. Ultimately, the quiz gave some information to the librarian about the success of the instruction, but gave the student no feedback about their own degree of understanding. Additionally, it was cumbersome to grade. The lack of student computers in the classroom precluded online quizzing tools, so we had to hand-grade each quiz and tabulate any analysis or enter the data for each student ourselves.

Additional problems are inherent to multiple-choice and short-answer quizzes. These kinds of quizzes can easily assess knowledge on the lower end of Bloom's Taxonomy, such as remembering. Such questions might ask:

- What is the password to access databases?
- Do you use the catalog or databases to find books in the library?
- What are some ways you can contact a librarian for help?

We could determine, to some degree, whether students could recall the content of the library instruction session. But that told us nothing about how well-equipped they were to do college-level research with library resources. Designing questions that effectively measure higher-order thinking skills, such as evaluating and analyzing, is a challenge. Such questions can involve scenarios to which the student must respond, or present examples for students to assess. However, these kinds of questions usually require substantial time for the student to answer; five or ten minutes is not sufficient for students at a novice level to respond. Indeed, these were often the kinds of questions that had a low percentage of correct responses in our classes.

Of additional concern is the validity of multiple choice quizzes. Our observations were that quiz performance did not translate to true ability; students who passed the quiz would still ask us fundamental questions when they came to the library to do their research, while students who were capable researchers could miss questions on the quiz. Our experience is consistent with the findings reported by Schilling and Applegate (2012): quiz performance, student confidence, and performance measures have little correlation with one another.

6.1.2 Finding a New Way

Given our lack of confidence in the efficacy of quizzes and our concerns about managing instruction time, we wanted to find an authentic activity that would engage students and provide them with an experiential learning activity that the librarians could also use as an easy tool to assess student learning. In experiential learning, students are actively engaged, building on existing knowledge as they learn-by-doing with the support of the instructor (Lewis and Williams, 1994).

We tried a variety of techniques to address this challenge, with varying degrees of success. Experiential learning opportunities increased engagement and were effective in teaching some information literacy concepts. In the course of our experimenting, we found some of the following activities valuable:

- Students assessing various types of resources for authority, currency, and scope;
- Exploring and reporting to the class the contents of reference materials, popular, and scholarly articles;
- Having class discussions about the reliability of real and bogus websites.

However, actually teaching students to be able to "[a]ccess the needed information effectively and efficiently" remained elusive (ACRL, 2015).

One day, an instruction librarian was demonstrating a database to a class when the computer at the presenter station froze. Efforts for a speedy revival failed and time was running short, so she instructed the students to get out their smart phones and follow her instructions. The students responded to doing research on their favorite devices with enthusiasm. While the mobile database interface we were using wasn't fully featured, the fact that the students were engaged and were able to practice was inspiring to us. We considered doing more "library research on your phone" sessions, but while it may seem that every student has a smart phone, this is not indeed the case. What's more, some have limited data plans or may not be readily set up to use the campus wireless network, a potential stumbling block in a library instruction session.

The serendipitous success of the phone session led to the idea of using iPads in classes. While still a mobile device, iPads are large enough to use the full-featured desktop versions of the library website, catalog, and databases. In addition, they could be preprogrammed to connect to the student wireless network, and links to common sites (such as the library homepage) could be added to the iPad home screen. Most of all, iPads would provide an equal learning opportunity for all students, and the librarian was not challenged with providing technical support for unfamiliar devices.

6.1.3 Acquiring and Setting Up the iPads

When the library director inquired about a grant for iPads, she was informed that the college's Office of Information Technology (OIT) had a surplus of older-model iPads that were available for projects that met certain criteria. Because of having been funded by student technology fees, the iPads could only be used if they were placed directly in the hands of students. We were happy to find out that our project qualified, and we received ten iPads to use for library instruction classes in Spring semester 2015 and an additional ten for Fall semester. We only needed basic Internet access, making the older iPads adequate for our needs.

Prior to incorporating the mobile iPad lab into classroom instruction, the library conferred with OIT to ensure that the equipment would be fully operational once placed in the students' hands. This required both hardware and software set-up, as well as deciding how best to access the wireless network in the classroom. Given the age and prior use of the iPads, OIT employees updated any relevant system software, removed extraneous applications and data, and checked the batteries on all units. A link to the library homepage was bookmarked on the iPad's Home screen. The iPads had long, hexadecimal serial numbers, so librarians assigned them simple one- and two-digit numbers to make it easy to identify individual iPads.

6.2 USING IPADS IN THE CLASSROOM

6.2.1 Classes and Databases

When approached by faculty members for scheduled instruction in the spring of 2015, librarians suggested an alternative to the traditional one-shot instruction culminating in a multiple-choice quiz. The library now offered a mobile lab option wherein the students applied newly acquired research skills on an active digital platform immediately following the one-shot instruction session. Several instructors enthusiastically volunteered to try out the experiential classroom model. The positive reception to the iPad assessment model in the spring semester prompted the library staff to promote the program during the annual faculty meetings for the fall semester of 2015. In the past, some faculty members eschewed library instruction because of the lack of available lab space for students. The mobile iPad lab and accompanying assessment finally offered a viable alternative to those looking for a more experiential approach to the instruction.

As a two-year institution, Georgia Perimeter College's curriculum focuses on core classes, and the library instruction program's strongest partnerships are with introductory-level humanities professors. English Composition and Public Speaking classes are the library's most-taught subject areas, and consequently, the ones in which this assessment strategy has been most used. In most English Composition I and Public Speaking classes, students research a controversial contemporary issue, and write a paper or give a speech supporting one perspective on it. To support these classes, the library subscribes to the *Opposing Viewpoints in Context* and *CQ Researcher* databases. *Opposing Viewpoints in Context*, a GALE database also available in a print edition, provides a wide variety of sources drawn from reference works, academic journals, statistics, and additional resources on controversial issues. *CQ Researcher*, a product of CQ Press, provides similar content on current social and political issues written by professional journalists, including a pro/con argument section.

When instructing in English Composition I or Public Speaking classes, the librarian demonstrates both databases. The assessment requires students to use *Opposing Viewpoints in Context* to find and email an article on an assigned topic. Care was taken when developing the topic portion of the activity, which is shown in Fig. 6.1. It was important to balance a range of factors. Chosen topics were prescreened to ensure that student searches would provide viable results. It was also necessary to narrow the

Directions	Topics
• Your group number is on the back of your iPad • Find an article on your topic in Opposing Viewpoints • Email the article to **the email address on the board.**	2. Performance enhancing drugs in sports 3. Banned books 4. Gay marriage 5. Funding space exploration 6. Online bullying 7. Death penalty 8. Prayer in public schools 9. Cell phones and cancer 10. Legalizing drugs

Figure 6.1 Slide showing the assessment exercise used with *Opposing Viewpoints*.

Directions
- Your **group number** is on the back of your iPad
- Find an article on your topic in **Bloom's**
- Email the article to **the email address on the board.**

Topics
2. *Harry Potter* and the hero's journey
3. W. Somerset Maugham and the bildungsroman
4. *Native Son* and rejection
5. Emily Dickinson and capitalization
6. *Walden* and society
7. Toni Morrison and abolition
8. *Frankenstein* and the grotesque
9. Zora Neale Hurston and community
10. "King Lear" and tragedy
11. Arthur Miller and the American Dream
12. "Beowulf" and monsters
13. Jane Austen and society
14. *1984* and power
15. Franz Kafka and Realism
16. *The Hound of the Baskervilles* and the gothic

Figure 6.2 Slide showing the assessment exercise used with literary criticism databases.

focus of the search, or specify certain elements of the search in a way that discouraged the students from simply selecting a broad topic category and using the first available article to complete the assessment. This also structured the topics enough to provide students with a similar experience to what they would need to do to complete the assignment post-instruction.

In English Composition II, students research literary criticism and write a paper analyzing a work of literature. Depending on the professor's preferences and the amount of time allotted for instruction, the instructing librarian may choose one or several of the literary criticism databases to which the libraries subscribe; the current selection includes *Artemis Literary Sources* (GALE), *Bloom's Literature* (Facts on File), and *Literary Reference Center* (EBSCO). For the assessment exercise, the instructing librarian assigns each group a literary criticism topic and a specific work; the students then research and choose a relevant article to send via the database's email function.

Following a similar process to the previously discussed *Opposing Viewpoints* topics, the literature topics were thoughtfully developed. Using prior reference interactions with students, as well as assignment guidelines, and taking care to keep the topics focused, relevant, and interesting, the list was created to closely replicate the experience students could expect when completing the class assignment later on their own, as seen in Fig. 6.2. Again, librarians attempted searches with these topics prior to instruction to confirm that the student experience would produce useful results and reinforce proper beginning research skills.

6.2.2 Practice and Assessment

In-class practice and assessment using the iPads evaluates students' ability to search for articles effectively in the selected databases. "The use of authentic assessment offers librarians an analysis of how students apply the outcomes taught in a specific class," making it a good choice for assessment in one-shot instruction sessions (Carter, 2013). After demonstrating keyword selection and searching techniques in the databases, the librarian instructor puts students into small groups, ideally in pairs, and distributes the iPads; working in pairs, in our observation, means that both students are engaged in the experiential learning, while in larger groups, one student tends to complete the assignment while others do not participate. The total of twenty iPads available in the Fall semester of 2015 made it possible to pair students even in the larger classes. Instructions for completing the assessment are listed on a PowerPoint slide projected on a screen at the front of the classroom; this slide also lists assigned topics for each small group. The instructing librarian verifies that articles on these topics are available in the database prior to assigning them as part of the assessment.

Small stickers on the backs of the iPads assign each tablet a number. Students match their iPad's number with the numbered topics on the slide to discover their assigned topic. They then search for an article on the topic in the assigned database, and use the email function within the database to send the article to the librarian instructor. Throughout the assessment, the librarian circulates among the groups, checking for understanding and answering any questions that arise. Typically, this is an excellent opportunity to clarify details of accessing and using the database, as well as to reinforce the value of library resources. Many students are already familiar with the iPad or similar technology, but for those who are not, this time is also an opportunity to help troubleshoot technical issues or provide guidance on using a tablet and the iOS operating system.

6.2.3 Results

After the class, the instructing librarian checks her email for articles sent to her on the assigned topics during the class time, and evaluates them using a rubric. The authors developed the rubric based on three main principles: selecting an *article* from the correct *database* on the assigned *topic*. The rubric considers only these criteria. For each criterion, a maximum of two and a minimum of zero points are available, making six points a perfect score. The criteria are judged on a spectrum of accuracy for the task the learners are asked to complete; for example, a learner who selects an article from a journal or periodical receives the maximum two points available, while one who selects a different information resource such as a book or a statistical report receives one. Failing to select an information resource of any kind yields zero points. The rubric was designed to review the results both quickly and accurately.

During the Fall semester in 2015, ten Communications and English classes were selected for inclusion in this study. Seventy-one groups of one to three students participated in the experiential learning activity, with strongly positive results. The data indicated strong performance on all three individual criteria. In selecting the correct information source (an article), students scored an average of 1.96. In selecting the correct database for their class, performance was even better, averaging 1.99. And in selecting an on-topic information source, all participants scored a perfect 2. The average of all the participants scored 5.94 out of a possible score of 6. In the individual results, all groups that participated scored at least a 1 for each criterion. The results from students who were able to or chose to participate in the experiential learning exercise indicate a high degree of competence in navigating to the databases and selecting on-topic articles.

After completing the assessment activity, students were surveyed about their experience of the assessment using a brief survey instrument embedded in a LibGuide. We added an icon with a link to the survey on each iPad's home screen, making it easy for students to find. The survey asked the following three questions:

1. Which of these options do you prefer to help you learn in class?
   a. Practicing using library databases with iPads;
   b. Hearing lecture and watching a demonstration of using library databases (no iPads);
   c. No preference.
2. How prepared do you feel to navigate to the databases using the library homepage?
   a. Prepared;
   b. Somewhat prepared;
   c. Not prepared.
3. How prepared do you feel to use the database you practiced with (Bloom's, *Opposing Viewpoints,* etc.)?
   a. Prepared;
   b. Somewhat prepared;
   c. Not prepared.

Students found the survey easy to access and complete, and we received eighty-one survey responses. For the first question about their preferred way to receive instruction, fifty-six of those groups (69.14%)

prefer practicing using library databases with iPads. Eleven groups (13.58%) preferred the lecture and demonstration, and fourteen groups (17.28%) expressed no preference. For the second question about how prepared students feel to navigate to the databases, fifty-three groups (65.43%) felt prepared, twenty-three (28.40%) felt somewhat prepared and five (6.17%) did not feel prepared. Responses to the final question about how prepared students feel to use the database with which they practiced in class were similar, with fifty-four groups (66.67%) reporting feeling prepared and twenty-five groups (30.86%) reporting feeling somewhat prepared. Only two groups (2.47%) reported feeling unprepared to use the database they used in class. Overall, students express a clear preference for using iPads in class for experiential learning, and strongly believe that this practice made them more capable of performing these critical research tasks on their own.

Feedback from instructors of assessed classes, collected via email, was also positive. One lecturer in Communications said,

> [U]sing the iPad during library lectures is an effective way to educate students about library resources and on how to utilize the library and Galileo [authors' note: GALILEO is the name of the libraries' database portal]. Plus, iPad usage also helps to increase student participation during the discussion. Students today are very technically astute—so allowing them to use technology in the classroom is a clever way to get them to learn about the library and its resources.

Another associate professor of Communications, agreed: "I thought both the info and the activities were great! [...] Please continue to do this presentation."

6.3 THE FUTURE OF AUTHENTIC ASSESSMENT

iPads are effective experiential learning tools in one-shot library instruction classes and have proven to be a successful way for students to learn to use library databases. Moreover, this strategy gained the support of the faculty, and of the students themselves; previously, while some faculty members were supportive of assessment efforts, students seldom were. Students are engaged and interested in using the iPads, and we found the class time dedicated to the exercise to be valuable both for them and for us. The rare complaints we received about the iPads indicated a preference for a different mobile platform or frustration with technical issues, rather than anger or stress about assessment. Learners also received feedback from the librarian during the exercise and from the database indicating that they have successfully sent an article via email, helping them to learn what successful research looks like.

Experiential learning also provides the opportunity for us as instructors to move past the lowest levels of Bloom's Taxonomy, to see more clearly what and how students are learning about the research process. Rather than relying on students' test-taking skills, we can see how they are applying (or struggling to apply, which is equally valuable to know) the skills of a college researcher. Using the iPads to find and select articles based on assigned criteria gives students a path to implement the skills they will need to use to complete their assignments. Additionally, they are evaluating the information that they find against a provided set of criteria, another skill they will need to successfully complete most research assignments. Moving into the higher levels of Bloom's Taxonomy allows students to practice these skills with the guidance of a librarian, to help to correct missteps and resolve misunderstandings before they begin the process on their own. Also, as we teach, correct, and guide, we learn more about what elements students find confusing or where in the process they get stuck. Experiential learning informs our instruction to better assist students in the future, both in the classroom and at the reference desk.

6.3.1 Lessons We Learned

Unforeseen issues included students not knowing their login credentials and a general unfamiliarity with the operation of the iPad itself. Forgotten passwords slowed down the start of the assessment portion, as groups scrambled to get logged on and engaged in the assignment. Similarly, significant time was sometimes needed to explain basic iOS user operation. It is also worth noting that the preparation of the iPads before and after instruction may require a substantial amount of time. Typical maintenance includes disconnecting student accounts from the wireless network, deleting bookmarked pages or cached data from browsers, and maintaining adequately charged devices.

Occasionally, technical issues arose that disrupted the flow of instruction. While these issues were intermittent and minor, others wanting to incorporate a similar instruction model may want to be aware of potential setbacks. The most notable situation was a wireless service outage in the classroom. Unfortunately, a quick fix within the class period was unlikely; however, many students in attendance brought their smartphones to class. The librarian redirected willing students to continue the assessment process on their mobile devices. This gave the students an opportunity to see the library's resources on a mobile platform and helped to minimize the disruption of the wireless network outage in the building. There was also an instance of a database service outage, and the librarian redirected the students to a comparable database for the assessment.

From our experience using iPads for IL assessment, we offer the following words of advice:

- Ask the instructor to require the students to bring their login credentials with them on the scheduled day of instruction.
- Work with the campus technology office to address any potential wi-fi connectivity issues and suggested work-around solutions prior to instruction.
- Suggest each group have at least one student familiar with using an iOS device and/or allow students to use their own wireless devices to complete the assessment.
- Develop a set of concise and explicit instructions for the students to follow for the assessment portion of the session.
- Have an alternate database in mind for the assessment portion, in the event of a vendor service outage.

6.3.2 The Future

In Fall semester 2015, the authors successfully submitted a grant proposal for forty new iPad Air devices, with covers, keyboards, and a charging cart; these new tools have been well received by students and faculty in instruction sessions. We are also considering expanding the exercise (and consequently, the rubric) to include additional criteria, such as requiring the selected article to be peer-reviewed, within a specific date range, or from a single journal or list of journals. In more advanced classes, the exercise could require that students select a database appropriate to the topic and format required.

In this study, students were not asked to provide their names or email addresses when emailing their article to the librarian, but, if supplied, the librarian had the opportunity to respond to the student. Some students asked questions or made comments in the email, such as asking if they had completed the exercise correctly, or expressing thanks for the opportunity to practice researching. Requiring students to supply their email addresses could be incorporated into the lesson to provide additional feedback to students.

Some students did not use the email feature of the database but, instead, copied the citation or article URL into the body of an email or emailed a pdf of the article. We did not explicitly require students to use the email function in the database, so we counted these responses as correct. However, we may consider adding using the email function in the database as a criterion in the future.

ACKNOWLEDGMENT

The authors wish to thank Leslie Drost for her help in collecting the data discussed in this chapter.

REFERENCES

Association of College & Research Libraries, 2015. Information literacy competency standards for higher education. <http://www.ala.org/acrl/standards/information literacycompetency> (accessed 25.08. 15.).

Carter, T., 2013. Use what you have: authentic assessment of in-class activities. Ref. Serv. Rev. 41 (1), 49−61.

Lewis, L.H., Williams, C.J., 1994. Experiential learning: past and present. New Dir. Adult Contin. Educ. 62, 5−16.

Schilling, K., Applegate, R., 2012. Best methods for evaluating educational impact: a comparison of the efficacy of commonly used measures of library instruction. J. Med. Libr. Assoc. 100 (4), 258−269.

PART II

The Experiential Library: Programs, Collections, Spaces, Staff Development and Training

CHAPTER 7

"Out of the Vault": Engaging Students in Experiential Learning Through Special Collections and Archives

C.J. Anderson and C. Brand
Drew University Library, Madison, NJ, United States

The Department of Special Collections and University Archives at the Drew University Library is committed to experiential learning as we connect our resources with both students and off-campus researchers. As a small liberal arts university that has faced budgetary constraints, we've elected to become more proactive with our programming, bringing our Special Collections and University Archives materials out of the vault and into the hands of our patrons. By thinking outside of the box, we have been able to implement a variety of initiatives and programs with little to no impact on the budget, resulting in multiple experiential learning opportunities for students.

This chapter examines how low-cost, engaging, and interactive programming using special collections and archival materials has transformed experiential learning for both graduate and undergraduate students at Drew University. Developed by the Department of Special Collections and University Archives of the Drew Library, these new events and programs include: the Out of the Vault series, library exhibits curated by students, and the enhancement of the student worker experience. These initiatives emerged out of departmental brainstorming sessions where each member of the staff was encouraged to think broadly and creatively to propose low-cost programming with the greatest impact. Each program involves our full-time and part-time staff, and all events are geared toward reaching out to the Drew campus as well as to the area towns of Madison, Chatham, and Florham Park, New Jersey.

However, the programs spotlighted in this chapter are only a small part of the total outreach that we do every year. We also regularly invite professors to bring in their classes to the reading room for interactive teaching and learning sessions, led by both Drew teaching faculty and librarians. Several graduate students found research projects as a result of these sessions. We curate exhibits regularly to showcase our materials. Recently, the department has begun collaborating with on-campus academic conferences and events as well as reached out to local historical societies and churches to enhance the attendees' experiences, through exploration of primary sources related to the conference or event theme.

Chris Anderson, coauthor and head of the department, uses his experiences with the Drew University baseball team and his weekly campus radio show to engage the student and alumni constituencies (Anderson, 2016). Coauthor Cassie Brand is both full-time staff and a graduate student at the university. Her immersion in the graduate school allows for informal conversations with fellow graduate students and professors at meetings, cocktail parties, classes, and the occasional road trip, which has resulted in greater collaboration and involvement with both students and faculty.

Through the integration of primary sources into the classroom, and various ways of engaging students with materials, the Department of Special Collections and University Archives furthers the student experience. Our programming, taken as a whole, attempts to connect the student with the Special Collections and Archival material. This engagement brings together a synthesis of student learning and experiential learning, while providing opportunities for students to gain hands-on practical skills they can use in their future careers.

7.1 EXPERIENTIAL LEARNING IN A SPECIAL COLLECTIONS AND UNIVERSITY ARCHIVES CONTEXT

Special Collections and University Archives are rich centers for experiential learning, because of the proliferation of primary source materials. By encouraging the use of collections and by welcoming students into the reading room, librarians and archivists create learning environments that enhance the student experience. The Department of Special Collections and University Archives at Drew University strives to increase the use of the collections by students, specifically undergrads who may face a degree of archival anxiety. Students may feel as though they are not welcome in the reading room because they are not serious scholars or do not have enough degrees to work with such special materials. However, like many other institutions, Drew University Library encourages the use of special collections by all of its students and by outside researchers.

One of the main ways in which we make students feel welcome is through inviting classes into the reading room to explore materials directly relating to the class topic. Introducing students to primary source materials in a classroom setting may help to alleviate any anxiety students have about using the reading room. Archival anxiety must be addressed because "negative emotions such as fear and anxiety can block learning, while positive feelings of attraction and interest may be essential for learning" (Kolb and Kolb, 2005, p. 208). Students who may have previously felt unwelcome because of preconceived notions of who is allowed to research in special collections will be welcomed by the librarian(s) hosting the class session and will be encouraged to return. Even this small gesture of welcome can relax students and make them feel as if they belong, allowing for a more positive experience and better learning outcomes.

Class visits are an important part of experiential learning in Special Collections and University Archives because of the unique opportunity they provide for students to get their hands on primary sources that most of them have never encountered. However, this chapter will spotlight the ways in which our department moves past class visits to further enhance the student experience and provide more opportunities for students to handle and learn from primary sources. The three programs highlighted below are the Out of the Vault series, student-curated exhibits, and the apprenticeship model used with student workers. These programs create room for conversation, collaboration, and reflection, all of which are essential to experiential learning according to David and Alice Kolb (Kolb and Kolb, 2005, p. 208). They invite students to learn and explore outside of the curriculum and provide opportunities for students and visitors to gain experience that may otherwise not be available to them.

7.2 OUT OF THE VAULT SERIES

The Out of the Vault program is a series of talks sponsored by the Department of Special Collections and University Archives of the Drew University Library. The title of the series was the result of our department wanting to create an image of bringing special collections and archival material out of its protected environment to be viewed, analyzed, and touched. As a result, each interactive session introduces attendees to one Drew Library Special Collection or University Archive Collection. The sessions provide opportunities for students and visitors to learn more about the collections of the Drew University Library including the provenance and content of specific collections. We are particularly interested in how students experience the materials and make it a focus of each session that students engage or interact with the collection. This provides a dual focus: students learn more about the specific collection, and they get to engage with and touch the materials. Each session takes place in the Wilson Reading Room of the United Methodist Archives and History Center and sessions are provided at no cost to Drew students and the outside community. There is no cost to the Library outside of staff time to prepare the showcase of materials.

The sessions are built around brief, informal talks prepared by Drew faculty, staff, and students, and occasionally researchers who use the collections. Each presenter is given up to fifteen minutes to speak on the collection. Their talks include basic information on provenance, notes about the donor of the materials, and an overview of the contents of the collection. We then reserve thirty minutes for attendees to interact with the collection which has been spread out on the tables of the reading room. While attendees engage with the materials, the staff and speakers are available for questions, or in some cases, translation of the materials. The entire session takes approximately one hour.

This past year, presentations included talks on and explorations of our Incunabula Collection, the "Tiny Books" at Drew, the Governor Thomas H. Kean Collection, the Robert Frost Collection, and the world-renowned Methodist Collection. The series has drawn significant interest on campus, especially with our graduate student population, and we've continued to book sessions up to one year in advance. Future events include talks on our George Fraser Black Collection on Witchcraft, the art of Jacob Landau, and the Methodist collections of LGBT materials housed at the archives center.

We've found the talks to be effective (and inexpensive) platforms to engage Drew students. The talks provide opportunities for both our undergraduate and graduate student workers to lead sessions on a collection they may have processed or researched, and it allows them to add a presentation line to their curriculum vitae. The talks also connect campus non-Special Collections and Archives Faculty and Librarians with our materials. They, in turn, learn more about our work as a department and it provides them with an opportunity for a public talk as part of their professional development and community outreach. Our intent is to broaden the speaker base to include persons from off-campus, including local persons from the Madison area, or even researchers who plan to spend time with a particular collection.

The Out of the Vault series provides opportunities for students to explore the collections without the need for a professor to bring them into the reading room. They can investigate the materials on their own, which removes several of the barriers that cause archival anxiety. The series acts as an invitation to interact with the collections, and we encourage attendees to handle the materials and to consider the items for their own research. But what Out of the Vault does best is to convey the message that John Overholt so eloquently stated, "Please touch. This is here for you. You are special enough for special collections." (Overholt, 2013, p. 19).

7.3 STUDENT-CURATED EXHIBITS

One of the ways we have engaged students with Special Collections materials is through student-curated exhibits. The department has sponsored several exhibits in which students either assisted the curators or were themselves curators. The departmental exhibit "Special Collections and Archives Recommends...An Exhibition of Favorites" invited student workers within the department to curate a single case. They were required to have a theme, write a context label, and a short biographical note introducing themselves as student staff.

Additionally, James M. Van Wyck, a graduate student at Fordham University and a regular researcher at Drew University, cocurated an exhibit with coauthor Christopher Anderson. Through this exhibit, Van Wyck was able to present his dissertation research to the public in a unique way. His ongoing research is based on Special Collections resources found at the Drew Library, which he used to contextualize the exhibit through labels and material objects displayed in the various cases. He, along with his doctoral advisor, gave talks at the opening reception. As a result of encouraging a graduate student from outside the university to experience our materials, the Drew Library was able to form a relationship with another nearby institution that assisted with PR for the exhibit and its opening event (Mercuri, 2015).

This past Spring semester our Library staff worked with students in Dr. Louis Hamilton's undergraduate Comparative Religion and History Honors Seminar, "The Reformation: Theology, Society and Devotion." Thirteen students from the course cocurated an exhibition of rare books from the 15th to the 18th centuries that had been used in the course during the semester. The students spent the semester researching the significance of these items and the ideas the volumes promoted. Books consulted and placed on display ranged from a first-generation European printing of the first *Book of Common Prayer*, to a history of the Inquisition, to a copy of the *Malleus Maleficarum* (*The Hammer of Witches*). This approach to experiential learning is the subject of a case study authored by Marianne Hansen on a student-curated exhibit at Bryn Mawr College (Hansen, 2012, pp. 237−241).

The exhibit was an optional extra-credit project that arose from a class assignment asking students to examine the books as material objects and to then write a paper describing them. The assignment made the reading room a lively place in which students examined books, asked questions of the staff, collaborated with the professor and librarians from different departments, exclaimed aloud about their discoveries, and collaborated with their classmates, often calling them over to share what they had found. The excitement of the undergraduates working with the primary sources is best expressed through the words of Nathan Williams, one of the undergraduates in the course:

> Working with the books in the archive made me feel genuine and connected to my subject matter in a way that is difficult to describe. Looking up articles on the internet and writing papers that way feels absolutely sterile in comparison. Books have a soul to them that can't be replicated by anything else. By working with these books I got to touch that feeling and that history a little bit.
> **Nathan Williams (2015, personal communication, 19 August).**

The course assignment helped students envision books in a different light, to learn about how the materiality of the book can affect the text and its reception. They also learned about the ways in which readers during the Protestant Reformation interacted with their texts, giving them further insight into the minds of the books' former owners.

Along the way, we met individually with the students and shared with them basic information on curating exhibits. We also asked them to consider how they wanted to display their book, which page should be opened, and how to write an appropriate text label to accompany the object. The Library hosted an opening reception for the exhibit and invited Dr. Hamilton and the student curators to discuss their experience working on the exhibit. Students were encouraged to invite their family and friends to the event, which drew several dozen people to the library. The event gave students the opportunity to share their experiences with the materials and also promoted collegiality and collaboration between the Library, faculty, and students.

Through their work on the exhibit, students gained a greater understanding of the books they were working with for their class project; they formed relationships with the Library staff members through emails and edits to their text; and they learned to deliver their research to a general audience. The undergraduates were also given the opportunity to have the essay they wrote for class published in a handout to go along with the exhibit. Haviland Atha-Simonton, a student who participated in the course, noted,

> When I was first informed that I had to work closely with a rare book, I was definitely excited by the fact, but in my head, a book was a book like any other and I didn't see anything special about it at the time that I was informed. It wasn't until I unwrapped my chosen book from its protective white cover and laid my eyes on its unique binding that I truly realized the privilege I had. From cigar burns, hand written calligraphy, and withering pages, I realized that I was able to see through the eyes of [another reader].
>
> **Haviland Atha-Simonton (2015, personal communication, 14 August).**

The students enjoyed the opportunity and the project continued a building relationship between the undergraduate faculty and our department at the Library. As a result, we have now strengthened collaborative programming with faculty and students, brought students to the Archives Center, and made positive impressions on the minds of both faculty and students. Through this undergraduate exhibit, we have been able to promote our collections, but also our role as educators in support of the faculty. In the Spring of 2016, Dr. Louis Hamilton was due to teach a similar course for which the final project would be an exhibit, rather than a paper. The department will be collaborating with this class throughout the entire semester.

7.4 STUDENTS WORKERS AS EXPERIENTIAL LEARNERS

Like many university libraries, Drew University relies heavily on student workers. At the time of this writing, Special Collections and University Archives employs six student workers and one volunteer. Five of the students are in graduate studies at the university and one is an undergraduate; the volunteer is an alumna of Drew University. In the past we have also taken on independent study students within the university, as well as both graduate and undergraduate interns and volunteers from other schools. For brevity's sake, we will use the term "student" to apply to all of our students, interns, and volunteers, despite their actual status.

The large number of student workers allows us to accomplish much more than would be possible as a department alone. However, as many supervisors have learned, managing student workers can be intensive and may take time away from other duties. While it is not always possible to determine a student's ability from an application, we have started requiring both a resume and a statement of interest from the students applying for positions within our department. Statements of interest are used to determine the student's ability to follow directions (e.g., did she/he cover what was asked for in the application?), past experiences with libraries or special collections and archives, and most importantly, their reason for being interested in the job. Many students are looking for a paycheck, but by looking for students with specific research interests and career goals, we have been able to collect an exceptional team of student workers.

We look for students whose goals match the department's and who will most greatly benefit from the work experience. For students within the university, we look to match collections with research interests and for students who are interested in special collections and archives as a future career or place for research. In addition, we take on interns and volunteers from outside of Drew University to extend the possibilities of experiential learning outside of the school. However, we are just as strict with volunteers as we are with our paid students. We only accept volunteers from outside of the university if they are highly motivated and interested in exploring librarianship as a potential career. Students whose goals are furthered through their work in the department are more highly motivated and more interested in the projects assigned.

In order to make the jobs even more beneficial to the students, we often extend their experiences beyond the normal job duties. For students interested in certain aspects of the profession, we aim to incorporate that into their work. For example, one of our graduate students was hired for a digital project, but wanted to learn more about archival processing. We were able to add processing a collection to his work load and he split his time between the digital project and processing. Of course, it's not always possible to assign job duties in areas where the students have interest. Volunteer Claire is interested in rare book cataloging. That training would be impractical, so instead she occasionally shadows the Special Collections Cataloger to learn more about the process. Claire described her experience in the following way:

> Through this modern-day apprenticeship I have been introduced to the day-to-day doings of an archival institution as well as some of the more nuanced philosophies and decisions concerning the running, promoting and maintenance of the collections. It is because of my experience here, the people I have met and the historical dialogues I have been invited to participate in that I have decided to venture into the archival field as a career. When I met with a college mentor to discuss my lack of direction after graduation, I never imagined that walking into the Drew archives would have such a profound impact. And yet every time I come to volunteer I am genuinely excited to see what objects and ideas, new and old await me.
> **Claire DuLaney (2015, personal communication, 14 August).**

Additionally, student supervisor Cassie Brand set up a series of three workshops for interested student workers and volunteers to introduce them to books as objects. They explored bindings, paper, and illustrations in each of the sessions which expanded their understanding of book history and the books that they work with on a daily basis.

Through allowing students room to explore areas within the department, but possibly outside their original job duties, we encourage experiential learning and personal growth. As Reg Dennick points out, "learning occurs in professional working environments where learners are working or shadowing and engaged in an educational programme at the same time" (Dennick, 2012, p. 620). Opening up possibilities for students by asking them what they would like to do and learn while working for the department gives them an opportunity to maximize their experiences.

One extreme example is undergraduate student Allie, who was originally hired for filing and scanning. However, through simple conversations, we learned that she is an art major who had taken courses in photography. We began asking for her to assist with photography requests and quickly realized her skills could be utilized to create a stronger website presence. We asked her to photograph the collections and create signature images that capture both the subject matter and materials in the collection. Her photography and artwork are now featured on the collection pages, which makes our website much more dynamic and acts as a portfolio of her work. By exploring Allie's strengths, we have created a more positive work and learning experience, where she is building her artistic skills. In turn, the department benefits through a more engaged worker and a more dynamic web presence.

In addition to looking for opportunities to engage students more fully through their work, we integrate our students into the staff in several ways. Dennick states, "If students feel isolated and not part of the group this may inhibit their learning, so ensure that interpersonal needs such as 'belonging' and being part of the group are met" (Dennick, 2012, p. 622). Integrating students into the workplace creates a sense of belonging, responsibility, and encourages learning in different ways. Integration of students into the staff relied mainly on treating the students with collegiality and respect. While it is necessary for the students to report to and get instructions from supervisors, it is also possible to treat them as colleagues at the same time. The department encourages communication at all times and furthers it through less formal means, such as weekly snack time, shared meals, and monthly meetings.

Informal get-togethers like snack time and potluck lunches provide a forum for staff and students to discuss their lives, their school work, and other things that take place outside of work. While these do not yield measurable results in the students' work, they do help to create an atmosphere in which learning and exploration can take place. Students and staff get to know each other better, become more comfortable with each other, and have a forum to express ideas informally. The monthly meetings have more of a formal feel with measurable outcomes. We gather staff and students in these formal meetings to discuss projects, progress, difficulties, and to ask questions. This meeting is usually scheduled for half an hour, but has a tendency to run long due to the flow of conversation and ideas.

The meetings create a higher level of collaboration among students, allow the students to discuss their work and progress, and have even brought about outreach ideas like the previously discussed Out of the Vault sessions. Paul Hodge et al. discuss the importance of storytelling and reflections to make learning concrete (Hodge et al., 2011). These meetings provide a regular forum through which students can assist each other to learn more and also concretize what they have learned through their work experiences.

Through proper training and supervision, our students take on professional-level job duties and are fully integrated into the running of the department. All students, interns, and volunteers are trained to manage the reading room, which involves registering patrons, retrieving materials, and assisting with reference and interlibrary loan requests. While this seems like a small thing, the impact can be great. Volunteer Gina noted,

> As an aspiring Special Collections Librarian, gaining hands-on volunteer experience was incredibly beneficial. I was able to experience the everyday duties and responsibilities, as well as explore new aspects of the profession to further define my career goals. This practical experience, combined with personal attention and direction, allowed me to see a side of the profession that research alone wouldn't have allowed. These opportunities provided a well-rounded perspective and unique access to valuable knowledge in my desired career path.
>
> Gina Modero (2015, personal communication, 16 August).

We also have students processing collections, writing articles for the Drew Library newsletter, and even assisting with class visits. Integrating students into the staff and treating them as professionals helps to prepare them for these challenges. As Pablo Alvarez reminds us, "the rare book librarian assumes the challenging and critical roles as both teacher and interpreter of the collection, which may deal with topics beyond his or her area of expertise" (Alvarez, 2006, p. 95). We must remember that our students become the expert on the collections they process and they may have additional expertise through their graduate studies and life experiences. Graduate student Brian has been responsible for processing the Drew University Center for Holocaust/Genocide Studies Collections, so he knows more than some of the staff about these collections. When a class comes in to view the Collections, we invite Brian to assist with the visit, to discuss the materials and contextualize them for the class. We use his knowledge of the collection to make it a better experience for visitors, while also giving Brian experience interpreting the collection. By treating our students as professionals—by asking their opinions, giving them responsibilities and reasonable decision-making powers—we in return get professional-level work.

When taking on any student worker, a supervisor must weigh the time it takes to train and supervise that worker with the benefits of employing that person. By being extremely selective about the students we hire and by maximizing their potential, we have been able to increase our productivity as a department and extend our outreach. Though things like shadowing staff members, meetings, and snack time take away from the assigned job duties, these help to integrate the students and enrich their experiences. The more positive the work experience, the more students will be motivated to work and learn.

7.5 CONCLUSION

Through providing students with opportunities to engage with Special Collections and University Archives materials, the Drew University Library has increased class and research visits as well as the visibility of our collections on campus and to the surrounding community. As Scott Walter confirms, "Campuses have recognized that public engagement is critical to their success because it is through engagement that institutions of higher education build communities of advocates for their cause beyond the traditional communities of teachers, students, researchers, and scholars" (Walter, 2010, p. 28). The programs highlighted above engage undergraduate and graduate students, faculty, staff, and the general public through opportunities to explore the materials in meaningful ways. This creates advocates for the Library and its collections, such as Fordham student James M. Van Wyck noted above. Even though he is not a student at Drew University, his participation in our programming, as well as his use of the collections and promotion of them over social media, has brought new visitors to the reading room. Van Wyck noted,

> Drew's Special Collections provide opportunities affording graduate students an unparalleled platform for publicly-engaged scholarship. Graduate students working at Drew can get involved in programs like Out of the Vault, which help [them] learn to pivot from knowledge creator to knowledge disseminator.
> **James M. Van Wyck (2015, personal communication, August 27).**

The development and promotion of programs that provide access to Special Collections and archival materials need not be expensive or taxing for libraries. With that in mind, we offer the following suggestions:
- Create an environment and friendly staff that welcome researchers and students;
- Invite classes for hands-on experiential learning opportunities;
- Create programming for the community at large, such as Out of the Vault;
- Explore curating exhibits using nonstaff members;
- Hire student workers carefully and strategically;
- Look for ways to utilize student talents while building their resumes;
- Integrate student workers into the staff and treat them as professionals;
- Always be open to new ideas without fearing failure.

Our experience with several Drew initiatives, including the Out of the Vault series, student-curated exhibits, and our mentoring of student workers, has demonstrated that initiative, brainstorming, and planning have been worth our time and can be implemented at little-to-no cost to the library. Library staff that work in a Special Collections and University Archives context can use work time to organize and plan events that allow for experiential learning in multiple ways. This may require modifying one's work schedule a bit to pull off successful outreach programs, but in the end the takeaway value far exceeds the inconvenience of working evening hours a few nights during the semester.

REFERENCES

Alvarez, P., 2006. Introducing rare books into the undergraduate curriculum. RBM 7 (2), 94−104.
Anderson, C., 2016. Welcome to the Drew Vault: educating students through college radio. In: DiBiase, A., Adamo, G. (Eds.), Education in Action: The Crucible of College Media. Peter Lang Publishers, New York, NY, forthcoming.
Dennick, R., 2012. Twelve tips for incorporating educational theory into teaching practices. Med. Teach. 34 (8), 618−624.
Hansen, M., 2012. Real objects, real spaces, real expertise: an undergraduate seminar curates an exhibition on the medieval Book of Hours. In: Mitchell, E., Seiden, P., Taraba, S. (Eds.), Past or Portal? Enhancing Undergraduate Learning Through Special Collections and Archives. Association of College & Research Libraries, Chicago, IL, pp. 237−241.
Hodge, P., Wright, S., Barraket, J., Scott, M., Melville, R., Richardson, S., 2011. Revisiting 'how we learn' in academia: practice-based learning exchanges in three Australian universities. Stud. High. Educ. 36 (2), 167−183.
Kolb, A., Kolb, D., 2005. Learning styles and learning spaces: enhancing experiential learning in higher education. Acad. Manag. Learn. Educ. 4 (2), 193−212.
Mercuri, J., 2015. Scholar traces evangelical anti-intellectualism to 19th-century reading habits. Fordham News. <http://news.fo;rdham.edu/arts-and-culture/the-story-behind-it-all-scholar-traces-evangelical-anti-intellectualism-to-19th-century-reading-habits/> (accessed 08.01. 15.).
Mitchell, E., Seiden, P., Taraba, S., 2012. Introduction. Past or Portal? Enhancing Undergraduate Learning Through Special Collections and Archives. American Library Association, Chicago, IL, pp. ix−xiii.
Overholt, J., 2013. Five theses on the future of special collections. RBM 14 (1), 15−20.
Walter, S., 2010. Advocacy through engagement: public engagement and the academic library. In: Welburn, W., Welburn, J., McNeil, B. (Eds.), Advocacy, Outreach & the Nation's Academic Libraries: A Call for Action. Association of College and Research Libraries, Chicago, IL, pp. 3−42.

CHAPTER 8

Game On! Experiential Learning With Tabletop Games

L. Hays and M. Hayse
MidAmerica Nazarene University, Olathe, KS, United States

8.1 GAMES GALORE: TABLETOP GAMING AS EXPERIENTIAL LEARNING

Tabletop games enrich so-called "traditional" approaches to classroom teaching and library services. The traditional classroom may conjure images of dutiful note takers, each an independent operator, attending to every word of the "sage on the stage." In contrast, tabletop games bring a more lively tone to classroom learning. Learners who play tabletop games immerse themselves in simulated worlds and manipulative models that come to life through face-to-face interaction with others. In this setting, tabletop games facilitate learning through direct, shared experience. Like the traditional classroom, the traditional library tends to divide learners from one another, each on a silent, solitary quest to locate hard-to-find resources, amidst imposing book stacks and labyrinthine catalogues. In libraries where tabletop gaming occurs, however, library patrons learn to collaborate and communicate about shared goals. They ask and answer each other's questions as they create knowledge together. Even though today's digitally saturated culture paradoxically renders us "alone together" (Turkle, 2011)—socially connected and socially disconnected at the same time—tabletop games counter that culture with the warmth and grace of physical presence.

We live in the midst of a tabletop gaming renaissance. Currently, the user-curated website BoardGameGeek.com boasts a listing of over 80,000 tabletop games—some quite ancient, but many brand new. For example, relatively new wargames such as Diplomacy (Calhamer, 1959) or Warhammer (Ansell et al., 1983) intensify the complexity of historic tabletop games such as the Chinese wargame Go, the European wargame of Chess, and the German *kriegspiel*. Similarly, the fantasy role-playing game Dungeons & Dragons (Arneson and Gygax, 1974) and its offshoots improvise upon the wargame (Peterson, 2012), inviting players to identify with and direct single wargaming figures for storytelling play, with gameplay sometimes spanning virtual and actual years. In contrast, collectible card games such as Magic: The Gathering (Garfield, 1993) remediate the fantasy themes of Dungeons & Dragons into a more complex combat-oriented system that requires only one evening to play. Finally, so-called "Eurogames" subvert the conventions of mass-market, family board games. Settlers of Catan (Teuber, 1994), for example, differs from a mass-market cousin like Monopoly (Darrow, 1933) by emphasizing player choice over chance, creating indirect rather than direct conflict, and sponsoring the play of collaboration rather than elimination (Woods, 2012). Tabletop game design has never been so popular and widespread.

Games serve many purposes. Some argue that games aim to entertain, distract, or aid in the temporary escape from more important concerns. McGonigal (2011) points to the Greek historian Herodotus as one of the first to argue this case. However, Herodotus also found profound meaning in the pleasurable distraction of gameplay. In The Histories, he tells the story of the ancient Lydians who endured an 18-year famine by playing games instead of eating on alternate days. McGonigal (2011) goes on to observe that this Lydian gameplay was anything but a trivial pursuit. She writes, "We often think of immersive gameplay as 'escapist,' a kind of passive retreat from reality. But through the lens of Herodotus' history, we can see how games could be a purposeful escape, a thoughtful and active escape, and most importantly an extremely helpful escape" (McGonigal, 2011, p. 6). If games can support purposeful, thoughtful, and active ends, might one of those ends be educational?

Researchers argue that digital games can serve educational ends—and those arguments extend to tabletop games as well. For example, Gee (2007) asserts that digital games facilitate learning through practice and interaction with cultural models that digital games represent. Similarly, a tabletop game such as Monopoly might teach economic development through cutthroat play, while Settlers of Catan might teach economic development through collaborative and mutually beneficial play. Each tabletop game reveals and represents a particular economic point of view. Squire (2011, pp. 28−29) describes digital games in terms of "ideological worlds"—simulated worlds that present a certain perspective upon life and culture. Likewise, as players explore and uncover the subtle rules and mechanisms that govern tabletop gameplay, their playful experience can give them insight into how life works.

Whitton (2012) argues that the educational power of gameplay has a lot to do with Kolb's experiential learning (EL) framework. Kolb (1984) describes the process of EL in terms of a four-step, iterative cycle: concrete experience, reflective observation, abstract conceptualization, and active experimentation. In other words, EL occurs as learners do something, reflect upon it, draw conclusions, plan their next steps, and proceed. All of these elements relate directly to the practices of tabletop gameplay. Tabletop game players must take action in order to play (concrete experience). Next, tabletop game players take a moment to reflect upon the consequences of their actions (reflective observation). Upon reflection, tabletop game players create new strategies (abstract conceptualization), test them out (active experimentation), and begin the EL cycle anew on the next turn.

21st Century Skill development, as presented by the Institute of Museum and Library Services (IMLS) (2015), relies upon the EL cycle that tabletop games utilize. The IMLS arranges its list of 21st Century Skills into four groups: Learning and Innovation Skills; Information, Media, and Technology Skills; 21st Century Themes; and Life and Career Skills. In the cooperative public health game Pandemic (Leacock, 2007), for example, game players learn a little bit about geography as they navigate a global map from city to city, but they learn even more about important life skills for the 21st century. During Pandemic, players must consider competing priorities while strategically balancing short-term and long-term gains. This requires the use of skills such as critical thinking, initiative, self-direction, productivity, and accountability. In addition, Pandemic players either win or lose as a team—the only success is shared success. This requires the use of communication, collaboration, social skills, and leadership skills. Most importantly, players must learn to overcome unexpected obstacles. This requires the use of flexibility and adaptability. In order to learn life skills such as these, players must engage in EL.

To summarize, tabletop games aim to entertain, but they can do so in a helpful, purposeful, and thoughtful way. Tabletop games require that players use 21st Century Skills in order to succeed. As players exercise these skills, they utilize the EL process: taking action, reflecting upon the consequences of their actions, creating new strategies, and testing them out.

8.2 LET THE GAMES BEGIN: TABLETOP GAMES IN THE LIBRARY

The introduction of tabletop games in libraries has primarily been for recreation (Nicholson, 2010). The Gaming Roundtable of the American Library Association has sponsored a library games day since 2007

(International Games Day, 2015) that has increased the profile of games in the library. Jenny Levine, one of the founders of National Games Day—renamed International Games Day in 2012—stressed the importance of games in libraries to bring generations together (Czarnecki, 2010). Robbins (2013) interviewed Wil Wheaton for Library Journal, and in the article, Wheaton emphasized the role of games for recreation. Wheaton extended the role of the game further, as being a way to bring people together who possess common interests. The social nature of tabletop games allows for increased interaction among patrons. Werner (2013) gives recommendations for library staff interested in starting a gaming program. Board games, or tabletop games, are one type of game Werner addresses for public libraries.

Increasingly, kindergarten through 12th-grade school libraries are adopting the use of tabletop games. These libraries do so in order to provide service and outreach in the areas of recreation and academic support (Copeland et al., 2013). Among postsecondary and academic libraries, however, tabletop games receive less attention. When postsecondary and academic libraries introduce tabletop games, they tend to do so for recreational reasons, as demonstrated in the article "Rolling the Dice in an Academic Library," by Blodgett and Bremer (2014).

Recreation and academic support are both important elements of the library's outward-facing services. Tabletop games can provide library patrons with opportunities to enjoy both. For those librarians who work in an academic setting, the main responsibility of the librarians is to support the educational community. Therefore, using tabletop games as an EL tool can serve a dual purpose: that of providing a pleasurable experience, as well as helping students learn and develop 21st Century Skills. With this in mind, academic librarians can learn a great deal by reviewing the work done by Harris and Mayer (2009) in the area of school libraries and games. The library use of tabletop games as learning tools is an area ripe for growth.

8.3 SETTING UP THE GAME: CENTER FOR GAMES & LEARNING

Librarians provide services and resources for the communities they serve, and often seek out opportunities on campus to support the broader interests of the community. Sometimes the seed of an idea starts from a conversation outside of the library, and grows from there. In fact, the authors of this chapter generated the concept of a library-based Center for Games & Learning during a discussion about tabletop games at a campus meeting. The authors asked themselves if there was a way to incorporate tabletop games into undergraduate coursework at MidAmerica Nazarene University and into the library. Out of this discussion, the authors wrote and received a Sparks! Ignition Grant from the IMLS to create a library-based Center for Games & Learning (see Fig. 8.1). In their grant application, the authors hypothesized that tabletop games teach 21st Century Skills such as collaboration, creativity, critical thinking, communication, flexibility, and adaptability. During the grant period, the authors gathered a cohort of additional faculty members to conduct case studies in courses across the undergraduate curriculum. Preliminary results from those studies are promising.

The mission of the Center for Games & Learning runs parallel to the mission of the library and the university. The Center addresses this mission through the avenues of faculty development and curriculum enrichment through EL. For example, the Center supports faculty who specifically want to incorporate tabletop gameplay into their courses, providing training and curricular guidance. In addition, the Center helps undergraduates to develop 21st Century Skills on an informal educational basis by providing game nights throughout the academic year. The Center also seeks to offer its service and support to external constituents—teachers, librarians, colleagues at other universities, non-profit leaders, and homeschool parents. All of these emphases reflect the broader mission of the library and the university.

The Center for Games & Learning also drafted a plan for strategic growth that included its own reassessment, a website launch, and conference planning. First, the library reassessed its strategies for facilitating 21st Century Skill development. Many current strategies focused on support

Figure 8.1 Center for Games & Learning Logo.

for traditional forms of instruction, and through student use of the physical library space. The Center allowed the library to expand its instructional modes through gameplay facilitation in the library, as well as game checkout by students and faculty for both academic and recreational use. Second, the Center launched a website (www.mnu.edu/games) shortly after the start of the grant period. The website broadcasts information on upcoming events and recommended resources. It also lists over 300 games in its collection, searchable by 21st Century Skills and game types (see Fig. 8.2).

Third, the Center hosted a conference on tabletop games and learning in July 2015. The conference brought together K-12 educators, public librarians, K-12 school librarians, academic librarians, college professors, and homeschool parents. The conference disseminated strategies for tabletop game use in classrooms and libraries. As a result of the conference, community outreach unexpectedly increased for the Center. Many excited librarians and educators wanted to learn more about using tabletop games in their teaching.

The Center for Games & Learning has enriched the opportunity for EL, not only at MidAmerica Nazarene University, but also at a number of local and regional libraries, schools, and universities. Classroom learners gravitate towards the hands-on, skill-based learning that tabletop games provide. Teachers and faculty members enjoy the opportunity to apply new teaching strategies in the classroom. Librarians also welcome the opportunity to provide valued resources and services to their constituents. The Center's work continues to expand as it explores new ways to align tabletop games with the various avenues of learning.

Figure 8.2 Center for Games & Learning Games List.

8.4 FACULTY AT PLAY: COMMUNITY OF PRACTICE

In addition to starting the Center, the authors also gathered a community of practice around tabletop gameplay and learning. The community of practice consisted of nine faculty members, drawn from across the university. They represented a range of disciplines across the curriculum, including composition, physics, economics, history, leadership, religion, education, and information literacy. Wenger and Snyder (2000) define communities of practice as "groups of people informally bound together by shared experience and passion for a joint enterprise" (p. 139). In this case, the community of practice met together throughout the faculty author's sabbatical semester that was set aside to launch the Center for Games & Learning. He shared his experience and passion for tabletop gaming and learning with the community of practice. Soon, the whole community of practice shared his conviction that "tabletop games can function as powerful learning engines" (Center for Games and Learning, 2015, para 2).

The Center for Games & Learning hosted meetings for the community of practice. These meetings allowed the community of practice to share their experiences of and feelings about using tabletop games in the classroom. The authors encouraged faculty to share in detail how they facilitated gameplay, how the students responded to the gameplay, and lessons they learned about tabletop games and learning. One faculty member felt ambivalent about participating. On one hand, he wanted to enjoy a collegial experience with the community of practice, and he wanted to try his hand at facilitating a case study. On the other hand, his prior tabletop gameplay experiences were not all positive—some of those experiences included relational stress in past relationships. In response, the community of practice lent support and encouragement to this faculty member throughout the case study process. The authors also helped him to learn and prepare the tabletop game that he planned to use in his case study. Through the support of the community of practice, he enjoyed a positive classroom experience with tabletop gameplay. He plans to continue to use the same tabletop game in future courses that he teaches.

8.5 STUDENTS AT PLAY: CASE STUDIES

The nine faculty members who joined the community of practice cohort each received a grant-funded stipend for their semester-long participation.

Each cohort member selected a course, identified a target 21st Century Skill, selected a game, and prepared to use it in class. Six cohort members selected commercial tabletop games. Two cohort members used classroom games of their own design. One opted to use a live, digital simulation. Throughout the semester, the cohort met and discussed best practices across three common teaching phases of (1) game instruction, (2) game facilitation, and (3) game debriefing. Three cohort members combined these phases into one learning session, while four divided the phases into two sessions. Two cohort members utilized three sessions for three phases—one session for game instruction, one for game facilitation, and one for game debriefing.

The authors gathered case study data in a variety of ways. Data gathering began with quantitative surveys. All undergraduate learners ($n = 129$) self-reported their varied gameplay activities during the past 4 weeks. Almost 100% of learners self-reported general gameplay participation during that time period, whether through sports or digital games or tabletop games. It is worth noting again that all game players are experiential learners. They learn through action, reflection, hypothesizing, and testing. They form their own unique communities of practice in which new players learn from more experienced players who function as mentors (Kolb and Kolb, 2005). Following the surveys, the authors video recorded and audio recorded each cohort member's classroom during all teaching phases. During the first two phases of instruction and facilitation, data gathering focused upon a single gameplay group among many others in each classroom. During the third phase of debriefing, data gathering widened to include all learners in the classroom. Finally, all cohort members completed the quantitative survey about their gameplay behaviors, also writing short answers to open-ended questions about their experiences.

Cohort members self-reported initial ambivalence during their experiences—yet, their overall assessment of classroom gaming was positive. At first, they wondered if learners would appreciate gameplay, and if learners would understand the relevance of gameplay for learning. Nevertheless, approximately three-quarters of cohort members perceived that most or all of their learners (1) enjoyed classroom gameplay, (2) positively connected classroom gameplay to learning course content, and (3) seemed more "engaged" when learning through gameplay. All cohort members observed that their learners used multiple 21st Century Skills in classroom gameplay, most notably, problem-solving (eight members), communication (six members), collaboration (six members), and critical thinking (five members). After completing the case studies, almost all cohort members testified that they were more likely to use classroom gameplay in the future.

These teachers also strongly affirmed the importance of the debriefing process as an essential part of classroom gameplay. One member wrote, "The 'make-it-or-break-it' of using games really comes down to facilitation and debriefing." Another wrote, "The debrief is probably the most essential component to effective teaching and learning through gameplay. Without this component, I don't think any of the skills or ideas would have been fully integrated into the students' habits and language." A third described her own experience as "intellectually stimulated, excited with the take-aways my students experienced." One member voiced a common tension felt by cohort members when he wrote, "Some students appeared to 'get it,' which made me feel good. However, some obviously did not, which was a bit frustrating." This observation affirms the importance of careful debriefing following EL, even while acknowledging that debriefing does not guarantee insight for every learner.

Scholars and practitioners across a variety of professional contexts echo the cohort's consensus on debriefing—from "serious (digital) game" design (Crookall, 2010), to medical school (Fanning and Gaba, 2007), to information science (Nicholson, 2012), to gifted education (May, 2005), to corporate training (Thiagarajan, 2004). David Crookall, a faculty member in the Higher Institute for Economy and Management at the University of Nice, and decades-longstanding editor of Simulation and Gaming: An Interdisciplinary Journal, argues that just as debriefing comes naturally to daily life, so serious gameplay should automatically include time and space for extended debriefing. Crookall (2010) summarizes "In my view, we will neglect debriefing at our peril... the real (solid, lasting, meaningful, and deeper) learning comes not from the game, but from the debriefing... Debriefing is the processing of the game experience to turn it into learning (to paraphrase Dave Kolb)" (p. 907).

8.6 CHOOSING A STRATEGY: TABLETOP GAME SELECTION

For those not well versed in tabletop game culture, the range of possible game selections can feel overwhelming. The authors recommend several web-based resources to guide librarians in this process. BoardGameGeek.com offers a vibrant "Games in the Classroom" forum, populated by helpful members who happily share their expertise with others. Dicetower.com features helpful reviews, as well as a wide array of helpful tabletop game "Top 10" lists that spans 10 years of posting. Playplaylearn.com recommends particular games that align with subjects taught in the K-12 classroom. The Center for Games & Learning website (www.mnu.edu/games) organizes its recommendations based upon subject alignment and 21st Century Skill development. For librarians, the Games and Gaming Round Table website (ALA.org/gamert/home) may be the most helpful starting point. Finally, those who select games should consider the *Spiel des Jahres*—the German "game of the year." This award is given to one game a year that the broad German community particularly enjoys, indicated on game boxes with the imprint of a red medal.

As librarians select tabletop games for their collections, they should remember the overlapping concerns that gameplay can address: curricular support, knowledge acquisition, skill practice, EL, and recreational play. For example, EL theory suggests that learning occurs through an emergent process rather than focusing solely on intended results (Kolb and Kolb, 2005). Nevertheless, librarians should consider the learning outcomes of courses and programs when selecting games to support the curriculum. Librarians need to work directly with faculty in order to understand those learning outcomes. Through their expertise, librarians can effectively align certain types of gameplay experience with certain kinds of learning needs. For example, some tabletop games lend themselves to social interaction or cooperative play, while others sponsor a more solitary form of play. Some require less than 30 minutes to complete, while others may require several hours. Some demand quick reflexes, while others allow for slow contemplation. Some only align with classroom topics thematically, while others align at points of deep simulation and knowledge acquisition. In all of these cases, librarians need to understand learning outcomes in order to provide tabletop games that integrate information, experience, and enjoyment.

For example, one of the authors used the social game Balderdash in her information literacy course. Balderdash requires players to identify correct definitions of obscure words, amidst a field of deceptive contenders. Adult learners played the game, followed by a time of discussion and debriefing about evaluating sources. The author asked the learners to describe the criteria that they used when deciding which definition was correct or incorrect. Then, the learners considered the CRAAP test (currency, relevance, authority, accuracy, and purpose) (Meriam Library California State Library Chico, 2010) as criteria for evaluating sources.

In the final analysis, this learning session integrated information and experience in an effective and enjoyable way for the learners.

8.7 HIGH SCORE: LESSONS LEARNED

In conclusion, the authors learned several lessons about tabletop game use for library-supported learning. We hope these lessons may assist readers in their own initiatives with tabletop games:

1. Assess the needs of your community. Who already uses tabletop games for learning? What types of tabletop games do students already play? How would a tabletop games collection fit into the strategic plan of the library?
2. Find a champion. The needs assessment will uncover those in the learning community who already feel passionate about tabletop gameplay. Capitalize on that passion—it will garner broader enthusiasm and support.
3. Seek strategic partners. This holds true especially if the main motivation for the project resides within the library staff. Strategic partners can build strong bridges between library services and a variety of constituencies. At the Center for Games & Learning, strategic partners include professors of teacher education, public school in-service coordinators, residential life representatives, student government representatives, faculty development coordinators at other universities, home school network directors, nonprofit directors, and a host of other educators and librarians.
4. Create flexible space in your library. Most libraries do not lack in shelf or table space. Nonetheless, deeper-than-average shelf space is often required to store the larger tabletop games. Standard library tables will work for some tabletop gameplay, but round tables can helpfully provide equal distance from the playing space and from other players.
5. Gameplay fosters shared experiences—sometimes loud or rowdy. Therefore, encourage gameplay in library areas where other social activities occur.
6. Remember that the power of tabletop gameplay rests in EL. Tabletop gameplay learners need to discuss their feelings, perspectives, hypotheses, strategies, and connections to other learning experiences that they have enjoyed (Kolb and Kolb, 2005).
7. Consider additional ways to foster EL in the library. For example, sponsor research forums, host recreational game nights, develop a maker space, and facilitate reflective discussion on campus initiatives.

8. Debriefing is vital for deep learning to occur. Thiagarajan (1992) identified steps for debriefing games. These steps include asking, "a) How do you feel? b) What happened? c) Do you agree? d) Déjà vu? e) What would you do differently f) What if…? g) Can you improve this activity?" (p. 162). It is important to work with faculty to encourage the inclusion of debriefing activities. Debriefing can occur in the class, as a discussion group in the library, or as even as a part of a group on campus that meets to play games together.

REFERENCES

Ansell, B., Halliwell, R., Johnson, J., Priestly, R., 1983. Warhammer. Games Workshop Ltd., London.
Arneson, G., Gygax, G., 1974. Dungeons & Dragons. Tactical Studies Rules, Lake Geneva, WI.
Blodgett, J., Bremer, P., 2014. Rolling the dice in an academic library. Am. Libr. 45 (11/12), 50–53.
Calhamer, A.B., 1959. Diplomacy. Avalon Hill, Renton, WA.
Center for Games and Learning, 2015. <http://www.mnu.edu/resources/center-for-games-and-learning.html> (accessed 20.08.15.).
Crookall, D., 2010. Serious games, debriefing, and simulation/gaming as a discipline. Simul. Gaming 41 (6), 898–920, <www.unice.fr/sg/authors/docs/Crookall-2010_Serious-Gs-debrief-discipline_898-920.pdf> (accessed 24.11.15.).
Copeland, T., Henderson, B., Mayer, B., Nicholson, S., 2013. Three different paths for tabletop gaming in school libraries. Libr. Trends 61 (4), 825–835.
Czarnecki, K., 2010. National gaming day. Sch. Libr. J. 56 (10), 20–21.
Darrow, C., 1933. Monopoly. Hasbro, Pawtucket, RI.
Fanning, R.M., Gaba, D.M., 2007. The role of debriefing in simulation-based earning. Simul. Healthc. Summer 2 (2), 115–125.
Garfield, R., 1993. Magic: The Gathering. Wizards of the Coast, Renton, WA.
Gee, J.P., 2007. What Video Games Have to Teach Us About Learning and Literacy, revised and updated ed. Palgrave Macmillan, New York, NY.
Harris, C., Mayer, B., 2009. Libraries Got Game: Aligned Learning Through Modern Board Games. American Library Association, Chicago, IL.
Institute of Museum and Library Services, 2015. Museums, Libraries, and 21st Century Skills. <https://www.imls.gov/impact-imls/national-initiatives/museums-libraries-and-21st-century-skills/museums-libraries-and-21st-century-skills-definitions> (accessed 03.10.15.).
International Games Day, 2015. <http://igd.ala.org/about/igd-history/> (accessed 14.09.15.).
Kolb, D.A., 1984. Experiential Learning: Experience as the Source of Learning and Development. Prentice Hall, Englewood Cliffs, NJ.
Kolb, A., Kolb, D., 2005. Learning styles and learning spaces: enhancing experiential learning in higher education. Acad. Manag. Learn. Educ. 4 (2), 193–212.
Leacock, M., 2007. Pandemic. Z-Man Games, Mahopac, NY.
May, D.G., 2005. Simulations: active learning for gifted students. In: Johnsen, S.K., Kendrick, J. (Eds.), Teaching Strategies in Gifted Education. Prufrock Press, Waco, TX, pp. 27–37.

McGonigal, J., 2011. Reality Is Broken: Why Games Make Us Better and How They Can Change the World. Penguin Press, New York, NY.

Meriam Library California State Library Chico, 2010. Evaluating information—applying the CRAAP test. <https://www.csuchico.edu/lins/handouts/eval_websites.pdf> (accessed 27.11. 15.).

Nicholson, S., 2010. Everyone Plays at the Library. Information Today, Medford, NJ.

Nicholson, S., 2012. Completing the experience: debriefing in experiential educational games. Proceedings of the 3rd International Conference on Society and Information Technologies. International Institute of Informatics and Systemics, Winter Garden, FL, pp. 117–121.

Peterson, J., 2012. Playing at the World: A History of Simulating Wars, People, and Fantastic Adventures from Chess to Role-Playing Games. Unreason Press, San Diego, CA.

Robbins, B., 2013. Wil Wheaton Talks Tabletop. Libr. J. 138 (13), 52.

Squire, K., 2011. Video Games and Learning: Teaching and Participatory Culture in the Digital Age. Teachers College Press, New York, NY.

Teuber, K., 1994. The Settlers of Catan. Franckh-Kosmos Verlags-GmbH & Co, Stuttgart.

Thiagarajan, S., 1992. Using games for debriefing. Simul. Gaming 23 (2), 161.

Thiagarajan, S., 2004. Six phases of debriefing for performance. <http://thiagi.net/archive/www/pfp/IE4H/february2004.html#Debriefing> (accessed 04.10.15.).

Turkle, S., 2011. Alone Together. Basic Books, New York, NY.

Wenger, E.C., Snyder, W.M., 2000. Communities of practice: the organizational frontier. Harv. Bus. Rev. 78 (1), 139–145.

Werner, K., 2013. Bringing them in: developing a gaming program for the library. Libr. Trends 61 (4), 790–801.

Whitton, N., 2012. Good game design is good learning design. In: Whitton, N., Moseley, A. (Eds.), Using Games to Enhance Learning and Teaching: A Beginner's Guide. Routledge, New York, NY, pp. 9–18.

Woods, S., 2012. Eurogames: The Design, Culture and Play of Modern European Board Games. McFarland & Company, Jefferson, NC.

CHAPTER 9

Building Knowledge Together: Interactive Course Exhibits in the Academic Library

S. Fralin[1], B. Mathews[1] and L. Pressley[2]
[1]Virginia Tech Libraries, Blacksburg, VA, United States
[2]University of Washington Libraries, Tacoma, WA, United States

Classrooms all across campus are filled with interesting ideas. Students and faculty regularly engage in conversations and debates. They participate in hands-on activities and explore important concepts. However, all this generally happens behind closed doors. As a library aspiring to support the creative, scholarly, and intellectual progress of our communities, we wondered: could we break down the walls and invite others to share the learning experiences?

9.1 THE BEGINNINGS

As an attempt to unleash learning from the classroom setting, we developed an intriguing proposal: what if we gave a class some space in the main library building for a few weeks? The intention was not for them to use it as study space or for instructional purposes, but rather, to create an exhibit showcasing what they were learning. We would offer them a designated spot in a high-traffic area, as well as an assortment of components. Students and faculty would work with librarians, technologists, and an exhibit curator to design their unique exhibit. Would people take us up on this "wild idea"? In this way, the Course Exhibit Initiative at the Virginia Tech Libraries was born.

As librarians become more engaged with pedagogical and curricular change, we felt inspired to make knowledge tangible and interactive (Lippincott et al., 2014). As we considered the different ways the library currently supports the learning enterprise, we recognized that there was a missed opportunity in our commons areas. Although you could glance around the building and observe students flipping through textbooks, designing content, or collaborating on assignments, much of their intellectual output is less visible. Students embark on a weeks-long learning journey, and we wanted to find better ways of revealing their effort. What if we could take the essence of these collective actions and make them more public?

In this manner, we would be celebrating academic achievement, and also visualizing it as a process. We would make the tools and concepts from various disciplines open and accessible to everyone. Our hope was that conversations would occur, as elements from one course might mix and match with another. The driving idea was that these exhibits would serve as immersive learning objects themselves. We should note here that the origin of this idea began at Georgia Tech. Charlie Bennett (then serving as Commons Coordinator) worked with an honors English course to explore homelessness in Atlanta. The students wrote essays, created documentaries, curated photo books, and designed other artifacts, including the construction of a temporary wooden shelter. This work culminated with a public reception and exhibit (A History of the Mad Housers, 2008). Our interest was in taking this concept and turning it into a scalable program.

9.2 THE IDEA TAKES SHAPE

We were confident that this was a feasible and even stimulating idea. It would offer students and faculty a platform for hands-on learning and integrate the library more deeply into knowledge practices. We amassed the tools and expertise to make this happen, now all we needed were a few enthusiastic faculty ready to try out the idea.

Over the course of a semester we spoke with 10 professors about the exhibit concept. They liked the spirit of it and found the premise compelling, but all of them declined to participate. Some were concerned with the amount of time it might take away from established classroom activities. Others were uncertain how students might react to the new assignment. And some struggled to imagine their course content manifested in this interactive format.

A breakthrough finally emerged when a colleague of ours, coteaching a religion and culture course, took us up on our offer (Variations of Practice Exhibit, 2013). We worked with her to stage an exhibit of physical and digital artifacts and to host an opening reception. This provided us with a working prototype to share with others. Faculty took notice and we gained some traction.

9.3 BUILDING THE PROGRAM

Soon we were hosting several exhibits each semester. To make sure the faculty members and classes involved have the most beneficial experience possible, each exhibit is tailored to them specifically. We start by considering what they want to express, and work backwards from there. We try to avoid encouraging students to format their content for digital screens just because we have them, and instead, start each exhibit from scratch. We prefer to build them organically out of the content and personalities of the students and faculty.

Many of the initial exhibits were built around course materials that existed from previous semesters. We would work with instructors (and students) to gather their material and create customized exhibits based on the available artifacts.

As the program grew, more people across campus have become aware of the benefits of exhibiting student work in the library. Today faculty members approach us with the desire to do an exhibit several months before their course gets started. This allows them to get accustomed to the idea of the public display of students' work, and it encourages the students to be deeply involved in the design process.

9.4 THE PEDAGOGY

The course exhibits invite students to think about course content in a different context. Not only are they learning-by-doing, literally "constructing knowledge," but they also encounter the difference between developing projects for class versus developing them for a broader audience. Their work becomes a form of personal expression instead of just an assignment to be graded.

Like many colleges and universities, our campus wants to engage students in diverse, hands-on learning experiences. In addition, many service units across the university advocate that faculty design their courses with educational theory and best practices in mind. The Virginia Tech Libraries built on this foundation by coupling a strong grounding in theory with the technical skills needed to work with students on exhibits. This allowed us to build a program that is a powerful learning experience for students and faculty, that is an impactful learning environment for our library users, and which allows the libraries to engage directly with the educational mission of the university.

The level of library involvement varies quite a bit. On the low end of engagement, assignments are given to the students with the expectation that the materials will be on public display. This often entails the students making posters or recording a presentation of some format. On the high end of engagement, the students take the exhibit concept into their own hands and do much of the conceptualization and building themselves.

9.5 CHICKERING AND GAMSON

The exhibits program makes use of the framework developed by Arthur Chickering and Zelda Gamson of good practices in undergraduate education (Seven Principles for Good Practice in Undergraduate Education, 1987). These practices have been widely embraced in higher education, and we found them relevant in our work with students as well.

1. *Good practice in undergraduate education encourages contact between students and faculty.*

    In producing an exhibit, the faculty member and students have to work together on the final outcome. The faculty member has an idea of what they hope the exhibit will look like, and is invested in the final product, because it will reflect on their work in the classroom. This investment encourages frequent discussion among the students and faculty about what the project should look like and about the shape it is taking.

    Similarly, most of our students have not completed a project like this in the past. Because the project is very different from a traditional assignment, students tend to have more clarifying questions for their professors than they would otherwise. In addition to collaboration with faculty, students also interact with the library team involved with each exhibit.

2. *Good practice in undergraduate education develops reciprocity and cooperation among students.*

    A course exhibit is a group project on a scale larger than traditional class work. Instead of small group reports and papers, students have to find a way to cooperate across the entire semester.

3. *Good practice in undergraduate education encourages active learning.*

    Exhibits definitely cultivate active learning. Students start from a place of understanding that they will need to create something based on the course content. This necessitates that they consider how to display and arrange course content, and/or produce something totally new, in a very active way.

4. *Good practice in undergraduate education gives prompt feedback.*

    As the exhibit is constructed, students receive prompt feedback from classmates, their professor, and the library team. In addition, students participate in an opening reception and receive feedback in that context on the final product.

5. *Good practice in undergraduate education emphasizes time on task.*

    Exhibits are time-intensive assignments. The more collaborative ones require students to schedule time to work together. There is little busy work, and the finished exhibits require cognitive "time on task."

6. *Good practice in undergraduate education communicates high expectations.*

    A public display of work carries with it inherently high expectations. Faculty know it will be viewed by their colleagues and others, and that the final product will reflect on their work as a teacher. Most students also understand the high expectations inherent in such a public work.

7. *Good practice in undergraduate education respects diverse talents and ways of learning.*

    Exhibits, more than any other library-based assignment that we have participated in, make space for diverse talents and ways of learning. There is a kinesthetic quality to putting together a physical project, design aspects, and communication (via text, graphics, and media) qualities as well.

9.6 BLOOM'S TAXONOMY

Bloom's Taxonomy (Bloom et al., 1956) is a way of talking about learning developed in the 1950s. A revised version was created in 2002 (Krathwohl, 2002). In both versions, shown in Figs. 9.1 and 9.2, the goal of instruction is to move students up the pyramid, from simpler cognitive tasks to more challenging ones. In both, basic memorization of facts is the foundation of learning, moving upwards towards more complex ways of using that knowledge. In the newest version, the pinnacle of the pyramid is creating, which is the outcome of the library's course exhibits program. In the act of creation, students show that they have learned course content, understood it, applied it, and thought of ways to use it in a new context.

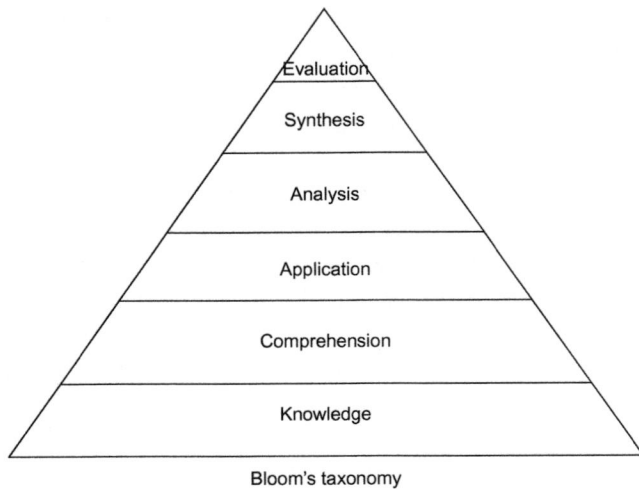

Figure 9.1 Bloom's taxonomy.

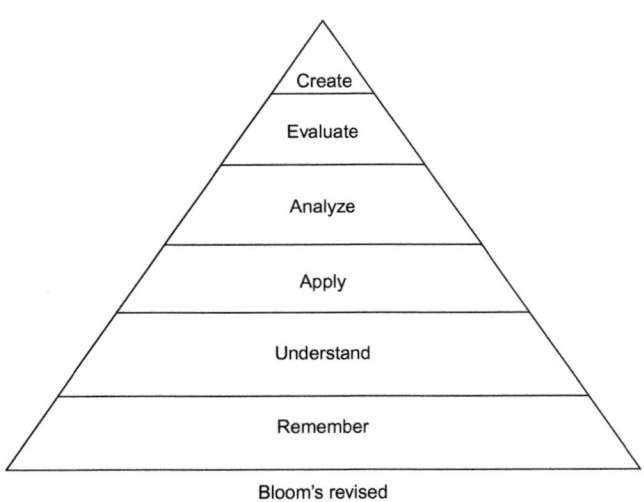

Figure 9.2 Bloom's taxonomy revised (2002).

9.7 LIBRARY'S LEARNING OUTCOMES

Course exhibits support the library's learning outcomes in a number of ways. As we strive to be an interdisciplinary hub on campus, this effort allows the library to more strongly support cross-disciplinary learning. The entire community is exposed to content from a variety of disciplines.

Students in a given discipline—for example, engineering—may encounter an exhibit on subjects that they cannot fit into their class schedule, such as the sociological aspects of cancer or Russian history. Furthermore, several exhibits have been interdisciplinary in nature, fitting in nicely with the libraries' aim.

The Libraries also seek to expose local scholarship. We do this through an institutional repository, events highlighting local scholarship, and events highlighting student work. Course Exhibits are the most impactful of this last category, as they remain available in library space for several weeks and are supported by a marketing campaign for each project.

Finally, the Libraries are interested in exploring the creation of learning environments. The Libraries have traditionally focused on collaborative spaces and recently developed a concentrated effort around online learning. Course Exhibits allowed the Libraries a new way to enhance learning environments and to experiment with ways to embed library services in the established learning environment.

9.8 THE DESIGN PROCESS

It is difficult to generalize the design process for Course Exhibits since it is tailored specifically for each class. Simply put, it consists of research, ideation, and iteration. Throughout this process ideas rise and fall, conflict crops up and gets resolved, and at some point the project gels together. Up until the point at which the project comes together, it often feels chaotic and on the verge of collapsing. If this sounds like a difficult, frustrating process—that's because it is. But at the same time, it is very rewarding and exhilarating to work through an exhibit from start to finish.

Below you will find two case studies of how course exhibits came to be. We rely heavily on design thinking processes, which provide the necessary structure to pull off such complicated projects successfully. IDEO, a global design firm, has produced a toolkit for libraries that advocates creating projects with design thinking in mind (Design Thinking, 2015).

9.9 CASE ONE: SOVIET HISTORY FOR THE NETWORKED AGE

Soviet History for the Networked Age (2014) was an exhibit formed around a history course taught by a seasoned faculty member who was looking to change the way students interacted with the course material.

She decided to take a blogging approach and the library supported this by purchasing a WordPress theme that allowed her to operate the site as she needed. The course had gone through two semesters with this new approach when we connected about presenting the materials students were creating as an exhibit. From the first conversation to the opening reception, the process of creating this exhibit lasted less than 4 weeks.

We began by talking about the scope of the project. It is essential to define expectations as early in the design process as possible to make sure threads don't get crossed and tasks don't fall through the cracks. In this case, we picked important dates for the project, talked about the budget, about the materials that were going to be exhibited, and about the objectives we intended to accomplish by creating an exhibit.

The major obstacle for this project was how to share what the students had done. All of the student work was made available through blogs, so we had no physical artifacts to show. At the time this slowed down our process because we weren't sure what to do with completely digital content. However, it did serve as a good anchor problem that we solved via the design process.

Once the scope of the exhibit was defined the research began. We asked for the course syllabus, access to the materials being shown, and any other relevant resources. We read the materials, figured out what the class was about, how the instructor approached teaching in this particular class, and began to explore ways in which to present the materials.

Depending on the type of project, you may need to expand your research beyond seeking relevant materials, to seeking relevant people and stories. If you want the exhibit to feel like an art gallery, visit an art gallery and takes notes on the experience, so you can replicate some of the elements to create your own experience. Or visit a retail store, a museum, a box office; whatever is appropriate for your exhibit. This expands your vision and prepares you to enter the ideation phase in full force.

This research process leads you into the beginnings of the ideation process. This is the point in the project when you should "shoot for the moon" and let the sky be the limit for your ideas. It is the time to amass as many ideas as possible, no matter how wild they may seem. (One of the most memorable ideas that didn't make the final cut was one to build a replica of the Berlin Wall, to make the exhibit more noticeable.)

We didn't have the equipment or the budget to share the work of the students on their blogs, so we took another direction and decided to make it tangible. After many revisions, we chose a design for the space

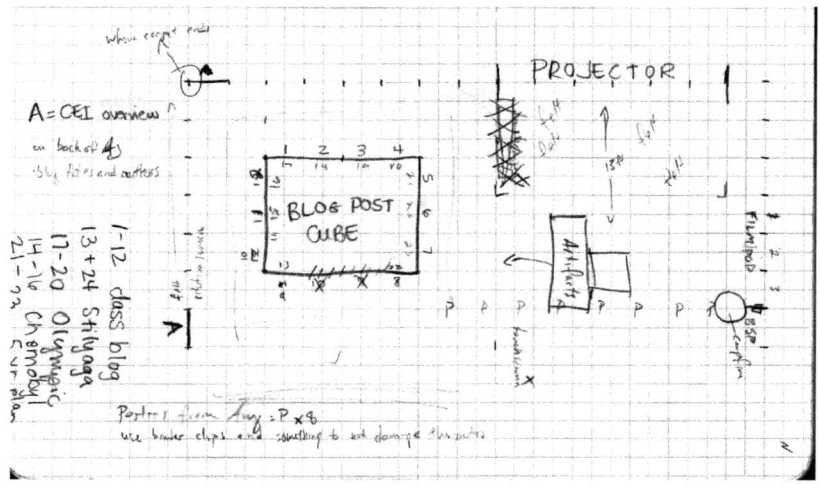

Figure 9.3 Schematic drawing of "Soviet History for the Networked Age" Course Exhibit.

that preserved some digital aspects of what the students had done and created an experience with tangible representations of their work. As you can see in Fig. 9.3, the space was divided into two parts.

On the left is the "blog post cube." It was made up of selected blog posts that we hand-picked from the course blog and formatted for large-format printing. We ended up choosing 24 posts for the cube, and a few others to be placed elsewhere. Each post was printed on a 2 × 6 ft. sheet of paper and hung from the ceiling.

This created a space within the exhibit space that immersed the visitors in the content the students had created. An ottoman was placed in the cube so visitors could sit and explore the Soviet materials that surrounded them as shown in Fig. 9.4.

On the other side of the exhibit space we placed a projector connected to an iPad so that visitors could explore the entire course blog at their leisure. Next to this was a mobile monitor playing a classic Soviet film, *Battleship Potemkin*, which several students wrote about in their blogs.

The final piece was another mobile monitor that allowed visitors to explore some of the sources students used when doing research for their blog posts.

As you can see in Fig. 9.5, couches and chairs were placed in the exhibit space so that students using the library did not lose study space. This allowed them to work directly in the space and be surrounded by the scholarship of their fellow students.

126 The Experiential Library

Figure 9.4 The "Blog Post Cube."

Figure 9.5 Exhibit space for "Soviet History for the Networked Age" Course Exhibit.

All told it cost around $600 for the exhibit. This cost was mainly paper and an iPad case, plus other miscellaneous hardware and software. The expense was reduced significantly due to the ability to use in-house large format printing and the availability of computer equipment. If all the materials used to create the Soviet history exhibit had been purchased outright the cost would have been around $10,000.

Printing all of the materials for the exhibit, preparing them, and building the exhibit itself took more than 30 hours. This total does not include time spent designing the blog posts and posters, programming the computer equipment used, and the untold hours of pre-preparation. As you can see, putting on exhibits like this is not a small investment.

9.10 CASE TWO: PHOTOGRAPHY IN FOCUS

Photography in Focus (2014) was an exhibit that came about when the neighbor of a librarian, a faculty member in photography, asked if she could mount an exhibition at the library. This kind of approach was common for early exhibits, since the program was young and people weren't sure what was possible and whether or not they could participate.

The Photography in Focus exhibit was based on an introductory digital photography course open to anyone in the university. While there were some in-class meetings and walks around campus to talk about different camera settings and lighting conditions, there were also virtual meetings, in which each student had an avatar and could explore a virtual gallery constructed by the instructor.

The faculty member was interested in showing off this virtual space and was also eager to share the students' work with the public. It is extremely rare to have a public showing for photography students and she wanted her students to have this experience. It was also a great way for her to incorporate a section on printing photographs in a digital photography course.

This exhibit differs from the Soviet History for the Networked Age exhibit, because we planned on using the materials the students created in the same semester they created them. In the Soviet history exhibit, the materials were from a previous semester.

Again, the first part of the process of creating the exhibit was to meet with the faculty member and discuss her expectations and to set the context that would help shape everything that followed. The exhibit was 3 months away, but we still sat down and selected the dates by which the photographs would be due, when the show would open, and when we would hold the reception. Without these anchor dates, a project of this scope can easily get off-track. We also spent some time discussing how we wanted the exhibit to look and how we wanted the visitors to feel.

Other requests the faculty member had were that visitors have a way to interact with the virtual class space, and a way to share photographs in addition to the selected photographs that would be printed and shown.

The research phase for this exhibit was very different to that of the Soviet history one. In this case we researched art-hanging systems and looked for structures that met the requirements we had talked about in our first meeting. As we continued to flesh out what we wanted the exhibit to be and feel like, we came to several conclusions. We wanted it to be open and welcoming, allow good light for the photographs, and easily fit into the student workspace it was destined for.

These requirements led to some specific designs, such as a small footprint on the floor, an open structure, and being easily movable. The first iteration was mocked up based on some other display structures we had researched, as seen in Fig. 9.6.

This structure had all the qualities we were looking for, except being easily movable. But for the stage we were at in the process, it was perfect. Then an unexpected thing occurred. We were a few weeks into the semester and students began to drop the course. In response to this we

Figure 9.6 Initial mock-up of "Photography in Focus" Course Exhibit.

Figure 9.7 Revised mock-up of "Photography in Focus" Course Exhibit.

had to re-evaluate the amount of space needed to show the photographs and in turn had to redesign the exhibit to accommodate the new attendance numbers, as shown in Fig. 9.7.

The size was reduced and the structure was reshaped to fit the new scope of the project, and we were on track again. Soon after this change, more students dropped the course and within 2 weeks of redesigning the exhibit design we had to once again rethink it. This was a simple change: one of the three panels planned for in Fig. 9.7 was reduced to two panels, ample space to hold the 18 photographs we would show.

Now that the design was finalized and the show a few weeks away, the necessary supplies were ordered and we got to work. Lumber was cut and painted, hanging systems were tested, and the final product came together over the course of about 2 weeks. The complete structure and exhibit space are shown in Fig. 9.8A and B.

This complete exhibit cost around $700. The hanging system holding the photographs was the majority of the cost, with the remainder being the lumber, paint, hardware, and Raspberry Pi computers used to power the monitors sharing all the students' photographs.

Between all of the woodwork, painting, assembly, wiring, and finish work it took around 40 hours to make this exhibit a reality. Again, creating something like this is no small investment.

Figure 9.8 (A, B) Final "Photography in Focus" Course Exhibit.

9.11 TIPS ON THE PROCESS

Even though the two projects described above are very different, there were constants in the process used to create each one. Here are some guidelines we've found helpful:
- Define expectations and scope of the project at the beginning;
- Define a goal that you wish to achieve by creating the exhibit;
- To manage progress, set deadlines for tasks such as:
  - Design idea review date
  - Final design due date
  - Installation day
  - Opening reception
  - De-installation day;
- Don't skimp on researching your topic or method of display;
- Consider experiential methods of research, such as visiting analogous settings or setting up a guided tour through a space you would like to emulate;
- Be open to a wide variety of ideas as research winds down and you start to put ideas to paper. It is important to let this process unfold, because bits and pieces of little ideas can fit together in a meaningful way to form a larger idea that may be the solution you're searching for;
- Be open to iteration on the ideas you generate. This is a reviewing and revision process that involves returning to a work and improving it based on feedback or insight. Often, in a project like those described above, an iterative cycle is kicked off when a project runs into a roadblock, like the shrinking class size for Photography in Focus. Regardless of the cause, iteration will always be a large part of these projects;
- Class involvement in exhibit design varies based on many factors. For lower-level undergraduate classes we will typically do the lion's share of the exhibit design, but for higher-level classes and graduate courses, the students in the class design the exhibit and even construct it in some cases.

9.12 COSTS/SUPPLIES

Each year we allocate $5000 for Course Exhibits. This amount has worked well to cover up to four large exhibits and five or six smaller exhibits in one year. The cost of each exhibit ranges from $500 to $1000, depending on the complexity and demands of the subject matter.

We have been able to keep costs down by taking advantage of materials that we have in-house. For example, when using monitors to share content, we use old monitors that have been removed from service by our IT department, instead of purchasing new ones. To power the monitors we often use Raspberry Pi computers which, at $35 each, are very cost-effective.

While we do have some expensive equipment used in exhibit construction, we have found that it does not take flashy technology to make a nice exhibit—just time and careful consideration of the subject matter. The Soviet History exhibit described above was constructed mainly out of fishing line, binder clips, and ceiling hooks.

Whenever possible we pull items directly from the courses being exhibited and put them on display. For example, in early fall 2015 we had an exhibit based around a computational thinking course. Instead of reinterpreting the tools that were used in the class and trying to format them for a wider audience, we simply included the tools in the exhibit for visitors to play with. The result was that visitors got a direct window into what daily life in the course was like and could experience it for a short time.

The exhibits are built in-house using our loading dock and offices as workspaces. Our main workspace, shown in Fig. 9.9, has become a de facto makerspace due to the nature of the different kinds of work that take place there.

Figure 9.9 Course Exhibit "Makerspace."

9.13 ASSESSMENT

Assessment is difficult for this type of project, and the exhibits are not assessed in the manner of a typical library service. The exhibits are not placed in closed spaces where we could easily count the number of visitors. And really, keeping track of how many visitors view the exhibits and increasing those numbers is not our goal. Instead, the goal is to foster a learning environment that is beneficial to students, whether they interact with the exhibit or not. We are more interested in the nontangible, atmospheric value that the exhibits provide. For example, many students commented on how much they enjoyed the Soviet History exhibit, and when the Photography in Focus exhibit was taken down, students were asking if they could purchase prints of the photographs.

An exhibit in early fall 2015, based on a music course (Digital Sound Manipulation), resulted in several students inquiring with the professor about enrolling in his course. Later that same semester, a graduate-level public history course designed and built their own exhibit based on one previously built by the library. Students and faculty are seeing what we're doing and want to get involved, whether that is by being featured in an exhibit or helping behind the scenes.

9.14 FUTURE

As we move forward, we are looking at other areas of the library in which to exhibit student- or faculty-created materials. In a recent renovation we installed a video wall, which has the potential to be an eye-catching space in which to exhibit digital materials. This allows us to exhibit more materials than we could previously handle.

Looking even further forward, we hope to expand the Course Exhibit program beyond the library and across campus. A new classroom building is being constructed as of this writing and we hope to stake a claim in it for an expansion of the Course Exhibit program.

We are also exploring the possibility of using student workers to help design and build exhibits. Currently, we are only able to do about six exhibits per year with one person working on the exhibits, but with more help we could expand the program.

9.15 CONCLUSION

We began this program with a simple question: what would a class do if we gave them some space in the library? Our aim was to encourage active learning through a project-based, experiential pedagogy. We wanted to facilitate the creation of knowledge for a public audience by making it interactive. We wanted to build on the library as the intellectual heart of campus, adding new forms of interdisciplinary sharing of information.

We entered this effort with an experimental mindset of "let's see what happens." We discovered that this concept resonated with many people across campus. Students felt proud of their work, and faculty felt proud of their students. People lingered in the library to look at the work.

We discovered that an exhibit program isn't a simple process. It requires a lot of time and creativity, and lacks the hallmarks that more scalable programs feature. But for us, and our campus culture, the outcome has been invaluable. Not only do these exhibits create a multilayered learning environment for our library commons, but they also signify to students and faculty that the library is deeply invested in partnering to support pedagogy and knowledge practices. In this manner, we are exhibiting ourselves and what an engaged library looks like.

REFERENCES

A History of the Mad Housers, 2008. <https://smartech.gatech.edu/handle/1853/20521> (accessed 12.01.15.).

Bloom, B.S., Engelhart, M.D., Furst, E.J., Hill, W.H., Krathwohl, D.R., 1956. Taxonomy of educational objectives: the classification of educational goals. Handbook I: Cognitive Domain. David McKay Company, New York, NY.

Design Thinking for Libraries, 2015. <http://designthinkingforlibraries.com/> (accessed 12.01.15.).

Krathwohl, D.R., 2002. A revision of Bloom's taxonomy: an overview. Theory Pract 41 (4), 212–218.

Lippincott, J, Vedantham, A, Duckett, K, 2014. Libraries as enablers of pedagogical and curricular change. EDUCAUSE Review Online. <http://er.educause.edu/articles/2014/10/libraries-as-enablers-of-pedagogical-and-curricular-change> (accessed 12.01.15).

Photography in Focus, 2014. <http://www.lib.vt.edu/events/course-exhibits/digital-photo/index.html> (accessed 12.01.15.).

Seven Principles for Good Practice in Undergraduate Education, 1987. <http://www.lonestar.edu/multimedia/SevenPrinciples.pdf> (accessed 12.01.15.).

Soviet History for the Networked Age, 2014. <http://www.lib.vt.edu/events/course-exhibits/soviet-history/index.html> (accessed 12.01.15.).

Variations of Practice Exhibit, 2013. <https://www.youtube.com/watch?v=Xq-r2c1pRUo> (accessed 12.01.15.).

CHAPTER 10

Going Vertical: Enhancing Staff Training Through Vertically Integrated Instruction

E.N. Decker[1] and J.A. Townes[2]
[1]Georgia Institute of Technology Library, Atlanta, GA, United States
[2]Georgia College & State University, Milledgeville, GA, United States

While collaboration and staff development are essential to the overall strength of the modern academic library, an experiential approach to staff training is less often discussed—despite the proven power of experiential methods to support and enhance workplace training. This chapter discusses our library's unique staff development and training program, wherein librarians and paraprofessionals alike alternate between being the teacher and the student. While every library has staff with specialized skills, this method of training ensures that we "spread the wealth" by sharing these skills through a hands-on, cross-training model.

This chapter describes the ways in which two librarians harnessed the talent of their respective teams to create quarterly instruction sessions to allow all staff to teach each other in a supportive setting. This experiential learning program has helped to build teams and has fostered an environment of enhanced collaboration within the library. Library staff not only benefit from learning from their colleagues, but staff teachers also benefit from and enjoy being recognized within the library for their unique strengths. Although this practice is not yet commonplace in the academic library, this chapter will provide considerations and hard-won knowledge about implementing such a program that can be replicated in any library.

10.1 WORKPLACE LEARNING

Workplace learning is an ongoing process, one that supports a wide range of career development needs. With the current workforce, these issues now include transitioning into or within the job, potentially losing work, and adjusting to changed circumstances (Parker et al., 2008). Learning and work "must now be integrated into a continuously supportive process" throughout an employee's career. The study of workplace learning is strongly associated with social theories of human behavior and methods of organizing within groups (Armson and Whiteley, 2010). Therefore, we can understand the outcomes of teaching and learning within peer groups by investigating the larger social behaviors at play in these encounters. Social behaviors such as verbal communication, experimenting as a group, and collegial approaches to problem-solving all positively influence workplace learning.

10.1.1 Learning Strategies

In the workplace, there are a variety of learning methods available to employees to help them enhance their skills and engage in problem solving. Geertshuis and Fazey (2006) categorize three types of learning approaches: deep, surface, and strategic. Those who adopt a deep approach to learning actively engage with their material and endeavor to understand the whole of it. Those who engage in surface learning may not see the need for ongoing development, and are content with such activities as rote memorization. Finally, strategic learners are those who plan their development to coincide with the achievement of personal goals. Each of these approaches requires a nuanced view of formal training. For example, with deep learners, who tend to learn for learning's sake, formal training is perceived positively. Not so with surface learners, for whom some kind of incentive is needed (Geertshuis and Fazey, 2006). In short, the various learning strategies employees use must be considered when conceptualizing any training cycle.

In addition to considering learning strategies, it is also important to understand learning patterns. Baert and Govaerts (2012) describe learning patterns as "the configuration of a variety of formal learning activities and the conditions at the workplace that are used for informal learning." Specific learning patterns identified by Baert and Govaerts include "helpdesk" and "agora" learning patterns. With the "helpdesk" learning pattern, "employees are unceasingly confronted with new and complex questions since the situation of their clients is highly variable and, to some extent, unique." The "agora" learning pattern relies on face-to-face communication in order to share ideas and discuss problems as a team. Examples of the "agora" learning pattern are informal consultation, team meetings, work groups, telephone contacts, emails, etc.

10.1.2 Formal and Informal Learning

Learning takes place in multiple formats and locations. These can be described by two umbrella terms: formal and informal learning. The differences between formal and informal learning are "most obvious in the areas of control, physical location, and predicting of learning outcomes" (MacNeil, 2001). Individuals are active agents of their learning (Armson and Whiteley, 2010), and when employees take control of their own learning, the result is likely to be informal. Conversely, when a manager or supervisor is in control of an employee's learning, the result is most likely to be formal. Physical location is also an important distinction. Most informal learning can be done at the desk, such as "e-mail, reading information on the Internet, 'fingertip' knowledge (e.g., Google), and casual, unplanned encounters" (Noe et al., 2010). Formal learning usually takes place in a separate location and in a group setting. The typical view of formal learning in the workplace is an organized and structured learning situation, "such as training programs and job-related training" (Armson and Whiteley, 2010). Formal learning often involves learning objectives and "off-the-job classroom or online course work, workshops, and seminars" (Cunningham and Hillier, 2013).

Though organizations spend "billions of dollars each year on formal learning," it has been suggested that more than 70% of learning in the workplace is informal (Cunningham and Hillier, 2013), and that "…informal interactions with peers are predominant ways of learning and that the impact of formal training on practice can be quite marginal" (Boud and Middleton, 2003). In order for informal learning to be effective, however, it is imperative that employees share their knowledge with their colleagues: "An effective informal learning process is one that enables the team members to make a transition from this 'solitary' state into that of team-based communications and sharing of learning" (MacNeil, 2001). Thus, informal learning moves into the realm of formal learning.

Formal and informal learning are often "inextricably entwined" (quoted in Armson and Whiteley, 2010), though informal learning is often not acknowledged by management (Boud and Middleton, 2003). MacNeil (2001) argues that instead "when senior management plan their employee development approaches, they should consider and implement not only formal but also informal learning processes." Informal learning better enables employees to gain "the skills and competencies which the organization has identified as being important to its success" (MacNeil, 2001).

10.1.3 Experiential Learning

Experiential learning occurs at the point where formal and informal learning meet. Experiential learning is participatory—the value of experiential learning is immersion into the experience (Benander, 2009). It is predicated upon the belief that learners have to be actively engaged if they are to gain applied knowledge (Yardley et al., 2012). In general terms, experiential learning "conceives of the adult learner as participating in an activity, then reflecting on the activity to make generalizations that he or she can then apply in new situations" (Benander, 2009, p. 36). For example, most "on the job" learning is experiential. The employee learns by doing, and the core condition of learning is participation. "There is no 'neutral' position: learners who do not feel legitimate (a mandate to be present) in workplaces will experience a sense of exclusion that hinders their learning" (Yardley et al., 2012).

10.1.4 Engagement Strategies

Promoting learning, growth, and development for employees underpins the manager's success (Parker et al., 2008). Three workplace conditions are necessary for positive psychological engagement: meaningfulness, safety, and availability (Cunningham and Hillier, 2013; Noe et al., 2010). An organizational climate that promotes active learning is important in promoting employee engagement in learning activities (Noe et al., 2010). MacNeil (2001) explains these conditions as an organizational culture that (1) allows for questioning in order to find meaning in directives and tasks, (2) understands how rewarding or punishing the behavior of individuals has a powerful influence on reinforcing or impeding individual learning, and (3) expresses positive forces in the norms and values of the learning environment. These tenets of active learning were considered in the implementation of our vertically integrated instruction program at the Atlanta University Center, Robert W. Woodruff Library.

10.2 GOING VERTICAL: VERTICALLY INTEGRATED INSTRUCTION

The Atlanta University Center, Robert W. Woodruff Library, provides service to four separate historically black colleges and universities: Clark-Atlanta University, the Interdenominational Theological Center, Morehouse College, and Spelman College. The Information and Research

Services Unit (IRS) is comprised of nine professional librarians, one part-time librarian, and the unit head librarian. The E-Learning Technologies Unit (ELT) is comprised of three paraprofessionals and the unit head librarian. During the summer of 2014, two librarians, working as unit heads for the IRS and ELT units, determined that more collaborative training was needed. In an attempt to foster departmental cohesion and to enhance teaching and technology skills, the unit heads designed a vertically integrated instruction pilot program.

Vertically integrated instruction, as described in this chapter, refers to a well-organized and purposely designed training program, combining both formal and informal learning, wherein library staff participants receive training from their colleagues that will help them to fill in gaps in their knowledge and skill-sets. It draws upon Peter Senge's (1990) theory about learning organizations, in that the participants are connecting with each other and learning together as a team. This feeling of being "part of something greater than oneself" benefits the individual as well as the organization.

Prior to the implementation of the vertically integrated instruction program, there had not been much collaboration between the ELT and IRS units on training and skills building. While the teams were used to working together toward accomplishing shared goals, the staff members on these teams were not accustomed to training each other. As with many other academic libraries, there is a divide in our library between the work done by professional librarians and the paraprofessionals; in this program, we made a concerted effort to bridge that gap and bring staff members in these units to the table together. In doing so, we created training opportunities that were hybrids of formal and informal approaches (MacNeil, 2001) and which took advantage of both classroom instruction and "agora" learning strategies (Baert and Govaerts, 2012).

Between them, the librarians in the IRS unit had logged hundreds of hours of instruction experience teaching classes in their respective subject areas. Each semester, the ELT unit offered a slate of workshops for faculty looking to incorporate technology into their teaching. The unit also offered technology workshops for library staff. ELT also offered students training in the use of the technology in the Technology Design Studio (TDS). The art of teaching was not new to any of the staff members who participated in this pilot program. That said, we found that instructing our own colleagues with whom you work every day is a different matter from teaching student and faculty users of the library!

The first workshop offered to the IRS librarians was on using Camtasia software, and was taught by the three ELT paraprofessionals. Camtasia is a user-friendly software that allows the user to capture videos or screencasts and provides basic editing functionality. In the library, faculty members often make use of Camtasia to create videos for flipped classes, while students use it to create videos for course assignments. Librarians use Camtasia to create short instructional videos for their classes, for posting on their LibGuides, and for assisting library users in navigating the software. While some of the librarians were already familiar with Camtasia, the workshop served as a refresher at the beginning of the semester.

On "training day", the librarians and paraprofessionals gathered in one of the library's classrooms, and the sense of participants eager to learn something new was in the air. The three ELT paraprofessionals first gave the IRS librarians an overview of Camtasia software. The librarians captured simple videos and learned the basics of editing and pairing the audio track with the video. The unit heads encouraged librarians already familiar with Camtasia to share tips and tricks with the group. After this initial training, we divided the librarians into two groups and had each of the groups work in the library's two presentation practice studios. The librarians were excited to do some hands-on work, and you could hear the conversations bubbling from each of the labs, as they worked together to create and edit a simple video. The paraprofessionals (pictured in Fig. 10.1) were enthralled with their role as teachers, and asked the librarians (students) to create a 1-minute video that could be used for instruction purposes. Instead of simply lecturing the librarians on the use of Camtasia, they had an engaging, hands-on experience. In other words, we ensured that the participants would be engaged in experiential learning (Yardley et al., 2012). At the end of the hour, the teams reconvened in the classroom to share what they had learned. They debriefed the process by sharing reflections and other thoughts they had. Librarians were overheard saying "this was fun," "you're good teachers" and "thanks for the opportunity to work with the software in the studio."

After the ELT paraprofessionals taught the IRS librarians the basics of Camtasia, the "tables were turned," and IRS librarians hosted a workshop for the ELT paraprofessionals on using the ProQuest Research Library database. This workshop combined both "agora" learning and "helpdesk" learning (Baert and Govaerts, 2012). Rather than simply

Figure 10.1 Paraprofessionals introducing librarians to Camtasia software.

being a demonstration of searching in ProQuest, the session began with a brief overview of the databases, recent changes and additions, and the essentials of how it is used. After this introduction, they allowed the ELT paraprofessionals to steer the search and discover the effective use of the databases on their own. By working through actual student questions received at the Information Desk, the paraprofessionals were able to build their confidence in using ProQuest. Brookfield (1991) advocates for this type of "simulated" experience in adult learning, because it requires the participants to work through the issues, dilemmas, and crises they might encounter in an authentic situation. This hands-on training turned out to be extremely well timed; shortly afterwards, a staffing shortage within the library necessitated using members of the ELT unit to serve a few hours per week on the Information Desk. Having gone through this training, they were able to quickly pick up the slack at the Information Desk.

The next workshop in the vertically integrated instruction series was hosted by the ELT paraprofessionals, where they taught the librarians how to create voice tracks in GarageBand (see Fig. 10.2). This learning experience explored using the software to create voice tracks over PowerPoint presentations and PowToon instruction cartoons, or as narration for any video. While GarageBand software offers a wide range

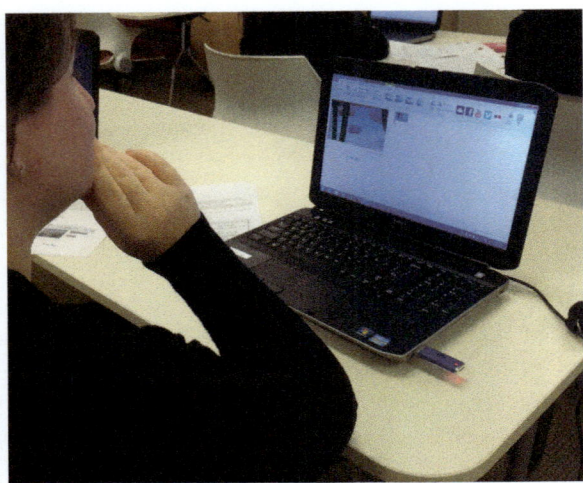

Figure 10.2 A librarian works on a project in GarageBand.

of options, for the purposes of this workshop, the ELT staff taught only the basics of how to record a voiceover. Librarians then gained familiarity and confidence with the microphones, having fun recording and editing their voice tracks in the recording studio. One librarian excitedly mentioned that she could now record voiceovers on videos in her subject LibGuides. While these resources (GarageBand, mixing boards, etc.) may not be available in every academic library, many technology-driven topics easily lend themselves to taking a peer-to-peer training approach. In our session, we discovered that one of the IRS librarians plays in a band, and had direct experience with creating voice tracks in GarageBand. As Brookfield (1991) recommends, we took a risk in diverging from our stated workshop agenda by asking him to share his experience. He did so, and at the spur of the moment, joined his ELT colleagues in instructing his colleagues and answering their questions. This experiential learning activity—with impromptu audience participation—created a casual and fun learning environment, where all participants had the chance to engage in authentic learning.

In the next workshop, the IRS librarians facilitated a tour of WorldShare Management System (WMS) for ELT staff. While the ELT unit had experience using WMS to find library materials, they noted that they "hadn't really had a chance to work in depth with it." By conducting a search in front of the IRS librarians, they were able to explain the rationale for the search approach they chose, and librarians could then give them feedback on their method. Librarians were patient, doling out praise for the efforts of their "students." This was an example of experiential and "agora" learning. It is a common misconception that the main "Search" box on the Library's homepage searches all of the library's holdings. When one participant attempted a search in this fashion, an IRS librarian was able to step in and explain this misconception, recommending that separate searches of databases be performed. By working in this "hands-on" style, the ELT student's familiarity and skill in using WMS was solidified.

In the final vertically integrated workshop of the semester, the ELT paraprofessionals hosted a workshop on digital drawing tablets the library acquired. This session taught IRS librarians how to take notes and draw basic diagrams on the tablets, and also included information on ways to promote their use to faculty departments. As there were three drawing tablets and nine librarians, ELT set up three different drawing tool workstations in a library classroom and the librarians took turns using the tablets. Since it takes some practice to get used to drawing on a digital tablet, ELT initiated a "drawing contest" for the librarians. The workshop was fun and had a "Pictionary" game feeling to it, with librarians competing to draw the best representation of a concept.

10.3 SOLUTIONS AND RECOMMENDATIONS

When implementing a vertically integrated instruction program, it is helpful to consider the following:
- Scheduling—while 100% attendance is unrealistic, make a concerted effort to schedule these workshops when the greatest number of library staff are available to participate;
- Motivation—consider hosting trainings at regular intervals, to keep the momentum up and get staff accustomed to a regular training schedule;
- Skill level—there is going to be an inevitable difference in skill levels among staff members. If the library staff are numerous enough, consider offering these workshops in a tiered system corresponding to pre-existing skill level;
- Leadership—this is an opportunity for staff to learn a bit about leadership; ask staff which topics they feel they are able to teach to other staff members, and encourage them to take a lead role in sharing their knowledge.

Furthermore, the following logistics will be helpful when implementing a vertically integrated instruction program:
- Look for hidden talents within your pool of staff;
- Survey library staff to determine training needs and topic interests;
- In particular, identify technology-driven topics available for peer-to-peer training;
- Review service desk staffing to identify cross-training opportunities.

10.4 FUTURE DIRECTIONS IN LIBRARY WORKPLACE LEARNING

Moving forward, we think it is worthwhile to investigate "learning teams" as an innovative option for experiential and collaborative training of library staff. A learning team could be comprised of two or three library employees (preferably of different rank and departments), who would work together to hone their skills on the use of a software package, database, or new technology. Afterwards, the learning team would then develop and present a training session for their colleagues. The learning team model promotes collegiality and, perhaps more importantly, puts the responsibility for developing the training squarely on the team itself. The act of creating this training session would be "experiential," in that the team would learn by doing and the session would have direct relevance to the participants' work lives, a hallmark of experiential learning.

Since the vertically integrated instruction program allowed for library colleagues—both paraprofessionals and librarians—to come together, work together, and learn from one another, a learning team model also has the potential to further promote cross-departmental cooperation. The success of the initial program is demonstrated by the way that it fostered teamwork and collegiality, and provided an opportunity for both learning and teaching new skills. A learning team model makes it possible to further this success, by shifting a larger portion of responsibility onto the staff to acquire and teach needed skills together.

Surprisingly, despite the well-known reduction of academic library budgets nationwide, there are not many examples in the library science literature of programs where library staff help develop their own colleagues' professional competencies. Though experiential training and peer-to-peer learning are used frequently in the business world, they also have their place in academia, too, as strong options for staff development.

While this study explored group-to-group peer training in the academic library, it would be interesting to consider questions such as:
- Does the experiential model work as well in one-to-one training?
- Do employees feel the same edification in teaching one person a skill as they do a group within a workshop setting?
- Is there the same level of accountability for the "teacher" and the "student" in a one-to-one setting as there is in a group setting?

Employee feedback is critical, too, in measuring the impact of peer-to-peer teaching and learning. During the first iteration of the vertical instruction program, we relied upon our own observations of the workshops and staff participation to measure their success. We also received word-of-mouth feedback from presenters and attendees on the perceived efficacy of the program. Future iterations, whether following the vertical instruction model or the learning teams model, will require a more formal assessment process.

Overall, we've seen that creativity, collaboration, and a willingness to "step outside the box" of everyday work routines allowed the vertically integrated instruction program at Atlanta University Center Robert W. Woodruff Library to support the professional development of its staff. Initially, it seemed unlikely that the library could directly address technology training needs, but employing experiential learning methods proved to be a strong and cost-effective model for training and for developing staff teaching abilities.

It is often the case that the strongest training resource in the library is the library staff itself. When library staff are empowered in their professional development, the library as a whole is better able to adapt to changing work demands and new and emerging technologies. Undoubtedly, they must develop strong skill-sets, but more often than not, these skills are not communicated to other staff members in different departments. Most academic libraries could benefit from having staff members teach each other aspects of their work, in order to de-silo their skills, to build their own sense of accomplishment, and, finally, to help other library staff members learn and develop new skills. In our library, staff benefitted from teaching and learning from each other, in a simulated environment of "how would you proceed?" scenarios. This allowed them to work their way through problems and to directly apply the training they had received.

Moving forward, we see it as imperative that libraries create new models, infused with experiential learning methods, such as the ones described in this chapter, for supporting library colleagues' professional development. While academic librarians are adept at collaborating with each other and with faculty, we believe that the bigger challenge (and opportunity) is to identify emerging training needs within the library, and to address those needs through vertically integrated instruction.

REFERENCES

Armson, G., Whiteley, A., 2010. Employees' and managers' accounts of interactive workplace learning. J. Workplace Learn. 22 (7), 409–427.

Baert, H., Govaerts, N., 2012. Learning patterns of teams at the workplace. J. Workplace Learn. 24 (7), 538–550.

Benander, R., 2009. Experiential learning in the scholarship of teaching and learning. J. Sch. Teach. Learn. 9 (2), 36–41.

Boud, D., Middleton, H., 2003. Learning from others at work: communities of practice and informal learning. J. Workplace Learn. 15 (5), 194–202.

Brookfield, S., 1991. The Skillful Teacher: On Technique, Trust, and Responsiveness in the Classroom. Jossey-Bass Publishers, San Francisco, CA.

Cunningham, J., Hillier, E., 2013. Informal learning in the workplace: key activities and processes. Educ. + Train. 55 (1), 37–51.

Geertshuis, S., Fazey, J., 2006. Approaches to learning in the workplace. J. Workplace Learn. 18 (1), 55–65.

MacNeil, C., 2001. The supervisor as a facilitator of informal learning in work teams. J. Workplace Learn. 13 (5), 246–253.

Noe, R., Tews, M., Dachner, A., 2010. Learner engagement: a new perspective for enhancing our understanding of learner motivation and workplace learning. Acad. Manag. Ann. 4 (1), 279–315.

Parker, P., Hall, D., Kram, K., 2008. Peer coaching: a relational process for accelerating career learning. Acad. Manag. Learn. Educ. 7 (4), 487–503.

Senge, P., 1990. The Fifth Discipline: The Art and Practice of the Learning Organization. Doubleday Business, New York, NY.

Yardley, S., Teunissen, P., Dornan, T., 2012. Experiential learning: transforming theory into practice. Med. Teach. 34, 161–164.

CHAPTER 11

From Training to Learning: Developing Student Employees Through Experiential Learning Design

H. Bussell[1] and J. Hagman[2]
[1]The Ohio State University, Columbus, OH, United States
[2]Ohio University, Athens, OH, United States

Learning in libraries: the phrase may conjure up images of students working with a librarian to find information or poring over library materials as they write a paper. When we consider learning in the library, however, we should also call to mind a sometimes-overlooked group: student employees. In many libraries, students work across departments and help with a wide range of vital tasks, both behind the scenes and in the public eye. The library literature offers much advice for training student employees with the goal of providing effective service within the library. Less often is there guidance for framing student employment as a learning opportunity that fits into the student's overall academic experience. Regardless of the type of work assignment, we think student employment is an opportunity for libraries to go beyond training and explicitly encourage student learning.

In this chapter, we describe an effort to take an explicit experiential learning (EL) approach for students working in our library's outreach program. While the students in these roles had previously been actively engaged in the library's social media and educational video production, their positions lacked an intentional focus on student learning. By framing their work as a learning experience, the student employees were able to set their own learning goals and use their work as a means of meeting those goals.

11.1 STUDENT EMPLOYEES IN LIBRARIES: AN EMPHASIS ON TRAINING

The library literature is replete with articles describing strategies for working effectively with student employees. Their work has become increasingly vital to many academic libraries, as the number of full-time staff members has decreased in the wake of budget cuts and positions left unfilled after retirements (Manley and Holley, 2014, pp. 76–77). With their growing importance to the daily work of academic libraries, many librarians have described their approach to recruiting, training, motivating, and retaining student employees for effective library services (see Farr and Valentine, 2011 and McInnes, 2009, for examples of entire outlines of the hiring, training, and the student employee retention process).

Many writers have offered up examples of their own training programs for students working in a range of roles. For example, Guerrero and Corey (2003, pp. 99–100) described a card-sorting exercise to help students learn to correctly shelve books. Drewitz (2013) advocated for a mentoring approach and modeling expected customer service behavior when training students for public-facing work. Hillyard and Whitson (2008) recounted the development of a collaborative training program for students who worked in a variety of academic services units. The new training program brought students together for an interactive session where they were introduced to the many academic services units, discussed customer services scenarios and public safety issues, and provided feedback on the overall training process to develop future training offerings. Starkel (2014) described a training program for students working in Butler University's Information Commons. Starkel and colleagues deployed the University's Learning Management System for training, which helped the students progress from basic training in library services to more advanced skills they would need to address research-related questions.

Articles such as these provide insight into the student training processes for student employees. Any student employee who comes to the library will indeed need to receive training in order to do their work. If we leave the conversation at training, however, we fail to consider the student employee as a learner who gains more from their work experience than income and a line on their resume. If we think of the student employee as a learner, we can go beyond training and help the students to develop skills that transfer to life beyond the library (Kern, 2009).

11.1.1 A Learning-Focused Approach

Some libraries have intentionally incorporated learning opportunities into their student training programs. Thomsett-Scott (2012) developed a program of training and mentoring for library and information science (LIS) graduate students working in library reference services. Students in this program received hands-on training that Thomsett-Scott identified as a form of EL. Participants were provided with training in areas of personal interest and need. For example, after realizing a need for public-speaking skills training among the graduate students, library staff offered opportunities for students to develop a public presentation. Similarly, Evanson (2015) described a peer research advisor program at Davidson University, having decided to "focus on the students as learners, not just employees" to help with motivation (p. 30). The training program for peer advisors included learning outcomes tied to information literacy threshold concepts. Each student worked with a mentor and developed their own long-term project that both supported the work of the university and served as a project they could reference in their post-graduation job search.

York et al. (2010) have discussed the incorporation of EL into library services at Middle Tennessee State University. They note that most examples of EL programs in libraries consist of marketing or advertising classes creating library promotional material for a class project. The authors recount several collaborative examples at MTSU, including a partnership with an art class to develop thought-provoking artwork intended to reduce paper consumption in the library (p. 195). These projects provided students the opportunity to engage in EL in the library with projects that helped the library meet its own goals. Such projects, however, came out of coursework, rather than student employment in the library.

Markgraf (2015) has described an effort at the University of Wisconsin-Eau Claire Libraries to turn student employment into a "high impact practice" (p. 770) through which students gain skills and experience in areas related to their academic work. Library supervisors at UW-Eau Claire drew on the IOWA GROW (Guided Reflection On Work) program from the University of Iowa to help students draw connections between their work and academic lives through a series of reflection questions (Office of the Vice President for Student Life, 2015). While UW-Eau Claire's program does not explicitly incorporate elements of EL, the program does include a focus on reflection, to help students make sense of how their work experiences "fit" into their overall academic career.

From these examples, we can see that some libraries' student employee programs treat the student worker as both a learner and an employee. One way that libraries can enhance student workers' experiences is to encourage them to reflect on their work and to consider how it fits into their academic life in college.

11.2 CURRENT STUDENT EMPLOYMENT PRACTICES AT THE OHIO UNIVERSITY LIBRARIES

At the Ohio University Libraries, we employ several students who produce social media and video content to support the Libraries' marketing and outreach efforts. Some of the students who do this work are funded through a special university-sponsored program that encourages significant work experience and career exploration opportunities for students. We have employed a Social Media Content Developer through this program since 2011 and a Multimedia Production Specialist since 2014.

The Social Media Content Developer works with Jessica Hagman, the Libraries' Social Media Coordinator, to create the Libraries' social media content. The student position was envisioned as a way to help the library develop additional content for its social networks, at a time when such work was not part of any full-time staff member's assigned work. In recent years, social media communication has become increasingly important for a wide variety of fields in which students might work after graduation, making the Social Media Content Developer position a valuable opportunity to learn how to translate an organization's communication into social content.

Similarly, the Multimedia Production Specialist works with the eLearning Librarian to create library promotional videos, as well as educational and other multimedia to promote specific information literacy outcomes. Ohio University librarians have created short videos for a number of years, which are used in classes and embedded in the FAQ section of the Libraries' website. We have found it increasingly time-consuming to keep existing videos updated and to create new ones that have a high production quality and meet accessibility standards (such as closed captioning). We hired a Multimedia Production Specialist student who has knowledge of video production and editing, and who can lend a fresh, student-centered perspective to our video content.

While these student positions contributed greatly to the Libraries' overall social media and video outreach strategies, their training was much like what other librarians have described in the literature: heavily focused on training, and highly directed by the student's supervisor. In the Fall of 2015, however, we sought to reconceive the positions in terms of student learning and to intentionally incorporate EL for the two students assigned to this work for the new school year.

11.3 ADAPTING STUDENT EMPLOYMENT PRACTICES TO INCORPORATE EL

11.3.1 Instructional Design Principles for EL

In considering how to incorporate experiential elements formally into our student employment practices, we found it useful to apply the instructional design principles described by Lindsey and Berger (2009). Drawing on John Dewey, David Kolb, and other educational theorists, Lindsey and Berger provide a set of guidelines for educators and instructional designers to implement EL in an instructional context.

Their first design principle is *"framing the experience"* (Lindsey and Berger, 2009, p. 125). Just because a student is engaging in an activity does not mean this is automatically EL. In order for it to become so, certain objectives and relationships should be discussed at the beginning in order to set the tone and help students engage more intentionally with the experience. Elements involved at this stage include communicating learning goals and establishing criteria for authentically assessing the experience. A list of learning goals for the Social Media Content Developer and Multimedia Production Specialist positions is shown in Box 11.1.

It is also important to discuss the social structure and types of interactions expected between learners, and between learner and teacher

---

BOX 11.1 Learning Goals for the Social Media Content Developer and Multimedia Production Specialist Positions

Learning Goals

Social Media Content Developer
1. Learn to use and analyze data from Google Analytics
2. Develop and implement a consistent content plan for the library's Tumblr page
3. Effectively use Trello to manage social media content
4. Create and successfully execute library social media contests and events

Multimedia Production Specialist
1. Brainstorm ways to improve marketing of the library videos to allow them to reach more students (try to create something that will go viral)
2. Experiment with creating animated videos
3. Get experience working more with motion graphics
4. Acquire skills and experiences that will help with future internships and jobs

(Lindsey and Berger, 2009, pp. 125–6). We believe this latter element is particularly important to consider when the EL happens in a student employment context, where the teacher is also the work supervisor. EL "involves a shift in the power base between instructor and learners such that the learners assume more of the responsibilities for what is learned and how learning occurs" (Lee and Caffarella, 1994, p. 44). In order for this shift to occur, it is vital that the learner sees the teacher as someone who can be challenged (Lindsey and Berger, 2009, p. 129). As tricky as it is to establish this level of trust between learner and teacher in a normal classroom, it can be even more difficult when the learner/teacher relationship is also an employee/supervisor relationship. This is especially the case when learning is taking place in a work environment where there are pre-established practices and procedures, challenges to which might meet with some resistance. Thus, we believe it is important that supervisors work hard to cultivate an environment of safety and respect, where the student employee feels comfortable voicing what might be seen as challenges to their supervisor or existing practices of the organization. This is not something that can be established just at the outset; rather, the supervisor must be conscious in maintaining it throughout the experience.

At the same time, there are situations where some didactic instruction during the initial framing stage of EL is appropriate. This may be especially true where there are ethical or legal issues involved (Lindsey and Berger, 2009, p. 132). In our case, for example, our student employees are creating public, digital outreach and instruction materials that must adhere to certain legal guidelines, such as accessibility and copyright. This is something that needs to be communicated to the student at the beginning of their training, because there can be real-world, detrimental consequences for everyone involved if the guidelines are ignored. Even in this situation, however, we think it is important not just to tell students they must follow the rules "because we say so," but to help them make sense of the guidelines by helping them relate them to their own prior knowledge and experiences.

Lindsey and Berger's next design principle is *"activating experience"* (p. 126). This is the "meat" of the experience itself, and as such there is less for the supervisor to do here to actively direct the process. Nevertheless, there are certain characteristics of the experience that the supervisor should help facilitate. For one, the experience should be as authentic as possible, so that the decisions the student employee makes and actions they perform provide them with realistic feedback.

The Social Media Content Developer, for example, receives regular feedback from the library's social media followers as their engagement—or lack thereof—indicates whether the content has been valuable to its intended audience.

Rather than giving the student employee directions for specific tasks to carry out, it is better to take a problem-oriented approach, with the student employee given an issue or scenario to analyze and resolve. Frequently, the Multimedia Production Specialist is given a topic for a video and perhaps a loose outline, but it is up to them to decide how to best design the video. In addition to working with the eLearning Librarian, they develop videos that are commissioned by other librarians for use in their classes and events, collaborating with the librarian to turn their vision into a final product. This collaboration is part of the learning experience in itself, since people working in video production are often commissioned to work on projects and must learn how to effectively balance the desires of the client with constraints set by time and resources.

By approaching the learning opportunity as a situation to be analyzed and figured out rather than a set of predetermined tasks to be completed, students have the opportunity to receive authentic feedback for decisions they make based on their failures and successes, and to incorporate this information into their knowledge base. Since "individuals do not simply absorb knowledge in authentic learning experiences," but rather "utilize their prior knowledge in the interpretation, retention, and revision of incoming, new information," learners should be encouraged to draw on their previously acquired skills and knowledge in solving the problems they are presented with in the learning context, thus creating new knowledge from the experience (Jackson and MacIsaac, 1994, p. 22). Most students who have come into the Social Media Content Developer position have taken classes in social media use or have used social media marketing for a student organization. Communicating on behalf of the library, however, requires that they use this experience as a basis for learning how to speak on behalf of an official university-sponsored account that has a specific "voice" it needs to maintain. They must also learn to build social content around a wide range of library-related topics and services. At the start of the school year, this requires extensive support from their supervisor to ensure that they have sufficient information to do their work. Throughout the academic year, however, they grow to know more about the library and eventually are able to develop content independently.

Finally, it is important to help create a learning experience with the right level of difficulty for the student employee. The experience should present enough challenges that the student employee is stretched to develop their skills and knowledge, but shouldn't be so difficult that they are likely to fail. For example, in creating videos about specialized resources that the Multimedia Production students may not be familiar with, the librarian tends to be more directly involved in developing the video and writing the script, so that the student can focus on the technical and design aspects.

The final design element we strive for is *"reflecting on experience"* (Lindsey and Berger, 2009, p. 128). This means that student employees are asking themselves the questions, "What happened? Why did it happen? What have I learned from this? Would I do something differently in the future?" In the fast-paced work environment of a library's outreach and social media area, moving from one project to another in quick succession is commonplace. Thus, it is important to incorporate reflection into the students' EL process, so that they have the opportunity to step back and consider what they have learned, helping to build their knowledge into the future.

One method for reflection, particularly when there are multiple students, is to have a group discussion or "debriefing" after an activity (Lindsey and Berger, 2009, p. 128). In our environment, where there are one or two student employees working independently, the supervisor might not always be physically present when the student finishes a project; thus, a verbal debriefing is supplemented by written reflection. Having the student employee write in a journal or blog gives them opportunities for reflection throughout the experience, and gives the supervisor the chance both to assess the project as it occurs and to ask the student employee additional questions to spur on more reflection. We have found that the use of a project management system can help to facilitate student work and reflection on their performance. We have used the free tool Trello for tracking student work for several years, and have seen that it enables efficient communication between the supervisor and student working at different times. When we decided to incorporate EL into students' work more explicitly, we developed a "project" for each student, in which they were able to track their progress towards individualized learning goals. Alternately, the student could keep a journal on a shared platform like Google Drive, which lets them track and reflect on their learning experience in collaboration with their supervisor.

An additional method for reflection we are implementing this year is a reflective portfolio. In addition to having student employees highlight the best representations of their learning and work, this portfolio will feature reflections written by the student about what they learned from the experience. MacIsaac and Jackson write, "Constructing reflective portfolios moves the learner beyond a description of the portfolio contents to an examination of the learning documented in the portfolio through a discussion of what the portfolio reveals about the learner's level of accomplishment" (1994, p. 66). Reflective portfolios thus give student employees a chance to reflect back on their entire experience over the year, and give the supervisor the opportunity for summative assessment. It also provides the student employee with a tangible representation of their work to show potential employers, and the experience of presenting their work in a professional way.

11.4 CHALLENGES AND ISSUES TO CONSIDER
11.4.1 Allowing for Failure

Working with students to develop library outreach materials poses a challenge, given that EL encourages students to have the opportunity to fail. The students' work in this case may be public and reflect poorly on the library's public image, if not done well. This is not only an issue faced by students working in outreach positions, however. Many student employees perform their work in the public eye and with patrons who may not differentiate between student employees and full-time staff. Supervisors must balance students' need to grow through their learning experiences with the library's need to maintain a consistent, appropriate, and accurate public presence.

We've approached the issue of failure for outreach student work by asking the students to draft their content for approval before it appears publicly on the library's social media accounts. Drafts are posted on a Google Drive spreadsheet that serves as an editorial calendar. Drafting content ahead of publication allows the librarian to ensure that the content is accurate and is consistent with the library's established social media tone and content guidelines. Any problems can be addressed in a way that lets the student make their own changes and learn from the experience.

A recent example: a student who sought to inject a bit of levity into the library's Twitter content proposed a message that included a meme photo. This widely shared image features an unflattering photo of a young woman who, presumably, did not intend to become the subject of many online jokes. While it is not officially part of our policy to not use memes featuring ordinary people, such images can be interpreted as bullying behavior (Franklin, 2015) and fall outside of the friendly tone we seek to exude via our social media communication. Having discussed this concern with their supervisor, the student was able to find a meme image that did not include an ordinary person who unwittingly became the subject of an unkind meme.

In terms of library communication, failure may also include messages that simply do not resonate with their intended audience, or that fail to engage followers on the social networking site. To address this element, we have incorporated more regular reviews of our social media content to determine what types of messages lead to higher levels of engagement and to help us develop future messages. Similarly, we have started to track the number of views for videos, comparing views on YouTube with views when videos are posted directly to Facebook. While we have always kept an eye on analytics, the process has not been intentional. By regularly reviewing our content and the available data for message effectiveness, students receive valuable feedback about their work. We are also seeking to expand our assessment to include instructional goals for library video content. To this end, we have begun assessing the effectiveness of videos created for a specific class or assignment, by seeking feedback directly from students, faculty, and subject librarians.

11.4.2 Scaling Up

We would be remiss to leave out issues of scale. The two authors directly supervise a single student each during the academic year, while many other libraries are working with a larger group of students performing a broad range of tasks. Incorporating EL training in a larger cohort of student employees will inherently be less efficient than traditional training practices (Wurdinger and Carlson, 2010). A library employing a fleet of students who shelve books or answer questions at library service points, for example, will have to devote significant resources to incorporate EL into the students' training.

11.4.3 Allowing Time for Reflection

Part of the challenge in scaling up the EL approach is to allow time for students to reflect upon their work, and for supervisors to engage directly with employees in the process. The library may need to budget for additional student hourly time and funding for students to reflect on their work, while supervisors will need to budget their own time as well. Students could be asked to keep a journal or portfolio that their supervisor can view, or employees could engage in a peer reflection process with their fellow student workers.

11.4.4 Higher Expectations for Student Workers

Deploying this type of approach means that the library will be asking more of the student employee than just doing their work. Depending on the individual student and the culture of the library, incorporating EL may be a change from previous practices. Deciding to move in this direction means that supervisors need to communicate new expectations and why they matter. Previously hired students will likely need some time to adapt to the new approach. In our experience with the EL approach, the potential for student learning and productive work is sizable, and worth the investment.

11.4.5 Deciding to Invest in EL

None of these issues are trivial. Going "from training to learning" will require the commitment of library resources, including one of the most precious: staff time. Any library considering an experiential training program will have to recognize that this is an investment of scarce resources. We would argue, however, that high-quality student employment is worth the investment, for those libraries interested in making it more than just a work experience for students.

In describing the changes made at the UW-Eau Claire, Markgraf (2015) noted that student employment in the library became a "high impact practice" (p. 770). This framing allowed UW-Eau Claire librarians to point to the library as a place where students not only find information, but have the opportunity to gain valuable work and learning experiences. Student employees at Eau Claire's libraries reflect on how that work influences their development throughout their college experiences. This has become increasingly important in a state where colleges and universities are often under attack for not preparing students for the workforce (Markgraf, 2015). For the students working in the library's social media and video development, we've decided that this approach is worthwhile. While they are earning money and learning job skills, the students also have the opportunity to learn an approach to problem-solving that will serve them well beyond their college years.

11.5 CONCLUDING THOUGHTS

Our goal in writing this chapter has been to try to expand the concept of "learning in libraries" beyond what happens at the reference desk, in the library classroom, or in informal study spaces, to the learning that takes place in student employee positions. Specifically, we believe the EL model offers libraries the chance to provide students with the opportunity to not only gain workplace experience, but to set and achieve authentic learning goals which complement their academic experiences. Taking this approach helps students develop learning strategies that they can apply throughout their postcollegiate lives and careers. A student who has worked in an environment that embraces EL has a model for personal growth and development as well.

In the end, libraries can help students come away with concrete job skills as well as a way to make their work more meaningful in the long term. From this perspective, student employment programs do more than help the library accomplish its work; they become a value-added service that contributes to the overall institutional mission. In outlining this model of library student employment, and how we have put it into practice in our own library, we hope to inspire other libraries to shift their emphasis from training to learning, by incorporating EL design into their student employment program.

REFERENCES

Drewitz, J., 2013. Training student workers: a win-win. AALL Spectr. 18 (2), 22–24.
Evanson, C., 2015. We aren't just the kids that sit at the front. Coll. Res. Libr. News 76 (1), 30–33.
Farr, M., Valentine, A., 2011. Yes, this is a real job and you do need to show up on time! Pa. Libr. Assoc. Bull. 66 (2), 15–20.
Franklin, K., 2015. The post-9/11 John Wayne vs. bullying: a tale of schadenfreude obsessed culture. In: Scheg, A. (Ed.), Bullying in Popular Culture: Essays on Film, Television and Novels. McFarland, Jefferson, NC, pp. 176–188.
Guerrero, T., Corey, K., 2003. Training and retaining student employees a case study at Purdue University Calumet. J. Access Serv. 1 (4), 97–102.
Hillyard, C., Whitson, K., 2008. An LA&M case study: a multi-unit approach to interactive training of student employees. Libr. Adm. Manag. 22 (1), 37–41.
Jackson, L., MacIsaac, D., 1994. Introduction to a new approach to experiential learning. In: Jackson, L., Caffarella, R.S. (Eds.), Experiential Learning: A New Approach,

New Directions for Adult and Continuing Education. Jossey-Bass, San Francisco, CA, pp. 17—28.

Kern, M.K., 2009. Teaching reference: ten questions from a first attempt. Ref. User Serv. Q. 48 (4), 330—333.

Lee, P., Caffarella, R.S., 1994. Methods and techniques for engaging learners in experiential learning activities. In: Jackson, L., Caffarella, R.S. (Eds.), Experiential Learning: A New Approach, New Directions for Adult and Continuing Education. Jossey-Bass, San Francisco, CA, pp. 43—54.

Lindsey, L., Berger, N., 2009. Experiential approaches to instruction. In: Reigeluth, C.M., Carr-Chellman, A.A. (Eds.), Instructional-Design Theories and Models, Volume III: Building a Common Knowledge Base. Routledge, New York, NY, pp. 117—142.

MacIsaac, D., Jackson, L., 1994. Assessment processes and outcomes: portfolio construction. In: Jackson, L., Caffarella, R.S. (Eds.), Experiential Learning: A New Approach, New Directions for Adult and Continuing Education. Jossey-Bass, San Francisco, CA, pp. 63—72.

Manley, L., Holley, R.P., 2014. Hiring and training work-study students: a case study. Coll. Undergrad. Libr. 21 (1), 76—89. Available from: http://dx.doi.org/10.1080/10691316.2014.877739.

Markgraf, J., 2015. Unleash your library's HIPster: transforming student library jobs into high-impact practices. In: Proceedings of the ACRL 2015 Conference.

McInnes, R.A., 2009. Hiring and training student employees. J. Soc. N. C. Arch. 6 (2), 75—85.

Office of the Vice President for Student Life, 2015. IOWA GROW. <https://vp.studentlife.uiowa.edu/initiatives/grow/> (accessed 10.11.15.).

Starkel, A.D., 2014. Investing in student employees: training in Butler University's Information Commons program. Indiana Libr. 33 (2), 83—86.

Thomsett-Scott, B., 2012. Creating a formal program to train LIS students for reference services. Ref. Libr. 53 (1), 41—59.

York, A., Groves, C., Black, W., 2010. Enriching the academic experience: the library and experiential learning. Collab. Libr. 2 (4), 193—203.

Wurdinger, S.D., Carlson, J., 2010. Teaching for Experiential Learning: Five Approaches that Work. Rowman & Littlefield Education, Lanham, MD.

PART III

The Experiential Library: Innovation and Multi-Library Collaborations

CHAPTER 12

Home Grown: Lessons Learned From Experiential Learning Partnerships in an Academic Library

C. Groves and A. Shealy
Middle Tennessee State University, Murfreesboro, TN, United States

12.1 SETTING THE STAGE FOR EXPERIENTIAL LEARNING AT WALKER LIBRARY

Libraries have been in transition to meet demands of modern clientele for over two decades. Gone are traditional bricks-and-mortar structures housing print collections. Many libraries today house collaborative, flexible, and technology-rich gathering spaces designed for patrons to rearrange as they want. Recent phases of libraries' transition are taking flexibility a step further: we have begun collaborating with our patrons in the design of services and spaces, encouraging them to interact with us as we continue our evolution. No longer are we simply studying and surveying users. Through the development of sustainable partnerships with stakeholders and focus groups, and through usability testing, we now more than ever include users in library planning and decision-making.

Several critical issues contribute to the need for patron-included library planning:
1. Staffing; many libraries are perpetually short-staffed.
2. Relevance; libraries consistently (and tirelessly) demonstrate to governing constituencies our importance to an organizational mission. What better way to demonstrate relevance than to include our clientele in the design process?
3. Specific/unique expertise; libraries are innovating to meet a myriad of patron needs, often ripe with complex technologies. To keep up, we tap into experts outside the field of librarianship.

Since 2007, Middle Tennessee State University's Walker Library has partnered with patrons. We sought out and engaged in experiential learning (EL) activities with students to enhance our relevance to the MTSU community. Similar to other libraries, Walker's experience with staff shortages proved challenging, so what started out as a pilot project in 2007 evolved into a valuable opportunity for students, as well as vital support for the Library. Thus, we quickly became much more reliant upon EL activities than originally intended. This chapter will describe Walker Library's EL initiatives and how we utilized them to achieve Library and MTSU goals. We will also provide examples of how we merged these projects into ethnographic studies of the Walker Library user experience.

12.2 STAFFING AT WALKER LIBRARY
12.2.1 Doing More With Less—Where We Were

Libraries have been troubled by staffing shortages for years. Similar to others, when the recession of the late 2000s hit, Walker Library witnessed a 10% reduction in personnel. Our clientele, however, increased, as more people came to college with the hopes of ultimately landing higher-paying jobs. As a result, the Library had to cover increased use with less staff. The Library administration approached the daunting task of "doing more with less" through a series of staff discussions. We identified "mission critical" services as well as those that could be reduced and/or eliminated. Personnel were provided with opportunities to migrate into areas of identified need, thus undertaking new skills and responsibilities. Many individuals became revitalized and re-engaged in their work, as they had new challenges to thrive on. The Library continued to thrive and remained a cornerstone of the MTSU campus.

However, we still had visible—at least to us—holes. Librarians are well-meaning stewards of information access, and we continue to seek ways to improve our service. Our librarians believed we could do things more efficiently. We also recognized that we were primarily keeping above water. Our streamlined "doing more with less" approach, while sustainable for the short term, was not a long-term solution. We had many projects "on hold" that would improve our ability to connect with users, most notably, the development of an Information Commons.

In 2009, the Library opportunistically received trickle-down America Recovery Act funding, so we jumped at the opportunity to launch a Commons. The funding covered modest renovations of our first-floor space, including new furniture and technology. Funds were also utilized to create a multimedia lab (the Digital Media Studio), which was integrated into our aging Microtext area on the second floor. What was not included in this funding was dollars for permanent full-time staff. Thus, we had new services to provide our students and fewer personnel than ever. We quickly sought opportunities to capitalize on funding from other campus sources. We had a strong relationship with the History Department, which voluntarily funded two 20-hour/week graduate assistantships. Our History Department-funded GAs provided much needed assistance in not only staffing our DMS, but also in helping us to become more comfortable with the hardware and software we offered users.

Second, we reached out to the University of Tennessee, Knoxville (UTK), which currently has the state's only American Library Association-accredited MLS program. As a result of the growth of distance education across the nation, we observed that a number of UTK MLS students were pursuing their degree from the middle Tennessee area. Those students were seeking practicum opportunities as part of their degree completion, and we needed help from eager and qualified individuals.

This was not an official partnership between Walker Library and UTK. It was, however, UTK professor-approved, and we utilized these students to engage in several valuable and timely Library projects. One student's practicum work resulted in the migration of nearly 100 online subject guides to the LibGuides platform. Another's work was instrumental in launching several Walker Library digital collections. Yet another practicum student worked in the Digital Media Studio's inaugural semester. Finally, a fourth practicum student provided valuable Reference Desk assistance and led a number of library instruction sessions. The practicum students were overseen by the Department Chair and Reference/Instruction Team Leader. They were scheduled into the daily workflow of the User Services department and included in all departmental meetings and communications. Their input and feedback were solicited throughout the practicum experience. Each student was thought of and treated as an employee. As a result, they experienced a "day in the life" of a professional MLS librarian, gained relevant skills, and earned credit toward their degree. The Library benefited from up-and-coming professionals working on these important projects. It should also be noted that all four of the practicum students quickly landed a professional role after their graduation. It is no doubt that the skills they gained while working with us helped toward that end.

However, we wondered about more fully embracing the concept of true EL. Our Administrative Services Librarian—now retired—had been actively involved with the development of the Experiential Learning Program at MTSU. That program was established in 2006 as a pilot project in support of the MTSU Quality Enhancement Plan.

Within a few short years, the program had charted some impressive numbers. Thus, if the Library could tap into this, what would be the mutual benefit? After some brainstorming, we decided to establish a 1 credit-hour course in the MTSU EL Program. At first, we designed the course so that the students would serve as an advisory board, with an "opportunity to help improve library services by reflecting on current practices, engaging in research projects, and reviewing other libraries' services" (York et al., 2010). Unfortunately, the class ended up with only four students. We retooled the course to focus on a research project to capture building usage data. Unfortunately, "the outcomes of the project were mixed" (York et al., 2010). Scheduling face-to-face meeting time among the four EL students and the librarians proved cumbersome (after all, this was only a 1 credit-hour course), so most of the class communication occurred online. There appeared to be a fundamental lack of understanding about the nature of the data collection project, as these students were representative of a wide variety of subject concentrations within the MTSU EL program, not in any relation to librarianship whatsoever. In retrospect, the EL class would have been more lucrative for the Library had there been more students enrolled. Nonetheless, "the raw data that was gathered has been useful for further analysis by librarians" (York et al., 2010). We have utilized these data multiple times in library space deliberations (most notably, the creation of the DMS) and plan to model future space usage studies after this one.

12.3 LIBRARY RELEVANCE AND INNOVATION

12.3.1 EL in Action—Developing Technology-Rich, Patron-Desired Services

Another example of EL at Walker Library is our Research Commons student focus group of 2009–10. For this project, we turned to our undergraduate and graduate students for guidance on what services would be most desirable for our Research Commons. Building logistics dictated some limitations, but overall, our first-floor Reference Desk and public computer stations were the ideal for collaborative computing spaces. Because our small-group study rooms were so popular, we were interested in providing additional options for larger groups to gather around technology. But, we had some questions about what to include and where in the building to locate the larger group spaces.

Our Marketing Specialist reached out to the Student Government Association President and invited him to meet with us about our interest in developing student focus groups. We explained that we wanted to solicit ideas and suggestions from students on how they used the Library, how we could better serve them, and what sorts of services, technology, and collections they wished to see in their "ideal library." The SGA President expressed interest and quickly gathered members of the SGA administration to join us. Additionally, we asked him to solicit volunteers from his peers outside SGA. The result was a group of 10–15 students, all eager to contribute to the development of a student-centered Library Commons.

As with most college students, a great way to entice voluntary meeting attendance and participation is to promise food. Thus, we provided pizza, snacks, and drinks. We spent the first part of the meeting talking and getting to know each other. We then shared our interest in their feedback, explaining our needs. We took them on a physical tour through the Library spaces so that they could provide "in the moment" suggestions of what might work where.

We designed our Commons and Meeting Places 2 and 4 as a result of their suggestions. The Meeting Places, on floors two and four, are the Library's largest technology-enabled group spaces. Each has a projection screen, laptop connectivity, is reservable—and they are extremely popular and well-utilized.

Additionally, the student focus groups helped us determine furniture arrangements and styles for the Research Commons. We invited our student focus groups to handle the chair selection. A number of chairs were loaned to us from our campus Contract Furniture Alliance for evaluation. During the week-long "Chair Fair," students were invited to sit in each chair and rate their preference on a survey card. They were also asked to share their fabric preference. Library personnel tallied the results, and the winning chairs and fabrics were selected for bulk order.

Our overarching goal with the Research Commons development was to seek out direct input from our users. Thus, it was important for us to follow through. If the majority requested it, we did our best to follow the recommendation—even though we didn't completely agree with each majority decision.

12.4 LIBRARIES EMBRACE ETHNOGRAPHIC STUDIES
12.4.1 If We Build It, They Will Come—Right?
Librarians have observed the rapid shift from collection-centered services to user-centered services, largely due to technology and a growing demand for electronic access to materials. Twenty years ago, the library was seen by users as the place to physically access information and resources. Now, the physical spaces inside the library are viewed as learning destinations, places where users gather to interact and collaborate. As this focus has shifted, so too have the research methods for understanding and analyzing how libraries are used. Though traditional data sources like circulation numbers, gate counts, and reference question tallies reveal a great deal about the frequency with which library services are utilized—and are valuable in their own ways—they provide little detailed insight into user behavior inside the library. We might know the aggregate number of students who used study rooms in a given semester, but what do we know about *how* these rooms were used? Did the students who used them find them easily in the building? Did the room itself meet their study needs? If not, why? To this end, simply noticing where students gather to collaborate on group projects provides insight into how spaces are utilized. From the vantage point of the reference desk or any highly trafficked service area, library staff can informally observe and measure how students use certain spaces, how they navigate the building, and where they seek help. These valuable methods are no-cost, low-risk, and provide vital feedback about user behavior to be shared anecdotally throughout the library.

Qualitative research on library spaces is also incredibly valuable in improving their use. Surveys, interviews, focus groups, and other methods of ethnographic data collection have all been used by libraries to formally assess and analyze research habits and usage. The first and most comprehensive ethnographic study of this kind, conducted by the University of Rochester, included not only surveying users, developing advisory groups, and holding workshops, but also partnering with a faculty member in Anthropology to analyze library use (Foster and Gibbons, 2007). This was a groundbreaking approach that "applied ethnographic and anthropological techniques to better understand" user behavior (Foster and Gibbons, 2007). Since the publication of that ethnographic study, many institutions have recognized the value of such an approach, and have sought to replicate it in their own libraries.

However, though these methods of formal assessment are extremely helpful in understanding user needs and behaviors, they can sometimes prove challenging to manage, especially due to staffing and/or budget constraints. As such, some libraries have merged the ethnographic approach to library research with the recent interest in EL. Within this combined approach, students assume the roles of principal investigators, and through hands-on experience, explore how library spaces are utilized, and assess what can be changed to better meet the needs of their peers in the areas of both information access and physical spaces.

But why recruit students to study their peers? How could academic libraries benefit from student-led research studies? More importantly, how do these studies allow students to learn experientially? A review of relevant library literature uncovers three benefits that libraries, librarians, and students alike experience through student-led ethnographic library studies.

One benefit consistently highlighted in library ethnography literature is student researchers' sheer proximity to their research subjects: in age, experience, and location. Hunter and Ward (2011) assert that students occupy a unique position when it comes to assessing their peers, as they possess "native expertise" about their own campus environment, and in turn, "may be able to establish easy rapport with research participants" (Hunter and Ward, 2011). Students "also have relatively easier access to other students than administrators or faculty" (Hunter and Ward, 2011). First-hand knowledge of the campus, the library, and the institutional environment—plus easy access to peers—makes students near-ideal investigators of student use of the library. Within our first student-led library ethnography research project at MTSU, we experienced and benefitted from this fact. In spring 2008, Walker Library partnered with an Anthropology class (ANTH 4120: Practicing Anthropology) and served as the focus of the students' research project. Students in this particular class were interested in learning more about the library's role in the student experience at MTSU, and decided to conduct "a study on how MTSU students use the library and its resources to complete research assignments" (York et al., 2010).

The student researchers selected focus groups as their method of ethnographic research, hoping to inspire discussion and gain honest feedback from their research subjects. As current students, the researchers possessed keen insight into the multifaceted makeup of the MTSU experience, realizing that the most valuable and robust data would come by soliciting input from other students on campus. Eventually, they recruited members for six student focus groups: "non-traditional students, Student Government Association Members, Geology majors, Anthropology majors, Honors students, and graduate students" (York et al., 2010). Undoubtedly, our students were able to quickly populate their focus groups due to their intimate knowledge of MTSU's student culture. Additionally, because they wanted to learn as much as possible about their peers, the Anthropology students had no specific or clearly defined outcomes for their study; they were mostly interested in the act of learning about other MTSU students through methodical research and study.

Even at this early stage of their ethnographic research, our Anthropology students were engaged in EL, whether they realized it or not. In his foundational work on EL, David A. Kolb outlines the various characteristics of EL, one of which describes EL as a process, not merely moving from desired outcome to desired outcome. Within true EL, he writes, "[i]deas are not fixed and immutable elements of thought, but are formed and re-formed through experience ... no two thoughts are ever the same, since experience always intervenes" (Kolb, 1984). As such, learning becomes more of a developing process rather than a checklist of results. As we saw through our experience, students involved in the ethnographic study of Walker Library approached their learning as a process: they selected their focus groups and their location of study, but beyond that, they really had no fixed outcomes for their research. They approached their research with open minds, allowing data collection and knowledge gathering to occur naturally, and allowing their learning to be impacted by what the study ultimately revealed.

Another advantage of student-led ethnographic research is the potential for collecting a larger amount of data, often through multiple research methods or at critical times in a semester. For example, in their student-led ethnographic study of the library at Brigham Young University (BYU), Washburn and Bibb (2011) note that their undergraduate student researchers utilized a variety of methods to collect data on student behavior in the library, including face-to-face and email surveys, interviews, photo diaries, and focus groups (Washburn and Bibb, 2011). Using varied methods of data collection allowed these student researchers to amass greater quantities of data, thereby providing them with a broader understanding of student needs and holistic library usage. The authors also point out that the sheer number of student researchers involved in the project (25 total) "provided a larger pool of available researchers ... who were able to carry out the research requirements ... within a minimal time frame" (Washburn and Bibb, 2011). Here, student-led research can be seen as another "win—win" for the library and students: students gain practical and valuable knowledge in their chosen academic field, while the library benefits from the students' ability to complete an ethnographic study within a short time. Again, from our experience, we found that a student-led ethnographic research project provided us with a large, rich amount of timely data, most of which was gathered and collected by the students during a critical and often incredibly busy time during the semester: final exams. During the final exam window, MTSU librarians (like all academic librarians) are busy with a flurry of end-of-semester activities, and our librarians might have found it difficult to fulfill the requirements of research on this scale then. In this respect, the ANTH 4120 students were a huge benefit to us, conducting the bulk of their research, focus group interactions, and data gathering during this busy, yet fruitful time. Here, too, the benefit of collecting larger amounts of data translated into experiential, real-world learning for our Anthropology students. Kolb characterizes EL as a process, particularly one that is continuous and ongoing, not just limited to one interaction or one moment. He states, "To focus so sharply on continuity and certainty is to risk dogmatism and rigidity, the inability to learn from new experiences" (Kolb, 1984). Our Anthropology students were able to collect such large quantities of data because they did not limit themselves to one focus group meeting, one afternoon observation, or one set of questions over the course of their ethnographic study. Essentially, they kept at it over the course of an entire semester, refining questions, asking as many students as possible about their library use, and observing student behaviors in the library at varied times throughout the semester. This dogged devotion to the project ultimately resulted in authentic learning, as the study became a continuous, unfolding process.

Additionally, as seen in student-led ethnographic library studies, library-use data gathered by students often proves to be more authentic than similar data collected by librarians or library staff. This is true for many reasons. Bedwell and Banks (2013) conclude at the end of their student-led research study that participant observation (students studying fellow students) allowed for the collection of robust data that painted a true picture of user behavior in the library, asserting that "[s]tudents would have been less likely to act naturally ... if they felt that an authority figure was observing them" during their time in the library (Bedwell and Banks, 2013). In their BYU study, Washburn and Bibb also found that this approach strengthened the integrity of the data gathered by their student researchers: "The collected data reflected what informants actually did [in the library], most times with a detailed explanation of why, rather than what they thought they should say to an adult, especially a librarian, asking them for the same information" (Washburn and Bibb, 2011). In both studies, the students who were interviewed about their library habits were real, honest, and forthcoming with the student researchers, more than likely feeling less intimidated than they might have around "adults."

Our 2008 study was no different in this respect. Without the perceived intimidation or persuasion that might have come from librarians or other "adults" conducting research and posing questions about library use, the focus groups provided open, honest feedback about Walker Library and its services. Many students voiced concerns about our hours of operation, the need for more group study spaces, and a desire for more technology. It is doubtful the groups would have responded as candidly to librarian researchers. This aspect of the project allowed our librarians and library staff to gain real insight into our students' wants and needs. In the end, our assumptions about library spaces and services were challenged; the data collected allowed us to innovate, based on real wants and needs.

At this stage in the project, our Anthropology students were able to learn through hands-on experience in possibly the most potent way: by creating, collecting, and revealing new knowledge. Kolb asserts that EL is the process of creating knowledge, of uncovering or cultivating new information through experience. Through their ethnographic study and focus group inquiries, our students revealed a wealth of new, previously unknown, and actionable knowledge. Furthermore, based on the feedback we received, we revised some of our services and even policies—such as our hours, food and drink rules, and study room policies. Through the students' honest feedback, and the new knowledge collected by our ethnographic researchers, we learned how we could better assist our student population during their time in the library and at MTSU.

Ultimately, as many libraries have found (and as we too discovered), these student-led ethnographic studies often produce results that are mutually beneficial for librarians, faculty, campus administrators, and current and future students, and can also spur "home-grown" library innovation. Students possess a unique perspective when it comes to assessing their own campus, academic services, and library spaces, and an ethnographic approach is a unique opportunity for authentic learning to occur.

12.5 FUTURE DIRECTIONS

12.5.1 User-Led Library Studies are Here to Stay

Walker Library has engaged in such EL endeavors to not only bolster minimal staffing, but also to seek relevant user input, and ultimately to innovate its collections and services. In retrospect, the Library's intersection of EL and library ethnography has been successful. However, the importance of embracing future innovation remains critical. The lessons we learned over the past several years are valuable tools for us as we continue to evolve. We have several new services and initiatives underway that will be less daunting as a result of our experience. Here are a few of our upcoming projects:

- The Walker Library Listening/Viewing Center—The Library recently launched a Media Listening/Viewing Center in support of our recently acquired print and audio Music Collection. We plan to collaborate with the College of Music students and faculty regarding surveys and usability studies to determine their ideal listening/viewing space.
- The future of the Digital Media Studio—The Digital Media Studio has been successful—largely due to EL engagement. With the evolution of makerspaces, Walker Library is now investigating how to migrate the DMS into a new frontier.
- MTSU has successfully launched a Master's of Library Science program, although not yet accredited. Plans are underway to establish a formal partnership between the Library and the MLS program. This lays the groundwork for practicum opportunities with MLS students.
- We also plan to continue our partnership with students and faculty in future sections of ANTH 4120. This partnership has the potential to both improve student learning and benefit the library, as the class requires students to study culture change theory and the practical dimensions of anthropology in a real-life setting. We also plan to partner with another upper-level Anthropology class, where students will be trained on ethnographic research techniques and may choose to fulfill a field experience requirement in the Library.

12.6 FINAL LESSONS

Walker Library has been engaged in EL with our students for many years. During that time, we developed student focus groups, partnered with

MLS practicum students, and created an MTSU EL course. What started as a critical need for assistance with staffing evolved into viable means to collect valuable data, upon which we could better understand our users and innovate the Library. Along the way, we gained insight into the views our users have of us. On the flip side, the students with whom we partnered gained skills that they could apply to their own careers.

The days of libraries housing closed stacks and discouraging talking, food, and drink are long past. Rather, as the evolution of numerous academic libraries' information commons suggests, users seek advanced technology and flexibility—an extension of their personal sense of space. If academic libraries do not provide such offerings, users will go elsewhere. Thus, our future depends on our willingness and ability to engage with users and interpret their needs. Librarians must regularly seek out users' valuable input for guidance in future directions. As suggested by the work of educational theorists like David Kolb, and the continuing transformation of academic libraries reported in the library literature, it is no surprise that EL is becoming an important part of any library's success in meeting user needs. And, as all libraries are different, there is no "one-size-fits-all" approach with EL. It takes a variety of shapes and forms, and is as individual as the participants, projects, and circumstances. We clearly saw this throughout the partnerships we engaged in, and the lessons learned from (and about) our users remain critical to their futures, as well as ours.

REFERENCES

Bedwell, L., Banks, C., 2013. Seeing through the eyes of students: participant observation in an academic library partnership. Partnersh.: Can. J. Libr. Inf. Pract. Res. 8 (1), 1−17.
Foster, N., Gibbons, S. (Eds.), 2007. Studying Students: The Undergraduate Research Project at the University of Rochester. Association of College and Research Libraries, Chicago, IL, <http://www.ala.org/acrl/sites/ala.org.acrl/files/content/publications/booksanddigitalresources/digital/Foster-Gibbons_cmpd.pdf> (accessed 04.08.15.).
Hunter, G., Ward, D., 2011. Students research the library: using student-led ethnographic research to examine the changing role of campus libraries. Coll. Res. Libr. News 72 (5), 264−268.
Kolb, D.A., 1984. Experiential Learning: Experience as the Source of Learning and Development. Prentice-Hall, Englewood Cliffs, NJ.
Washburn, A., Bibb, S., 2011. Students studying students: an assessment of using undergraduate student researchers in an ethnographic study of library use. Library & Information Research 35 (109), 55−66.
York, A., Groves, C., Black, W., 2010. Enriching the academic experience: the library and experiential learning. Collab. Libr. 2 (4), 193.

CHAPTER 13

Grasping a Golden Opportunity: Librarian Support for Students on Summer Internships

C. Seeman and S. Ziph
University of Michigan, Ann Arbor, MI, United States

Without question, the roles and functions of academic libraries have changed a great deal over the last 20 years. With the proliferation of electronic resources and the need to connect more directly with our users, the expected roles for 21st-century academic librarians are being transformed before our eyes. While we have seen dramatic changes in the academic library space, one place where this change has been especially salient is with the departmental or academic branch libraries. In the past, many academic schools or departments would have libraries or reading rooms of their own. In what might be the first "location-based service," departments would yield space for quicker access to their important print resources. Over the last quarter century, however, these departmental and academic branch libraries have been contracting and consolidating, as more work of the library becomes centralized and print resources are decreasing.

With this contraction comes a change in librarians' workload, and staff responsibilities have been increasingly taken up by tasks related to electronic resources and digital services. With this change, many libraries centralized operations and reduced staffing levels. Additionally, many libraries redeployed staff from reference services, assigning more of that work to student temporary staff. Many good articles in the literature report how the relationship has changed between the library and the campus, as the nature of our resources shifted from print to electronic (Rodwell and Fairbairn, 2008; Mozenter et al., 2000). This enabled some libraries to focus more on purchasing electronic resources over staffing needs. Other libraries took new directions, such as creating Makerspaces and teaching credit classes, especially those focused on information literacy. What is clear is that what the library stands for and the role it serves on campus has been slowly evolving into new areas. This is especially true in the context of the departmental library.

Contraction and consolidation has been very common for libraries serving graduate schools of business. During times of change, library directors, librarians, and staff have sought out new ways to return value to the school. Many of the academic business libraries have focused on providing research assistance for faculty and PhD students. The premise that students would be well covered with the information found in business case studies allowed libraries to move in this direction.

In an effort to distinguish themselves in the business education marketplace, many schools have moved to a situation where, paradoxically, students' needs for information were no longer being covered in business cases. The approach has taken different names over the years. These include action learning, experiential learning, and field-based experiential learning. The notion behind this development was that business students would be better prepared to face adversity and opportunity in the years to come if they do so in a controlled setting under the guidance of business faculty. One aspect of the standard business school curriculum that has not changed is the role of the Master's of Business Administration (MBA) internship, taken between the two full academic years. Many of these internships provide MBA students with "real-world" experiences, to match skills and knowledge attained during the first year of study (Sanahuja Vélez and Ribes Giner, 2015; Hergert, 2011; Knouse and Fontenot, 2008). Increasingly, business schools are offering structured internships with start-ups, nonprofits, and social enterprises to provide students with enriched learning opportunities. At the Ross School of Business (Michigan), these take the form of internships, available through a number of programs. Students are charged with solving an issue within an organization. Unlike business case studies, students rarely start with all the data and secondary information they need to assess the problem. These projects are information-intensive and provide business librarians with a great opportunity to support students.

13.1 BUSINESS CURRICULUM AND THE ROLE OF THE INTERNSHIP IN BUSINESS EDUCATION

The internship has long been an expected part of the standard MBA program. In the standard 2-year MBA curriculum, the summer between the two years is a time when the student will work as an intern for a company or organization. In many ways, internships reinforce the learning objectives of the business school curriculum, and provide the students with practice needed to become a more viable job candidate. Various studies note the benefits of internships for business school students, including providing students with an understanding of how classroom concepts can be practically applied, increasing student knowledge of industry and career options, and providing marketable job experience (Maertz et al., 2014). Internships, unlike team-based class projects, typically consist of individual project-work supervised by company sponsors or mentors. These positions can, and often do, lead to full-time employment offers.

Recruitment activities and applying for internships is a very intense and time-consuming aspect of a student's first year in the MBA program. There are many companies that offer highly sought-after internships, usually companies that students wish to work for upon graduation. At Ross, many students seek out internships at companies like Facebook, Google, and Amazon, as well as consulting firms such as PWC, EY, and Accenture (just to name a few). Students at Ross find internships through company recruiters, on-campus recruiting events, faculty and alumni contacts, and personal networks.

In addition, the School offers programs where students are placed into internships through one of the centers or institutes. The Tauber Institute at the University of Michigan places students in MBA and engineering programs into focused internship programs, where they are charged with looking at a specific issue from a major company, primarily related to manufacturing or machinery. These student teams work with campus faculty, communication consultants, and librarians to support them over the course of the summer internship. Additionally, the Center for Social Impact funds internships for students to work with nonprofits, NGOs (nongovernmental organizations), and social enterprises on very specific projects over the summer between the two MBA years.

The scope of the business students' projects ranges widely. In some cases, the interns are supporting an existing operation within a unit, sometimes with interns from other schools. In others, interns are working to support a new program or initiative that the company would like to pursue. Student internships usually consist of project-based work and the topics range widely across disciplines. Recent student queries for assistance have addressed such topics as language and race concordance between patients and providers in the healthcare industry, communication preferences for veterinarians (from food suppliers), the outlook for the cosmetology market in the Philippines, and a competitive analysis of the US video game streaming industry. Librarians provide research strategies and guidance in order to help students hone research skills developed during their experiential learning projects.

13.2 ACTION LEARNING AT ROSS SCHOOL OF BUSINESS

The Ross School of Business at the University of Michigan has long been a leader in action learning, a form of experiential learning. Since 1992, the MBA students at Ross have been participating in a program called Multidisciplinary Action Projects (MAP). In this core class at the end of the first year of study, all MBA students are pulled together into groups of between four and seven people, and are assigned to work with a sponsor on a real-world business issue. All told, there have been between 80 and 95 teams of MBA students each year in MAP seeking to solve business situations that vary greatly from project to project. This issue might be with an established company, an international company, a start-up, a governmental agency, a nonprofit, or an NGO. The goals of MAP, especially since it is placed during the end of the first year of the MBA curriculum, is twofold. First, the project is a live-action method for the students to practice what they have learned during the core classes from the first year of study. While the projects may have some predetermined focus in one of the areas, such as marketing or finance, the most successful projects involve a student's broader understanding of all the aspects of businesses that are taught throughout the core curriculum. Second, the project is intended to transition the student from the controlled situations that are documented in the traditional business case study, to the unpredictable environment that exists in the real world of business. In large part, these projects are designed to better prepare the MBA student for success during their corporate internship, taken right after MAP.

The support system that has developed over the years to support the MBA curriculum is fairly unique. Each team is assigned two faculty members, who not only provide guidance on the project and serve as liaisons with the sponsor, but also grade the final project. The teams also have access to a support team that includes an experienced second-year MBA student coach, a communication consultant (a Ross staffer to help with the final presentation/report), and a librarian or secondary research consultant.

The role of the librarian as a key member of the MAP support team has been a tremendous opportunity for Kresge Library over the years. The librarian plays an instrumental part in supporting the student teams; indeed, it is a recognized value that Kresge Library brings to the school, and it is central to the core mission of the library (Berdish and Seeman, 2010, pp. 208–224). Kresge Library Services currently has 10 staff members and 9 librarians. The majority of the librarians work with MAP teams, serving between 7 and 18 daytime MBA MAP teams during the Winter Term. The librarian acts as the guide to crucial information and resources, and the work at hand is very important for the overall success of the project. In business case studies, all the information is provided as part of the material that the students receive. This allows them to analyze the business situation and make recommendations on the directions the company should take to resolve the problem. Business cases are self-contained learning tools with all the information that the students need to assess the situation and "solve" the problem. MAP is the anti-case. Instead, with MAP projects, the students often start out with little or no information and it is up to the team, with the support from their librarian, to fill in the gaps. Each project has fairly unique information needs, and we have found that something beyond traditional library instruction is required to cultivate the needed information skills for students to successfully complete a MAP project.

The service provided by Kresge librarians during MAP has had two very profound outcomes. First, the value provided by librarians is regarded by both faculty and school administrators as an essential element in the program's success. This can be demonstrated by the similar role that Kresge librarians have as MAP expanded to other programs at the School (such as Part-time MBA, Weekend MBA, Executive MBA, and the Bachelor's of Business Administration programs). The MAP service created a compelling and widely understood reason for the library staff to continue at its size, despite a dramatic reduction in space in 2014 (Seeman, 2015, pp. 101–125). The second major outcome for the library is that we make very strong connections with MBA students during the program. The Kresge librarians who support MAP teams repeatedly hear from students when they are in need of information assistance during their second year. Through supporting this experiential program, the librarians provide value that is clearly appreciated by the students. Simply put, if it were not valued by the students, they would not seek out our assistance time and again. Many of the students also reconnect with the MAP librarians, as they work on their internships in their second year.

Since internship work is essentially similar to the work students do during MAP, the connection between the library and the students' information needs becomes very evident. This connection provides a unique and strategic advantage for libraries that support action learning or experiential learning programs. If a student has little interaction with the library, except as a place to study or occasionally find a reserve reading, they will not associate the library as an important resource for their internship work, or as they delve into subjects where greater information support could be useful. Experiential learning and action learning provide value to students in the "real-world" problems and information needs students are faced with. Indeed, experiential scenarios such as the MAP more closely mirror the professional contexts MBA students will encounter when they graduate.

13.3 SERVICE ORIENTATION OF KRESGE LIBRARY SERVICES

In its long history serving business education at the University of Michigan, the Kresge Library Services unit has always focused on providing strong user services. With this particular orientation, the Kresge librarians and staff have been well positioned to meet the diverse needs of the Ross user community. The value proposition that was put forward by our library over the years was not that the library was an essential source for business information, but that the library was an information partner, enabling the students, faculty, and others to make the best use of the information. Also, rather than seeing what services other business school libraries were providing, Kresge has long had a tradition of matching services to identified community needs. This has led to our unique MAP support model, a student-focused course reserves program, and other programs that are geared towards making the library a strong community partner. This has also led to an expansion of the staff over the years to support this program (Seeman, 2015, pp. 101–125).

A great deal of the service orientation that a library may (or may not) develop stems in large part from the size of the staff and its ability to deliver quality services to the community. A smaller library may be equally service-oriented, but potentially hampered in what it offers to the community, so as not to be overwhelmed. At Kresge Library, we are fortunate to have a total staff of 19 people, with 9 librarians. Additionally, the librarians and support staff work year round, so there are no periods where staffing size is down, as might be the case where 9 month contracts are common. This gives us great flexibility to support the diverse information needs of the Ross community, and has freed up the library to "do things differently": by shifting more staff into public service roles, we can now more strongly support experiential learning for graduate students than in the past.

At most academic libraries, especially ones with a central operation, only one or two librarians serve the students in the business programs. This alone make for a daunting task when a school has between 3000 and 4000 students. This is the primary reason why librarians in these situations are cautious about reaching out to schools when they have many students or programs to support. This phenomenon was touched upon in a study of Georgetown University graduate students who are potentially underserved by having a high student to librarian ratio (Gibbs et al., 2012, pp. 268–276). In this process of protecting their time (and sanity), walls and limits stand in the way of providing strong services to the community, and thus it is not surprising that such libraries may use a "one-to-many" system of support. While this will definitely protect the library, it may not fully support students' information needs in experiential learning programs. Additionally, without the individualized attention, it is difficult to make solid connections that improve the stature and respect of the library in the minds of the students.

Even in the context of career work and research, the library may have very distinct services to match the specific needs of business students. Often, the general needs of the students are well met with instruction sessions and one-on-one appointments. For example, Kresge librarians offer hour-long sessions on finding and using library career resources, including internship resources. General hints provided during the instruction sessions enable students to quickly use these resources for their career search. Most importantly to the students, they are introduced to librarians through these classes and often reconnect when specific questions arise.

Students may also schedule an appointment with a librarian for individual help on crafting job or internship searches tailored to their career interests and personal preferences (industries, companies, locations, etc.) So, while a student may learn the basic functionality of the databases, they might seek out assistance should they wish to focus on a very narrow field. Let's suppose that a student was interested in working for a consulting firm in Topeka, Kansas. They would likely reach out to the library for assistance and expertise. While this could be a great deal of work, providing assistance to the students at their point of need is a tremendous service opportunity for the library. This is doubly true when the interaction provides a clear and tangible benefit to the student, such as improved grades or finding an internship.

13.4 USING MATERIALS FOR ACTION AND EXPERIENTIAL LEARNING PROGRAMS: BEST PRACTICES

One of the most important considerations in supporting any action-based or experiential learning project is the understanding of how material may be used by the students. Academic libraries are able to purchase resources to support the business curriculum and research at significant discount to what commercial entities pay. The rationale for this is typically understood to be twofold. First, academic libraries are licensing resources to train students, not directly to make money (as would be the goal in a commercial enterprise). Second, students' name recognition for these information products could be enhanced when they join the workforce. Along with discounts come restrictions on how the materials may be used, especially when students are working with commercial enterprises that could license the material themselves. As libraries look to support the experiential learning of students, librarians and library staff need to be aware of these limitations, and act accordingly. The consequence of not being responsible stewards of these resources is that libraries could lose access altogether. If vendors and publishers feel that there is abuse at a college or university, they are not likely to renew a license for that school.

In particular, the business environment provides a number of use challenges for libraries. As stewards of licensed resources, Kresge has developed guidelines for database usage during action learning programs such as MAP; for an example, see: http://kresgeguides.bus.umich.edu/MAP/dbguidelines. While not comprehensive, these cover the main requirements and ensure that we are abiding by the agreements we have with our publishers and information vendors. These types of restrictions are more common in business than in other fields that academic libraries need to be concerned about. And, with the increasing number of students who are engaged in growing a business during school, the line between academic and commercial enterprises is blurring.

While these restrictions are a concern, they should not deter the library from supporting action learning programs. The challenge lies in a library's ability to ensure that these protections are in place, and that there is a good-faith effort to enforce them. No academic library can absolutely prevent material from being used for a commercial enterprise; libraries need to make reasonable accommodations. This may be through outreach efforts, splash pages that a student must acknowledge before getting to the resource, public guidelines, and other means. The types of library resources used to answer internship questions include the full range of resources offered. For the most part, students are allowed to freely share full-text journal articles with internship sponsors. Our industry and market research database contracts, however, preclude sharing full-text reports outside the Ross educational community, especially in cases where a company might profit financially from the information.

13.5 INTERNSHIP SERVICE OPPORTUNITIES FOR LIBRARIES

Kresge Library has been able to support students on internships by virtue of having a large reference librarian staff. Additionally, most internships take place when there are few classes on campus, providing more flexibility in the scheduling of the librarians. At libraries that are challenged with smaller staffs and academic year faculty appointments, opportunities still exist to support the students working on experiential projects. This may be done with part-time reference assistants or simply by connecting with students through email or chat.

One of the key elements in supporting internships is making connections with students that might not otherwise be made. Over the course of an internship, it is likely that the student will have a detailed research need that cannot be met easily on their own. While the student may have access to internal data through their project, the information needed to place that in a broader context is likely to come from the library. The student on an internship is witnessing first-hand the transition from an information-rich environment like an academic library to one where information is scarce or expensive (such as in commercial enterprises).

The complexity of the questions asked during MAP also provides a tremendous opportunity for librarians to help students with these projects. Students are not asking basic questions, but ones that are very narrow in scope and often difficult to track down. The questions that we have been asked from students on internships include:

- What is the market for hot tea in the United States? In particular, what is the market opportunity for hot tea in consumer food service?
- What are the industry best practices for aircraft maintenance programs from airlines and airplane manufacturers?

- What are the best practices for product quality management in e-commerce industries?
- What are companies in the New York Metropolitan Area who work with energy consulting or LEED construction?
- Where are articles on demand planning and forecasting across a company's supply chain?
- What are best practices of beverage containers, including returnables, in Latin American dairy distribution?

While the desire is always to have librarians teach students how to use the resources and become self-sufficient researchers, the reality is that these skills develop over years, not months. Very specific and narrow questions such as these also beg the question of whether the student has effectively assessed all the resources that are available to answer the question. This is a great opportunity for the library to position itself as a key element in the research process. And since typical business case studies do not require additional research, this is a real opportunity for the library to demonstrate value to the students and the school. But more importantly, it showcases the research abilities of the library as the student prepares for the rigor that will be required for their second year of study. In many ways, we have found that students who connect with the library over the summer usually have very positive experiences, and this translates to having more engaged and supporting members of the community. It also has the added bonus of keeping the librarians' information skills sharp during the quiet months of the summer.

As students proceed through their program and tackle greater and greater questions, the path forward should be focused on supporting their needs, rather than creating self-sufficient researchers. Academic business librarians have spent their careers mastering information retrieval and understanding. If they can use this to support students, then it is a benefit to the school. An interesting approach to this dilemma comes from Ari Weinzweig of Zingerman's Deli. He has crafted what he calls the "Twelve Natural Laws of a Successful Business." Ari's eighth law is simple and appropriate: "Success means you get better problems—but there will always be problems" (Weinzweig et al., 2010). The premise of this statement is that as you solve problems, you will be presented with more complicated ones. This will be particularly the case in libraries, where librarians play a critical role in providing clarity for students and faculty who may be unable to find the data they need. The enhanced reputation gained by the library grows as the questions become more complicated. Similar to issues facing reference desks in general academic libraries, students are not asking the easy questions they once brought to the desk, but the more challenging ones. As librarians successfully answer increasingly "tough" questions, the students and faculty are very happy to sing their praises and tell others about the library services. This is exactly what happened at Kresge Library over the years and how, when the physical library was closed in 2014, the service aspect of the group continued on at the pace that it had when it was a traditional library. Any organization wants the higher-level questions and problems that come with success. It may just well be the recipe for success in the library of the future.

13.6 CONCLUSION

Academic libraries right now are undergoing a great deal of change. Among the complex issues confronting libraries today are contracting space, changing formats, and greater demands from our patrons. While libraries have struggled to put into place mechanisms to remain relevant and demonstrate value in this environment, we run the great risk of disconnecting with our campuses if we move in directions that are not valued by our user communities. Academic libraries have implemented solutions that, while successful at other libraries, often do not meet the specific needs of the community. Instead, we believe that libraries should seek out opportunities on their own campuses, and address the unmet information needs of their own students and faculty. Indeed, we have found that supporting information needs for experiential learning programs is a tremendous opportunity—one that will pay dividends to the library. In our situation as a library supporting a business school, we have witnessed the move from business cases requiring little active research, to experiential learning that encourages students to seek out assistance from the library. Showcasing the library's skills in the academic enterprise can change (for the better) faculty and students' estimation of the library's important role. Going above and beyond simply providing a place for the student to work—and the resources to work with—will be key to the success of the library of the future.

REFERENCES

Berdish, L., Seeman, C., 2010. A reference-intensive embedded librarian program: Kresge Business Administration Library's program to support action-based learning at the Ross School of Business. Public Serv. Q. 6 (2–3), 208–224.

Gibbs, D., Boettcher, J., Hollingsworth, J., Slania, H., 2012. Assessing the research needs of graduate students at Georgetown University. J. Acad. Libr. 38 (5), 268–276.

Hergert, M., 2011. Student perceptions of the value of internships in business education. Am. J. Bus. Educ. (AJBE) 2 (8), 9–14.
Knouse, S.B., Fontenot, G., 2008. Benefits of the business college internship: a research review. J. Employ. Couns. 45 (2), 61–66.
Maertz Jr., C.P., Stoeberl, P.A., Marks, J., 2014. Building successful internships: lessons from the research for interns, schools, and employers. Career Dev. Int. 19 (1), 123–142.
Mozenter, F., Sanders, B.T., Welch, J.M., 2000. Restructuring a liaison program in an academic library. Coll. Res. Libr. 61 (5), 432–440.
Rodwell, J., Fairbairn, L., 2008. Dangerous liaisons? Defining the faculty liaison librarian service model, its effectiveness and sustainability. Libr. Manag. 29 (1/2), 116–124.
Sanahuja Vélez, G., Ribes Giner, G., 2015. Effects of business internships on students, employers, and higher education institutions: a systematic review. J. Employ. Couns. 52 (3), 121–130.
Seeman, C., 2015. "No one gets left behind": managing library human resources during dramatic shifts in academic libraries. In: Schmehl Hines, S., Simons, M. (Eds.), Library Staffing for the Future. Emerald Group Publishing Limited, Bingley, pp. 101–125.
Weinzweig, A., Nagy, I., Stiner, R., 2010. A Lapsed Anarchist's Approach to Building a Great Business. Zingerman's Press, Ann Arbor, MI.

CHAPTER 14

The New Hampshire Human Library Project: Breaking Barriers and Building Bridges by Engaging Communities of Learners

C.W. Gamtso[1], M. Mannon[2] and S. Whipple[3]
[1]University of New Hampshire at Manchester, Manchester, NH, United States
[2]Goffstown High School, Goffstown, NH, United States
[3]Goffstown Public Library, Goffstown, NH, United States

14.1 BEGINNINGS

In 2013, the Goffstown (NH) High School Information Center, the Goffstown (NH) Public Library, and the University of New Hampshire at Manchester (UNH Manchester) Library collaborated to present the first "Human Library" in New Hampshire. Seeking to strengthen community ties and gain support to propel their work, the institutions' librarians worked together to establish separate, but related, Human Library events. Working as a team, the librarians reached varied audiences and made use of diverse human resources. Their collaboration also provided an opportunity for their distinct constituencies—high school students, community members, and college students—to engage in a powerful experiential learning (EL) activity. This chapter will describe the planning and implementation of the New Hampshire program, including an explanation of the Denmark-based international Human Library Organization; a review of the literature regarding EL and its connection to the mission of a library; and a discussion of the New Hampshire Human Library's impact on participants' learning.

14.2 WHAT IS A HUMAN LIBRARY?

The Human Library Organization was formed in Copenhagen, Denmark, as a way to combat prejudice and discrimination in all of their forms. The organization's mission is "[t]o help build social cohesion and a greater understanding for diversity in the community, locally and on a global level" by facilitating Human Library events around the world (Human Library Organization Facebook Page, n.d.). In a Human Library (or "Living Library"), the "Books" are individuals from the local community who have been stigmatized for some aspect of their identity or experience (Garbutt, 2008). The program provides an opportunity for a participating "Reader" to engage in an open but respectful conversation with the Human Book, an encounter that may challenge attitudes and opinions.

The Human Library models itself on the operations of a "typical" library. Readers browse Book titles from a catalog that includes short descriptions provided by the Books themselves. The Reader selects a Book to "check out," and at the designated time, a librarian introduces the Reader to the Book. The two then engage in a respectful dialogue for 15–20 minutes, at which time the Reader may choose to check out another Book for the next check-out period. These conversations bring together community members who might never have had the chance to meet, much less talk deeply about issues that may at first appear to divide them, such as gender, race, ethnicity, culture, career choice, sexual orientation, gender identification, religion, or class. By bringing these issues to such a personal level, the Human Library breaks the barriers that separate people and seeks to bridge the gap that remains. (For this reason, the New Hampshire Human Library's title was "Breaking Barriers, Building Bridges: Diverse Community Voices.")

The Human Library ties directly to a library's core mission of inclusion and connection to its community members, while simultaneously expanding the library's influence through creative engagement with community organizations (Wentz, 2012). The Human Library also exemplifies the Association of College and Research Libraries' goal of "provid[ing] programs and services that are inclusive of the needs of all persons in the community the library serves" (Association of College and Research Libraries, 2012). As a program deeply grounded in a commitment to community cohesion and diversity awareness through direct, face-to-face interaction with another person, the Human Library also provided participants—from current students to lifelong learners—with an EL opportunity.

14.3 THE OPPORTUNITY OF EL

At its core, EL conceives of education as a hands-on activity wherein students gain practical experience and then reflect upon that experience, thus producing new understanding. In 1984, educational theorist David A. Kolb provided a now-classic definition of learning as "the process whereby knowledge is created through the transformation of experience" (Kolb, 2015). Kolb based his model of EL on those of earlier educators, among them John Dewey, who posited the existence of "an organic connection between education and personal experience" (Dewey, 1998).

In many high schools and colleges in the United States, EL is often conceptualized as service-learning or internship placements that occur outside of the traditional classroom, while still offering students an opportunity to reflect on how those experiences relate to theoretical coursework (Gresham, 2001). Libraries have an important role to play in these EL initiatives. In college and university libraries, this role may include providing the opportunity for student-led projects (York et al., 2010) or providing print and online resources that enhance EL, such as support materials for students engaging in cultural immersion programs (Shen, 2011).

However, EL encompasses far more than learning that happens "away from school," so to speak. It is also a method of teaching within the school or classroom environment: "Closely tied to the active-learning movement in undergraduate education, classroom-based EL advocates regard this educational approach as an opportunity to teach students how to become involved in their learning, relate theory to practice, and reflect upon what they are doing" (Gresham, 2001, p. 19). In this regard, the Human Library presents a venue for both Readers and Books to engage actively in a mutual learning process; to connect theories of "community" and "inclusion" to the lived experience of an open conversation with another individual; and to reflect—either through a teacher-led class activity or through their own personal reflections—on the meaning of that lived experience.

14.4 THE NEW HAMPSHIRE HUMAN LIBRARY COLLABORATION
14.4.1 Three Libraries, One Story

The Human Library arrived in the United States in 2008 with events held in Washington and California (Wentz, 2012). The New Hampshire Human Library event was the first held in the state. The project was initiated by the Goffstown High School (GHS) Information Center, in collaboration with the Goffstown Public Library (GPL) and the UNH Manchester Library. All three institutions approached the project differently: the librarians had different audiences, different types of books, and different goals. However, they prepared together, shared human resources (Human Books) when appropriate, participated in each other's libraries as Books and as Readers, and collaborated on publicity materials. They used each other's personal and professional networks to expand their influence and thus provide the chance for a larger community to experience the Human Library. Their professional camaraderie allowed them to guide one another through the process.

In each of the three library settings, the Human Library event provided participants with opportunities for EL. Together, the organizers explored the different models they could create within the Human Library framework, and by collaborating, showed how a specific EL concept could vary in different environments. The UNH Manchester Library tied the experience to the course curriculum of two specific classes. The GPL focused on a wide goal of community education. The GHS Information Center tied the event to the needs of high school juniors thinking about their futures.

The New Hampshire Human Library organizers discovered that there were many resources available to help them plan and implement the program. Many of these resources were provided by the Human Library Organization itself, which furnishes sample documents and logos for approved Human Library venues. The New Hampshire library partners were also aided by a Rhode Island colleague's support. This librarian had already been through the process of planning a Human Library at the Providence Public Library, and through a Skype conversation provided the New Hampshire librarians a model for how the Human Library might operate in a practical sense (length of "check-out," role of volunteers, logistics of the day, etc.). Inspired by the willingness of library colleagues to share their experiences with others undertaking a Human Library initiative, the New Hampshire-based librarians gave a presentation at a New England Library Association (NELA) conference after their own event, to similarly help others who wanted to take up the challenge. A key component of experiential education is for students to ground their learning in others' experiences as well as their own. Working to support others in the profession is key to the success of libraries looking to support their communities using the EL model.

The New Hampshire Human Library took place at the three locations—GPL, GHS Information Center, and UNH Manchester—on three separate dates. Each site varied in its audience and focus, but the sites shared a commitment to providing a deep learning opportunity for their community members, as we will see in the next section.

14.4.2 Goffstown Public Library

A library's mission statement lays the foundation for the manner in which its respective community is served. The GPL's mission is to "serve as a primary resource for community information needs" and "provide a comfortable place for citizens to access quality materials and programs, enhance cultural awareness and to explore issues of local, national and global interest" (Goffstown Public Library, 2015). The Human Library is one vehicle by which those explorations occur. Through Book/Reader interaction and dialogue, participants have the opportunity to learn and gain insight from the collective human experience.

Since 2013, GPL has developed a collection of 12 Human Books, drawing from the immediate town as well as the surrounding communities at large. In keeping with the Human Library's mission, the Books have represented a broad range of experience. With a diverse collection varying each year—including a gay female rabbi, a formerly homeless veteran, a Pakistani exchange student, a blind social worker, a transgender male, and a young woman in substance abuse recovery—Readers were exposed to perspectives and lifestyles quite different from their own (see Fig. 14.1).

As a kickoff to National Library Week, the public was invited to the library for the 3-hour event on a Sunday afternoon. Readers were provided with a copy of the catalogue, which included Human Book titles and descriptions. With the afternoon broken into seven 15-minute "checkouts," Readers chose the Books they were interested in borrowing and with whom they would like to interact. Ten-minute breaks were built into the schedule to allow for travel between floors and to provide the Books with respite from the conversations. Generic conversation starters were also provided to the Readers to be used as needed. Volunteers manned each floor, marking the beginning and end of each session.

In order to determine the impact of the event, surveys were given to both Readers and Books. The survey comments were overwhelmingly positive. Readers unanimously agreed that they learned something meaningful from the discussions and would continue discussions with friends and family outside the confines of the Human Library. All Readers responded in the affirmative when asked if they would attend future

Figure 14.1 Human Book Roger Beaudoin and a volunteer at the Goffstown (NH) Public Library's event. Roger's book title was "'Seeing' the World through My Rose-Colored Dark Glasses."

Human Library events. When prompted to share the most meaningful or memorable part of the program, one Reader included a quote from American folk singer Pete Seeger, who said, "Talk to people you don't agree with." This particular Reader also called the event a "mind-stretcher." Others commented on the openness of the books and their willingness to share their stories. One Reader was surprised by the breadth and depth of the collection of Human Books. Several of our youngest readers were quite engaged in talking to a blind man, but were particularly interested in the gender issues that were represented. Some found the Books inspirational. One Reader mentioned that putting faces and names to familiar labels was uncomfortable and eye-opening.

Responses from our Books were also quite positive. One Book expressed that it was an amazing experience, especially to have an inquisitive 9-year-old who attended with her parents, asking questions about life as a transgendered individual (see Fig. 14.2). Another Book responded that it was great to focus on redemptory power rather than residual pain. Yet another expressed that it had been a long while since he had experienced that level of open communication. Others shared the value of the conversations that took place between the Books themselves, which was an unanticipated positive outcome.

Figure 14.2 Human Book Porcia Chanel talks with a family of Readers at the Goffstown Public Library. Porcia's chosen title was "Look at Me Now!".

Providing a safe, nonjudgmental environment where these rich interactions could occur was integral to the success of GPL's Human Library event. Respectful questions were asked and answered. Curiosity was satisfied. Perspectives and preconceived notions were challenged. In putting real faces, names, and stories to commonly held stereotypes and misperceptions, the Human Library's purpose was fulfilled. In connecting patrons to the issues that are inherent in the human stories, the public library's mission was also fulfilled. By giving Readers an opportunity to learn directly from another person's experience, and then to reflect on the deep learning that had taken place, the goal of providing EL for the community was achieved.

14.4.3 Goffstown High School Information Center

School libraries should strive to be hubs for learning that unites disciplines and supplements classroom experiences (Young et al., 2014). GHS Information Center offers hands-on activities and student access to outside experts, connecting learning to real-world applications. The school's "learning commons" bridges disciplines and standards-based lessons by providing students with authentic learning experiences. The Human Library is a key component of this effort.

In its purest and original form, the Human Library "promotes an inclusive way to challenge prejudice through social contact...Book titles deliberately acknowledge and provoke the assumptions or common prejudices that we, or society may have, and Readers are empowered to choose from a broad range of titles, and challenged to engage with the people behind the labels during short and respectful conversation" (Human Library UK, n.d.). At GHS, the goal is to encourage students to reflect on their personal presumptions about careers and the people employed in various fields. The experience of talking to diverse professionals and considering the possibility of one's own future in a particular occupation helps students realize that they can pursue any path that interests them. Young people feel empowered to chase their dreams despite their background, race, religion, or sex.

The Human Library and career connection is an obvious one for secondary students. As young adults begin to think about life after high school, the opportunity to talk to adults in fields that interest them, and to gain a deeper understanding of various career paths, is invaluable. Students talk to individuals who have already experienced the challenges of the working world. The Human Library interaction allows students to really grasp the reality of entering this world, preparing them to better represent their own interests in a professional way after high school.

In keeping with the library's goal to connect to classroom learning at GHS, students are encouraged to take part in the Human Library event in the 11th grade. This extends the impact of a 10th-grade English Department-led "Passion Project," in which students begin exploring potential career paths in-depth. The Human Library encourages students to further consider their own futures when they listen to stories about life paths taken by others. According to a 2014 teen participant, the Human Library was a chance to hear how the path one chooses in life is not necessarily the path on which one remains. In informal exit surveys, students noted that the experience was "fun" and many said that they wished to chat with their Human Books for a longer time. One student wrote, "I really appreciated when Human Books were passionate in what they talked about. Speakers willing to share their wealth of information were immensely helpful!" All teen participants responded "yes" when asked if they learned "something meaningful through [their] conversation with the Human Book (s) about society, culture, or belief systems" (Goffstown High School, 2014).

It is important to note that the experiential focus of the Human Library also naturally fits within a new national emphasis on the Common

Core State Standards in primary and secondary schools. Even though this connection was not a prime consideration when GHS initiated their Human Library, the relationship is beneficial to any schools considering EL. Specifically, the Human Library strengthens student Comprehension and Collaboration, a prime component of the Common Core English Language Arts Standards in the area of Speaking and Listening. Through the Human Library, students have the opportunity to speak with experts, to "initiate and participate effectively in a range of collaborative discussions (one-on-one, in groups, and teacher-led with diverse partners)..." (CCSS, ELA-SSL11-12-1) (Common Core State Standards Initiative, 2015a). Furthermore, students "propel conversations by posing and responding to questions that probe reasoning and evidence; ensure a hearing for a full range of positions on a topic or issue; clarify, verify, or challenge ideas and conclusions; and promote divergent and creative perspectives" (CCSS, ELA-SSL11-12-1-c) (Common Core State Standards Initiative, 2015b). Students have the opportunity to "respond thoughtfully to diverse perspectives; synthesize comments, claims, and evidence made on all sides of an issue; resolve contradictions when possible; and determine what additional information or research is required to deepen the investigation or complete the task" (CCSS, ELA SSL11-12-1-d) (Common Core State Standards Initiative, 2015c). Finally, teens may "evaluate a speaker's point of view, reasoning, and use of evidence and rhetoric, assessing the stance, premises, links among ideas, word choice, points of emphasis, and tone used [by Human Books]" (CCSS, ELA-SSL11-12-3) (Common Core State Standards Initiative, 2015d).

EL is vital to the education of today's American teenager, who is looking for ways to better connect in-school studies to out-of-school opportunity. At GHS, the Human Library encourages respectful and professional interaction with adults. It offers an active, participatory experience that encourages deep personal reflection, promotes empathy, and encourages further exploration. Tied to 21st-Century skills, the Human Library makes learning more meaningful. It highlights the central purpose of school library learning as an extension of classroom lessons, and reflects the value of EL as a whole.

14.4.4 University of New Hampshire at Manchester Library

The University of New Hampshire at Manchester (UNH Manchester) is the university's urban, commuter college. Located in New Hampshire's largest city, the college serves a diverse local community and is committed to expanding its reach through student volunteer and service learning opportunities. The Human Library program was a perfect fit for UNH Manchester's academic goals and cocurricular priorities. UNH Manchester has a strong institutional commitment to celebrating diversity and promoting inclusivity. This commitment is evident in the college's Statement on Diversity and Inclusive Excellence, which asserts that the college "strives to create a collegial and supportive community that values differences of opinion and disagreement along with civility and consensus, and in which all of its members are valued for their contributions and are appropriately recognized and rewarded for what they do" (UNH Manchester, Diversity & Inclusive Excellence, n.d.). To support its mission of diversity and inclusion, the college provides faculty, staff, and students with experiential development programs such as Safe Zones Training—to build awareness of issues affecting lesbian, gay, bisexual, transgender, queer, and questioning colleagues—and Social Justice Educator Training—to raise awareness of social justice issues (UNH Manchester, Diversity & Inclusive Excellence, n.d.). Both the Human Library's focus on community-building and its aim of challenging prejudice and discrimination meshed with the goals of these existing social justice programs.

Because of this synergy, and because she saw a unique role for the UNH Manchester Library in the college's diversity initiatives, the librarian reached out to UNH Manchester's Diversity & Inclusive Excellence Committee to see if they would be interested in partnering to bring the UNH Manchester Human Library to fruition. The committee members were very enthusiastic about the project and decided to cosponsor the event on campus. Diversity & Inclusive Excellence committee members helped recruit Human Books for the library by reaching out to their personal and professional networks. They also served as volunteers on the day of the event, providing much-needed logistical support as greeters who explained the Human Library process to participants; "reference librarians" who helped Readers navigate the Human Library's catalogue of Books; and "circulation staff" who managed the check-out periods. A librarian also remained in the "reading room" during the check-outs to ensure that the dialogue remained respectful and that the Books were comfortable with the conversations. Our organizers also recruited Books that represented a wide range of backgrounds and experiences, including a Muslim student from Sudan, a transgendered man, a 21-year-old recovering alcoholic, a Tibetan exile, a breast-cancer survivor, an antibullying activist, a homeschooled student, and a member of the Deaf community (and many more). The overall—and somewhat unexpected—themes of the Book "collection" were resilience, pride, and the need to follow one's dreams in the face of all obstacles.

UNH Manchester has a strong focus on community involvement and EL. Located in the heart of New Hampshire's largest city, the college provides students with multiple opportunities for community-based projects, service learning placements, volunteer opportunities, and internships (UNH Manchester, Internship & Career Planning, n.d.). EL also infuses the pedagogy of the UNH Manchester faculty, most of whom strive to move learning beyond the classroom lecture and into real-world applications. These teaching practices include everything from role-playing and group discussions to hosting visiting experts and going on field trips. Seeing a unique opportunity to enhance student EL through the Human Library, the librarian contacted two faculty members whose course themes fit the diversity focus of the Human Library, and invited their classes to the event. Both faculty members were enthusiastic about the chance to have their students put classroom theory into practice. One of the classes, Political Psychology, had just completed a unit on social identity; the other, Narrative, spent the entire semester exploring the many ways people seek meaning and connection through storytelling. Through the Human Library, students directly experienced topics they had explored in their courses, and were able to reflect on the experience afterwards in class.

In addition to the Political Psychology and Narrative classes, the organizers of the UNH Manchester Library also invited students, faculty, staff, and the general public to the event.

Reactions of these various audiences to the UNH Manchester Human Library were overwhelmingly positive. Readers connected on a deeply personal level with some of the Books and expressed that the conversations shed light on their own experiences, fears, and hopes. For example, one Reader commented on how her dialogue with a young recovering alcoholic helped her to better understand the struggles of a relative struggling with addiction.

Faculty members who brought students to the Human Library were gratified by the extent to which the conversations connected to the learning outcomes of their courses. The professor who brought her Narrative students to the event indicated that it was "overall, a really valuable experience for students" that meshed nicely with her course, especially in the way that the personal stories we tell are relational and may change depending on an audience's perception of the stories. While the students related more to some Books than to others, they saw the Human Library as a "great experience" (Jago, 2015). The Political Psychology professor agreed that the event was beneficial for her students, stating that the Human Library was a "wonderful way for the students to engage in an activity that facilitated deeper thinking about the psychological theories [they] covered in class" (Negrón-Gonzales, 2015). These communications from Human Library participants indicate that the program was an active-learning experience for all involved, an activity that connected theory with direct personal experience.

14.5 "CLOSING THE BOOK": ENDINGS AND NEW BEGINNINGS

At all three sites, the organizers discovered unexpected outcomes and advantages to the Human Library. Many Books stated that they learned from the Readers as much as the Readers learned from them: the conversations were true dialogues in which the Readers opened up to the Books about their own lives. One Book expressed her appreciation for the "gratifying and humbling" experience of "open and honest conversation[s]" about issues of such personal importance to her (Dube, 2015). The Books also took the chance to talk to one another during break times or periods of "low check-out," creating a sense of collegiality and shared purpose. As a result, many of the Books realized that they are not alone, that the experiences they saw as isolating them are shared by others in the community, and that the Readers accepted them as individuals as a result of the conversation. In this sense, the New Hampshire Human Library achieved the ultimate aspirations of the global movement: "The idea behind the living library is that personal contact between people is very powerful in breaking down barriers—seeing the human being in the 'other' and realising that stereotype never does justice to a person" (Garbutt, 2008). The words of Books and Readers alike confirm that the three events led participants to see each other with fresh eyes and an open mind.

The organizers were particularly gratified to hear participants discuss ideas for future applications of the Human Library in various educational and business settings. A school administrator saw a role for the Human Library as a professional development program for teachers working with refugee students and families, while another participant envisioned using it as a training opportunity for businesses seeking to enhance employees' sensitivity to customers and clients.

During the process of planning, marketing, and presenting the Human Library, the organizers encountered unforeseen challenges and unanticipated benefits to the project. The following are ideas and tips for libraries and community organizations wishing to plan their own Human Library events:

- Get support and advice from others who have planned a Human Library—don't reinvent the wheel!
- View the project as an opportunity to help the community look at libraries differently; to help promote face-to-face interaction; and to understand that people are important resources, too.
- Try to host the event in a high-traffic area, to generate the curiosity of passers-by.
- Organizers may be overwhelmed by the number of participants and/or surprised by their responses to the experience. Be organized, and have a welcoming and open-minded attitude.
- Allow plenty of time for orientation and logistical questions for the Books. This is a new concept for most, so it is important for them to be comfortable with the format.
- Have ample staff and volunteers available to greet Readers and to provide logistical information. Again, this is a new concept, so most borrowers will be unfamiliar with how the Human Library works.
- Provide Readers with generic "conversation starter" questions. Sometimes the Reader and the Book need a boost to break the ice and get the conversation rolling.
- The New Hampshire organizers found that the Human Books liked to come back together at the end of the event to debrief. The conversations among the Books themselves were as meaningful as those between Readers and Books.
- A Human Library sparks many other interests and ideas. Be prepared to be a resource for others looking to do similar things!
- Keep in mind that "collection development" may be limited by the size or configuration of the available library space.
- Be sensitive to community needs and adapt "collection development" activities accordingly. For example, a career-focused Human Library works well in a high school setting.
- Organizers who are collaborating on a Human Library project should participate in each other's libraries. The New Hampshire organizers

found it instructional as well as fulfilling to be Readers and Books at the other sites.
- Consider the power of the experience. Human Books are not simply telling stories: they are sharing deeply personal and sometimes upsetting experiences, and they may be surprised to have Readers open up with their own experiences. Organizers should advise Books that the conversations could be intense (as well as gratifying), and provide time and space for Books to reflect after an emotional dialogue.
- Be open to the diversity and complexity of every individual's experience. Organizers may recruit a Book for one aspect of his or her identity, but the Book may end up talking to Readers about another, if moved to do so.
- No one Human Library can incorporate all the diversity that may exist in a community, and organizers may find constraints on their vision. Think about recruiting new Books for a future event!
- Advertise well. Use local resources to create logos, videos, and other publicity to generate interest in this unique project.

The New Hampshire Human Library met the goals of its organizers: by tapping into the wisdom of local individuals with unique experiences and expertise to share, the Human Library built a sense of community cohesiveness and pride. It extended the walls of "the library" beyond what many library workers and patrons alike may perceive as our traditional borders, reaching new audiences by providing a dynamic EL opportunity. Participants left the event with new ideas about the purpose and mission of libraries, understanding that libraries are dynamic spaces for learning and growth.

REFERENCES

Association of College and Research Libraries (ACRL), 2012. Diversity standards: cultural competency for academic libraries. <http://www.ala.org/acrl/standards/diversity> (accessed 07.10.15.).

Common Core State Standards Initiative, 2015a. English Language Arts Standards-Speaking & Listening-Grade 11-12-1. <http://www.corestandards.org/ELA-Literacy/SL/11-12/1/> (accessed 09.10.15.).

Common Core State Standards Initiative, 2015b. English Language Arts Standards-Speaking & Listening-Grade 11-12-1-c. <http://www.corestandards.org/ELA-Literacy/SL/11-12/1/c/> (accessed 09.10.15.).

Common Core State Standards Initiative, 2015c. English Language Arts Standards-Speaking & Listening-rade 11-12-1-d. <http://www.corestandards.org/ELA-Literacy/SL/11-12/1/d/> (accessed 09.10.15.).

Common Core State Standards Initiative, 2015d. English Language Arts Standards-Speaking & Listening-Grade 11-12-3. <http://www.corestandards.org/ELA-Literacy/SL/11-12/3/> (accessed 09.10.15.).
Dewey, J., 1998. Experience and Education, 60th anniversary ed. Kappa Delta Pi, West Lafayette, Indiana.
Dube, M., 2015. Email to Carolyn Gamtso, 3 December.
Garbutt, R., 2008. The living library: some theoretical approaches to a strategy for activating human rights and peace. In Garbutt, R. (Ed.), Activating Human Rights and Peace: Universal Responsibility Conference 2008 Conference Proceedings, Southern Cross University, Lismore, Australia. <http://epubs.scu.edu.au/cgi/viewcontent.cgi?article = 1526&context = sass_pubs> (accessed 27.11.15.).
Goffstown High School, 2014. Breaking Barriers, Building Bridges: Diverse Community Voices. (Survey).
Goffstown Public Library, 2015. About Us. <http://www.goffstownlibrary.com/about> (accessed 07.10.15.).
Gresham, K., 2001. Experiential learning theory, library instruction, and the electronic classroom. Colo. Libr. 27 (1), 19–22.
Human Library Organization, n.d. About Human Library Organization. <https://www.facebook.com/humanlibraryorg/info/?tab = page_info> (accessed 07.10.15.).
Human Library UK, n.d. What Is the Human Library? <http://humanlibraryuk.org/human-library> (accessed 14.11.15.).
Jago, B., 2015. Interview with Carolyn Gamtso, 30 October.
Kolb, D., 2015. Experiential Learning: Experience as the Source of Learning and Development, second ed. Pearson Education, Inc, Upper Saddle River, NJ.
Negrón-Gonzales, M., 2015. Email to Carolyn Gamtso, 12 December.
Shen, L., 2011. The role of multicultural information in experiential learning. Educ. Libr. 34 (1), 15–22.
University of New Hampshire at Manchester, n.d. Diversity & Inclusive Excellence. <http://manchester.unh.edu/student/diversity/> (accessed 07.10.15.).
University of New Hampshire at Manchester, n.d. Internship & Career Planning. <http://manchester.unh.edu/student/internship-career-planning> (accessed 07.10.15).
Wentz, E., 2012. The Human Library: sharing the community with itself. Public Libr. 51 (3), 38–40.
York, A., Groves, C., Black, W., 2010. Enriching the academic experience: the library and experiential learning. Collab. Libr. 2 (4), 193–203.
Young, C.L., Fiels, K.M., Grief, T., and Norton, S.K., 2014. School librarians: Leaders transforming teaching and learning. <americanlibrariesmagazine.org> (September/October 2014 digital supplement on school libraries) (accessed 07.10.15.).

CHAPTER 15

Conclusion: An Experiential Librarian's Creed

P. McDonnell
Bemidji State University, A. C. Clark Library, Bemidji, MN, United States

Personal experience, and indeed experiential learning in general, can often be likened to a journey through a landscape. The paths one walks may twist and turn, and it is not a straight line or linear progression, often looping back on itself in strange and unexpected ways. In the course of the chapters of this book are many examples of how academic libraries are, now more than ever, on a "learning journey" with the communities of which they are part (and vital to). The book has hopefully detailed some of the more exciting and replicable applications of experiential learning theory in the academic library setting. Or, to put it in terms of the model of the learning cycle developed by David Kolb, the reader has hopefully gained some insight into the topic by traveling "around" part of the spiral of the learning cycle—the areas of *concrete experience, reflective observation*, and *abstract conceptualization*—and is now perhaps ready for the *active experimentation* stage, of applying the knowledge in his or her own library context.

15.1 WHY A CREED?

For those wishing to take the journey of experiential learning a bit further, a "roadmap" to the landscape can be a useful tool. A teacher's creed, a personal statement of the educator's beliefs and vision about what education means (the why's) and in what way it should be conducted (the how's), is a time-honored activity of modern educators. It can serve as a reflective source for inspiration, as well as a guide to concrete action. One famous example, relevant to the purposes of this work, is John Dewey's *My Pedagogic Creed* (1897). Librarian-educators may benefit from the roadmap a teacher's creed provides, in seeking to live out their guiding beliefs. Thus, I humbly offer this "Experiential Librarian's Creed."

I hope to leave the reader with some ideas to take away as springboards for further application, ideas which will perhaps lead to more questions (inquiry being one of the major themes in the academic world today).

- **I believe that experiential learning has the power to both energize and greatly facilitate the continuing transformation of academic libraries.**

As we have seen, libraries are being proactive in becoming more responsive and relevant to the missions of their parent institutions, amid increasing calls for library involvement in assessment and student engagement. Experiential learning can enhance libraries' contributions to student learning, and can heighten libraries' visibility in and engagement with their parent institution's mission. For example, academic libraries that collaborate with faculty and students in active knowledge generation, rather than passive assimilation of information, may be seen as more vital partners in the academic enterprise, and more supportive of student growth.

- **I believe that academic libraries, beyond their role as a repository of knowledge, are dynamic places, where a community of scholars—students, faculty, staff, and the community at large—gathers to create and share knowledge, expertise, know-how, and wisdom.**

Dynamism is a key theme for academic libraries of the future. As shown by the maker movement and makerspaces in public libraries, libraries can indeed become hotbeds of knowledge generation. Academic libraries in particular are being called to actively partner in the production of knowledge, and can leverage spaces to strongly support experiential learning of students engaged in the research process—for example, see the Course Exhibits described in Chapter 9, Building Knowledge Together: Interactive Course Exhibits in the Academic Library. Academic libraries should also look to public libraries for relevant and exciting ideas that open up the library to the wider community, such as lifelong-learning events like the Human Library described in Chapter 14, The New Hampshire Human Library Project: Breaking Barriers and Building Bridges by Engaging Communities of Learners. As libraries continue to become more dynamic and relevant, communities are strengthened, scholarship is heightened, and wisdom grows.

- **I believe that changes in the ways students approach their learning demand a call to action in academic libraries, to bring the library closer to the cycle of teaching and learning.**

Research has suggested that Millennial students, as discussed in Chapter 5, Training Student Drivers: Using a Flipped Classroom Model for IL Instruction, are a bit different to students of other generations. They are sometimes contradictory, often being self-directed learners, yet needing structural supports in their learning. Depending on the student's life experiences and background, they are often more involved in their learning from a younger age, as compared to learners of previous generations. As reported in Chapter 5, Training Student Drivers: Using a Flipped Classroom Model for IL Instruction, employers desire employees who have information literacy and problem-solving skills, but are finding recent graduates are underprepared in these areas. This is where the power of experiential learning methods can shine, especially in the context of the academic library. Academic libraries are perfectly situated at the juncture of subject matter/discipline content and learners, and should accelerate the rate at which they are enhancing services, collections, and library spaces to support the widest possible range of learning styles and ways of knowing among today's students. Considering that the ACRL Framework for Information Literacy for Higher Education (Association of College and Research Libraries, 2015) views experiential learning as a best-practice and "reflective discovery of information" as a key aspect of student success, it seems likely that more academic libraries will effectively raise student success through enriched support of diverse learning styles.

- **I believe academic libraries are engines of inquiry, and can align themselves to inquiry-based teaching and learning at all levels, from faculty/student research collaborations, group projects for credit courses, all the way to internship and externship placements.**

The ACRL Framework for Information Literacy for Higher Education also states that "research is iterative and depends upon asking increasingly complex or new questions whose answers in turn develop additional questions or lines of inquiry in any field" (Association of College and Research Libraries, 2015). Inquiry is thus seen as a primary, motivating force, as students learn to navigate the world of academic and disciplinary information, under the guidance of—and now more often in collaboration with—faculty and librarians. Students' interest and passion for their chosen academic field is also important for libraries to keep in mind, as libraries create more tailored and responsive collections and services to support learning. As John Dewey (1897) wrote presciently more than 100 years ago: "The interest [of the student] is always the sign of some power below; the important thing is to discover this power." Academic libraries should work with faculty, campus departments, and student engagement staff to further encourage this "learning power" in students as they make their way in the world.

- **I believe libraries should step up and lead change in their parent organizations, by developing staff knowledge of experiential learning, thus further enhancing the library's role as a center of innovation.**

It's during times of great change, upheaval, and sometimes disruptive innovation that libraries can create a culture of lifelong learning. Now more than ever, there are rich opportunities for library staffs to engage in and reflect on best-practices in change management and organizational development. One of the goals of this volume has been to help foster experiential learning approaches in the visioning, planning, and implementation processes of libraries, and it has highlighted the contributions of experiential exercises in making those processes better and more impactful. This book has also highlighted a few proactive strategies for improving organizational development in libraries, through paying attention to developments in the experiential learning field and applying those developments, where appropriate, in the academic library setting.

Just as one example, as a librarian interested in staff professional development, I have merged together my experiential learning background (I have a Master's degree in Experiential Education) with faculty service to create group teambuilding experiences centered on group drumming. When I began facilitating group drum circles (also known as "percussion-based experiential exercises"), I wasn't sure how this would mesh with my work as a librarian, but I knew that I was attracted to it from a "gut-instinct" level. I thought that it could bring teambuilding, wellness, and community-building benefits to the groups of people I work with. (I also had to admit—drum circles are just plain *fun*.)

Through progressive experiences of facilitating drum circles with groups of students, faculty, and staff at my institution, as well as taking group drumming "on the road" to library conferences and reflecting on the progress in my "The Circle is a Circuit" blog (McDonnell, 2013), I came to see how group drumming could serve as a change management and teambuilding tool in the workplace. Staff development is really about change—change in both knowledge and attitudes (Stewart et al., 2013, p. 4). Activities such as group drumming help to accomplish change; they are simply tools in a flexible toolkit for engaging with students and staff. And, the more libraries innovate locally and share best-practices nationally and internationally, the more poised everyone will be to adapt to change in an uncertain future.

Furthermore, as Chapters 10, Going Vertical: Enhancing Staff Training through Vertically Integrated Instruction, 11, From Training to Learning: Developing Student Employees Through Experiential Learning Design, and 12, Home Grown: Lessons Learned From Experiential Learning Partnerships in an Academic Library suggest, libraries are developing unique approaches to continuous learning for staff, and are turning libraries into learning organizations in the truest sense of the phrase. These processes may have an experiential learning component to them, as many times they are focused on specific, practical skills which the staff member can apply immediately to their work. Readers interested in creating a library staff professional development plan would do well to consult the most recent edition of Stewart et al.'s guide on this topic (2013). Academic libraries wanting to do more to support the lifelong learning of their staffs may also find it valuable to reach out to their campus Human Resources (HR) office for assistance. Library staff could become "resident experts" on staff professional development for service departments, and could provide innovative services in this regard. As one example, the author of the Foreword to this volume, Keith Russell, had a shared appointment over 18 months between the University of Kansas (KU) Libraries and KU's Human Resources Employee Development unit. Russell collaborated on a project with campus training staff to incorporate a variety of best-practices and experiential approaches into workshops offered by the unit. At KU, the Libraries is one of the units that utilizes these programs the most, and some of the recommendations from the project were adopted by Human Resources; this unique joint effort is reflected in a published report by Russell et al. (2003). Examples such as this enable a wider view of librarians as staff development experts in their own right.

15.2 FINALLY... WHAT CAN LIBRARIES DO TO SUPPORT EXPERIENTIAL EDUCATION?

First, as we have seen, learning has to do with transformation, both for institutions and people; it is a complicated endeavor in its own right. A key part of the learning cycle is the transformational aspect. David Kolb's definition states it clearly: "Learning is the process whereby knowledge is created through the *transformation* of experience" (Kolb, 2014, p. 38) (italics mine). Learning is hard, learning is work, but through that hard work, comes transformation, both of the experience and the hard-won knowledge.

The question for libraries now is: What hard-won knowledge has been gained through the transformation? What does it contain, what does it mean/signify, and how does it change what libraries are and how they operate? One answer is to suggest that libraries can (and should) continue to be responsive to the contextualized needs of faculty, students, and the academic enterprise in general. As spotlighted by the practical examples in this book, libraries are integrating experiential learning methods into information literacy instruction, are transforming services and spaces, and are collaborating, innovating, and supporting student and faculty research, all in the service of deeper learning. As academic libraries strive to become ever more integral to the academic mission and student success, many will naturally transform themselves into true "learning organizations."

REFERENCES

Association of College and Research Libraries, 2015. Framework for Information Literacy for Higher Education [Homepage of ALA]. <http://www.ala.org/acrl/standards/ilframework> (accessed 30.03.16.).

Dewey, J., 1897. My Pedagogic Creed. E. L. Kellogg & Co, New York, NY.

Kolb, D.A., 2014. Experiential Learning: Experience as the Source of Learning and Development, second ed. Pearson Education Ltd, Upper Saddle River, NJ.

McDonnell, P., 2013. The Circle is a Circuit. <http://thecircleisacircuit.blogspot.com/> (accessed 09.04.16.).

Russell, K., Ames-Oliver, K., Fund, L., Proctor, T., Vannaman, M., 2003. Organizational development, best practices, and employee development. Libr. Adm. Manag. 17 (4), 189−197 (Fall).

Stewart, A.W., Washington-Hoagland, C., Zsulya, C.T., Library Leadership and Management Association (Eds.), 2013. Staff Development: A Practical Guide. fourth ed. American Library Association, Chicago, IL.

INDEX

Note: Page numbers followed by "*f*" and "*t*" refer to figures and tables, respectively.

A

Academic business libraries, 176, 184–185
Academic Library, xxvii, xxxii, 175, 181–185. *See also* Education Library; Walker Library
    EL in, xxvii–xxxi, 19–21
    OBL in, 32–34
    service learning and, 43–45
    subject matter/discipline content and learners, 204–205
Accommodator, xxix–xxx
ACRL. *See* Association of College & Research Libraries (ACRL)
Action learning, 180
    programs, 182–183
    at Ross school of business, 178–180
"Activating experience" principle, 152–153
"Agora" learning pattern, 136, 140–141
Anschauung, 29
Anthropological techniques, 168–170, 172
Archival community, 32–33
Archives
    experiential learning
        through materials, 89
        in university archives context, 90–91
    staff, 38
Archivist–faculty collaborations, 34
Art-hanging systems, 128
Artifacts, 27, 35, 118
Assimilator, xxix–xxx
Association of College & Research Libraries (ACRL), 58–59
    framework, 10–11, 58–59
    for Information Literacy for Higher Education, 204–206
    Standards, 11
Association of Experiential Education, 15
Atlanta University Center, 138–139, 145
Authentic assessment, 79–80
    efficacy of quizzes, 76
    future, 82–85
        lessons learning, 83–84
    iPads, 76–77
        acquiring and setting up, 77
        in classroom, 77–82
        quizzes, problem with, 74–76

B

*Big*6 model, 9
"Blog post cube", 125, 126*f*
Bloom's Taxonomy, 56–57, 75, 83, 121, 122*f*
Board games, 103–106
Brigham Young University (BYU), 170–171
Business
    curriculum, 176–178
    librarians, 176, 184–185
    school
        curriculum, 176–177
        libraries, 180
    students projects, 177–178
BYU. *See* Brigham Young University (BYU)

C

Camtasia software, 140, 141*f*
CCSS. *See* Common Core State Standards (CCSS)
Center for Games & Learning, 106–108
    games list, 108*f*
    logo, 107*f*
Class(es)
    classroom-ready technology skills, 18
    using iPads, 77–79
    visits, 91
Collaboration, 135, 187
Collaborative learning, 24
Common Core English Language Arts Standards, 194–195
Common Core State Standards (CCSS), 194–195
Community
    organizations, 188
    of practice, 21–22, 109

Compulsory SmartBoard, 18–19
Converger, xxix–xxx
"Conversation starters", 191, 199
Course Exhibit(s), 119–120, 122–123
  in Academic Library
    assessment, 133
    Bloom's Taxonomy, 121, 122*f*
    building program, 119
    Chickering and Gamson framework, 120–121
    commons coordinator, 118
    costs/supplies, 131–132, 132*f*
    design process, 123
    idea, 118
    library's learning outcomes, 122–123
    pedagogical and curricular change, 117–118
    pedagogy, 119–120
    tips on process, 131
  Makerspace, 132*f*
  Photography in Focus, 127–130, 130*f*
    initial mock-up, 128*f*
    revised mock-up, 129*f*
  "Soviet History for Networked Age", 123–127, 125*f*, 126*f*
CQ Researcher databases, 78
CRAAP test, 112–113
Creed, 203–207
  experiential librarian, 203–204
    academic libraries, 204
    ACRL framework, 204–205
    group drumming, 206
    libraries supporting experiential education, 207–208
    library staff, 207
    percussion-based experiential exercises, 206
    research, 204–205
  teacher's, 203–204
Cross-training model, 135

D

Design thinking, 18
Dewey, John, xxvii–xxix, 4, 151, 188–189, 203–206
Digital Media Studio, 164–165, 173
Discrimination, 187–188, 195–196

Diverger, xxix–xxx
Diversity, 187–188, 195–196, 200
Double-loop learning, 19
Drew University Library, 89, 93
Dynamism, 204

E

E-learning technologies (ELT) unit, 138–139
  paraprofessionals, 141–143
Education, Dewey's theory on, xxix
Education Library. *See also* Academic Library; Walker Library
  path to EL in, 16–19
    in academic library, 19–21
    in higher education, 15–16
    reflections, 21–24
EL. *See* Experiential learning (EL)
ELT unit. *See* E-learning technologies (ELT) unit
Employability skills, 54
Engagement strategies, 138
English as Second Language (ESL), 9
"Episteme", 59
ESL. *See* English as Second Language (ESL)
Ethnographic
  libraries embracing ethnographic studies, 168–172
  studies, 163–164, 172
  techniques, 168
"Eurogames", 103–104
Experience and Education (Dewey), xxviii–xxix
Experience-based practices and methods, xxvii–xxviii
Experiential education, libraries supporting, 207–208
Experiential learning (EL), xxvii, 15, 53, 55–57, 104–105, 138, 147, 172, 180, 187–189, 203–204. *See also* Handheld learning; Object-based learning (OBL); Service learning; Workplace learning
  for academic libraries, xxvii–xxxi
  application, 12, 60–62
  center for games & learning, 106–108, 107*f*, 108*f*

coauthor Cassie Brand, 90
through collections and archives, 89
in collections and university archives context, 90–91
community of practice, 109
defined, xxviii
EL theory, 3
in faculty of Education Library, 16–19
  in academic library, 19–21
  in higher education, 15–16
  reflections, 21–24
Free Dictionary online, 3
fun and games, 109–111
IL curriculum and EL at ZU, 6–12
  ACRL Information Literacy Competency Standards, 9
  ACRL Standards, 10–11
  Centre for Waste Management, 9–10
  collaboration of librarians, 7–8
  experience, 8
  "Learning Assessment Map", 11–12
  Public Health department, 11
  Zayed University IL curriculum integration, 7f
instructional design principles for, 151–155
investment in, 157–158
Kolb's theory of EL, 4–6
pedagogy, 55–56
preliminary observations, 62–63
prerevised and revised information cycle assignments comparison, 61t
programs, 182–183
project, 63–67, 177–178, 182
  application, 63–66
  preliminary observations, 66–67
  prerevised and revised bibliography assignments comparison, 65t
  prerevised and revised narrowing topic assignments comparison, 64t
student employment practices, 151–155
student-curated exhibits program, 93–95
students workers as experiential learners, 95–100
  synergy between flipped classroom and, 57–60
  ACRL framework, 58–59
  EL—course redesign, 58
  flipped classroom, 60
  flipped classroom LS102, 57–58
  threshold concepts, 58–59
tabletop games
  as EL, 103–105
  in library, 105–106
  selection, 111–113
out of vault series program, 91–93
at Walker Library, 163–164
Experiential Learning: Experience as the Source of Learning and Development (Kolb), xxix
Experiential Learning Theory (ELT), xxix
Experiential librarian's creed, 203–204
  academic libraries, 204
  ACRL framework, 204–205
  group drumming, 206
  libraries, 204
  libraries supporting experiential education, 207–208
  library staff, 207
  percussion-based experiential exercises, 206
  research, 204–205
  teacher's creed, 203–204

F

Faculty–librarian collaboration, 90
First Year Seminar program, UMM's, 43, 45–46
Flipped classroom model
  advisories, 69
  connecting IL, research skills, and employability, 53–55
  end of road, 70
  hits, 67–68
  for IL instruction, 53, 55–57
  misses, 68–69
  pedagogy, 56–57
  synergy between flipped classroom and EL, 57–60
    ACRL framework, 58–59
    expanding EL, 58

Flipped classroom model (*Continued*)
  flipped classroom, 60
  flipped classroom LS102, 57–58
  threshold concepts, 58–59
Formal learning, 137
"Framing experience" principle, 151
Free Dictionary online, 3

G

GarageBand software, 141–142, 142f
Georgia Perimeter College, 73
Goffstown High School (GHS)
    Information Center, 187,
    189–190, 193–195
Goffstown Public Library (GPL), 187,
    191–193, 192f, 193f
Google, 9–10, 53–55, 137, 177
  behaviors, 66
  finding articles via, 63
Google Drive, 154–155
GPL. *See* Goffstown Public Library (GPL)
Graduate schools of business, 176
Graduate students, 89–90, 96–97,
    148–149, 166–167, 169–170, 181
Group drumming, 206
Guided Reflection on Work (GROW), 149

H

Handheld learning. *See also* Object-based
    learning (OBL)
  efficacy of quizzes, 76
  future of authentic assessment, 82–85
    future, 84–85
    lessons learning, 83–84
  iPads, 76–77
    acquiring and setting up, 77
    in classroom, 77–82
  quizzes, problem with, 74–76
"Helpdesk" learning pattern, 136, 140–141
Heutagogy, 19
Higher education
  EL in, 15–16
  OBL in, 31–32
Home grown
  EL at Walker Library, 163–164
  libraries embrace ethnographic studies,
    168–172

library relevance and innovation, 166–167
  EL in action, 166–167
  staffing at Walker Library, 164–166
  user-led library studies, 173
HR office. *See* Human Resources (HR)
    office
Human Library, 187, 198–200
Human Resources (HR) office, 207
"Hypertext mindset", 55

I

"I believe" statements, xxviii–xxix
Ideal library, 167
IL. *See* Information literacy (IL)
IMLS. *See* Institute of Museum and
    Library Services (IMLS)
Informal learning, 137
Information and research services (IRS)
    unit, 138–139
Information literacy (IL), xxx–xxxii,
    17–18, 34–35, 53, 55–57, 76,
    204–205
  ACRL framework for, 205–206
  IL curriculum and EL at ZU, 6–12
    ACRL Information Literacy
      Competency Standards, 9
    ACRL Standards, 10–11
    Centre for Waste Management, 9–10
    collaboration of librarians, 7–8
    experience, 8
    "Learning Assessment Map", 11–12
    Public Health department, 11
    Zayed University IL curriculum
      integration, 7f
  instruction, 3, 43–44, 47–48
Inquiry-based learning, 16, 24, 30. *See also*
    Object-based learning (OBL)
Institute of Museum and Library Services
    (IMLS), 105
Instructional design principles for EL,
    151–155
  Multimedia Production Specialist, 151
  Social Media Content Developer, 151
Internship(s), 176
  in business education, 176–178
  service opportunities for libraries,
    183–185

iPad(s), 76–77, 82–83
   using in classroom
      classes and databases, 77–79
      practice and assessment, 79–80
      results, 80–82
      workshops, 18–19
IRS unit. *See* Information and research services (IRS) unit

K

Kolb, David A., xxviii–xxx
Kolb's theory of EL, 4–6
   forms of knowledge, 5*t*
Kresge Library Services, 179, 183
   service orientation, 180–182
KU. *See* University of Kansas (KU)

L

Learning, 58–59, 207–208. *See also* Experiential learning (EL); Object-based learning (OBL); Workplace learning
   approaches, 136
   learning-focused approach, 148–149
   organization, 207–208
   outcomes, 112
   patterns, 136
   strategies, 136
Learning cycle, xxix–xxx
Learning styles, xxix–xxx
"Learning Assessment Map", 11–12
Librarian, 179, 184–185
   action learning
      programs, 182–183
      at Ross school of business, 178–180
   support for students on summer internships
      business curriculum, 176–178
      experiential learning programs, 182–183
      internship in business education, 176–178
      internship service opportunities for libraries, 183–185
      service orientation of Kresge Library Services, 180–182

Libraries, 189, 193
   communication, 156
   EL in action, 166–167
   embracing ethnographic studies, 168–172
   exhibits curation, 89
   innovation, 166–167
   internship service opportunities for, 183–185
   planning, 163
   relevance, 166–167
   workplace learning, 144–146
Library and Information Science (LIS), xxvii, xxx–xxxii, 148–149
Lifelong learners, 188
LIS. *See* Library and Information Science (LIS)
Literacy, 43, 45–46
Living Library, 187–188. *See also* Academic Library; Education Library

M

MAP. *See* Multidisciplinary Action Projects (MAP)
Master's of Business Administration (MBA), 176, 178
Master's of Library Science program, 173
MBA. *See* Master's of Business Administration (MBA)
Middle Tennessee State University (MTSU), 149, 163–166, 169–174
Mind-stretcher, 191–192
MSCHE. *See* US Middle States Commission on Higher Education (MSCHE)
MTSU EL program, 166
MTSU Quality Enhancement Plan, 165–166
Multidisciplinary Action Projects (MAP), 178–180
Multimedia Production Specialist, 150–151, 153
My Pedagogic Creed (Dewey), xxviii–xxix

N

New England Library Association (NELA), 190
New Hampshire Human Library project collaboration
    Goffstown High School Information Center, 193−195
    Goffstown Public Library, 191−193
    libraries collaboration, 189−191
    UNHM Library, 195−198
    EL, 188−189
    endings and new beginnings, 198−200
    Human Library, 187−188

O

Object-based learning (OBL), 27. *See also* Service learning
    during 20th century, 29−30
    academic librarians, 27−28
    in academic libraries, 32−34
    carved stone, 31*f*
    educators, 28−29
    elementary education reformers, 29
    hands-on examination, 40−41
    in higher education, 31−32
    library instruction for, 34−40
    OBL theory, 30
    Omeka site creation, 39*f*
    student working with documents, 36*f*
    University College London, 40
OBL. *See* Object-based learning (OBL)
Office of Community Engagement (OCE), 43
Office of Information Technology (OIT), 77
Ohio University Libraries, student employment practices at, 150
OIT. *See* Office of Information Technology (OIT)
"Online campus", 73
Out of vault series program, 91−93

P

Pedagogy, 75, 119−120
Peer-to-peer learning, 144−145
Percussion-based experiential exercises. *See* Group drumming
Photography in Focus, 127−130, 128*f*, 129*f*, 130*f*
Piaget's theory, 4−5
PIL. *See* Project Information Literacy (PIL)
Political Psychology, 197−198
Portfolio, 58, 63
Practicum students, 165
Professional development, 145
Progressive education movement, xxviii
Project Information Literacy (PIL), 54
Project-based work, 177−178
ProQuest Research Library database, 140−141
Public Health department, 11

Q

QEP. *See* Quality Enhancement Plan (QEP)
Qualitative research, 168
Quality Enhancement Plan (QEP), 53
Queen's Education Library, 17
Quizzes, problem with, 74−76

R

"Real-world" experiences, 176
"Reference librarians", 196−197
Reference services, 175−176
Reflective portfolio, 155
Research Commons, 166−167
Research process, 184
Ross school of business, action learning at, 178−180
Rubrics, 80−81

S

Semester-long group project, 46
Sensory experience, 27, 29
Service learning, 3, 7−8, 10−12. *See also* Object-based learning (OBL)
    and academic library, 43−45
    about community, 48−49
    community partners, 51−52
    course, 45−48
    Morris community, 50
    students learning about themselves, 49−50
    upper-division students, 51

Social Media Content Developer, 150–151
"Soft skills", 55–56
Soviet History for Networked Age, 123–127, 125f, 126f
Staff development, 135
Staff professional development, 206–207
Staff training, 135
   future directions in library workplace learning, 144–146
   solutions and recommendations, 143–144
   vertically integrated instruction program, 138–143
   workplace learning, 135–138
      engagement strategies, 138
      experiential learning, 138
      formal learning, 137
      informal learning, 137
      learning strategies, 136
Student employees/student employment
   adaptation to incorporate EL, 151–155
   challenges and issues for consideration
      allowing for failure, 155–156
      allowing time for reflection, 156–157
      deciding to invest in EL, 157–158
      expectations for student workers, 157
      scaling up, 156
   through EL design, 147
   in libraries, 147–149
      learning-focused approach, 148–149
      practices at Ohio University Libraries, 150
Student(s)
   engagement, 35
   internships, 177–178
   student-curated exhibits program, 93–95
   student-focused course reserves program, 180
   students workers as experiential learners, 95–100

T

Tablet computers, 80
Tabletop game(s), 103
   as EL, 103–105
   in library, 105–106
   selection, 111–113

Technology design studio (TDS), 139
Technology skills, 138–139
Theory of heutagogy, 21–22
Threshold concepts, 10–11, 58–59
Tremendous service, 181–182
"Twelve Natural Laws of Successful Business", 184–185
21st Century Skills, 105–107

U

UAE. See United Arab Emirates (UAE)
UMM. See University of Minnesota, Morris (UMM)
Undergraduate
   education, 120–121
   students, 53, 89, 166–167, 170–171
United Arab Emirates (UAE), 6
University of Kansas (KU), 207
University of Minnesota, Morris (UMM), 43
University of New Hampshire at Manchester (UNHM) Library, 187, 195–198
University of Tennessee, Knoxville (UTK), 165
US Middle States Commission on Higher Education (MSCHE), 9
User-led library studies, 173
UTK. See University of Tennessee, Knoxville (UTK)

V

Vertically integrated instruction program, 138–143
   Atlanta University Center, 138–139, 145
   ELT paraprofessionals, 140–141
   implementation, 139
   librarians in IRS unit, 139
   paraprofessionals, 141f
   theory about learning organizations, 139
   workshop, 141–143

W

Walker Library, 173. See also Academic Library; Education Library Listening/Viewing Center, 173

Walker Library (*Continued*)
  staffing at, 164–166
  stage for EL at, 163–164
WMS. *See* WorldShare Management System (WMS)
Workplace learning, 135–138. *See also* Experiential learning (EL)
  engagement strategies, 138
  experiential learning, 138
  formal learning, 137
  informal learning, 137
  learning strategies, 136
WorldShare Management System (WMS), 142–143

Z

Zayed University (ZU), 3
  IL curriculum and EL at, 6–12
    ACRL Information Literacy Competency Standards, 9
    ACRL Standards, 10–11
    Centre for Waste Management, 9–10
    collaboration of librarians, 7–8
    "Learning Assessment Map", 11–12
    Public Health department, 11
    Zayed University IL curriculum integration, 7*f*
Zayed University Learning Outcomes (ZULOs), 6

CPI Antony Rowe
Chippenham, UK
2019-01-15 12:02